THE
ORPHAN
HEART

STEVE HEPDEN

Blessings,

Steve

Layout by Freedom Publishing
Cover by Esther Kotecha, EK Design
Printed in the UK by Bell and Bain Ltd, Glasgow

CONTENTS

DEDICATION

In memory of my mother who kept me

Endorsements

"Written with vulnerability and transparency, this powerful and pivotal book introduces us to an emotional pandemic that transcends culture, race and geographical boundaries - the orphan spirit (heart). The author who has addressed this subject with scriptural thoroughness writes out of a lifelong ministry of prophetic teaching that has been distilled in the crucible of rich experience. I recommend it to you"

John Glass
General Superintendent Elim Churches 2000-2016, Conference Speaker, Writer, Broadcaster

Over the forty years I have known Steve, he has always sought to walk with integrity whether his path has been on the mountain or down in the valley.

This book is a journey into the heart of the Father, that pulsates with revelation of God's goodness in Steve's life. Steve uncovers his heart of compassion which has been shaped by both experience and prophetic insight

The Orphan Heart brings both a clarity from the Scriptures and experience from Steve's testimony together.

The truth that Steve shares is a key to a door opening up new possibilities for you to enter into a life of acceptance and freedom. As you walk into the arms of a loving Father, you will be led into spacious places, designed just for you.

Trevor Baker
Senior Leader, Revival Fires

After supporting people as a therapist for nearly twenty years, I've come to understand well the problems that childhood pain causes. And sadly the world is populated by a great number of individuals who were emotionally wounded in their early years. Some of these wounds present as you might expect, such as a difficulty with vulnerability, a fear of intimacy, problems regulating thoughts and emotions, a struggle to form attachments, a deep distrust of anything you doubt you could control, or crippling self-doubt coupled with the craving for whatever helps you to feel seen and validated. These can create years of battling what is often more broadly defined as stress, depression and anxiety. However, some of these wounds do not always present in a way we might presume. Sometimes the wounds present as the 'seemingly' innocuous pursuit of excellence in one's employment, the consuming pursuit to clear all obstacles from out of our children's way, or an exceptionally high bar of expectation for the behaviour of one's significant other and zero tolerance for people's mistakes. I could go on.

For sure, some of these might be in some cases good sense or wise boundaries. But in other cases they are coping strategies that create inflexible and unrealistic ideals that set up the conditions for our pain and the pain of others. Therapists are limited in what they can do to help. But God is not! Steve's story is a powerful example of what God can do to heal and set people free from the pain that happens in life. Steve's experience comfort us to know we are not unique in our struggle and his wisdom is a balm we can apply to our wounds. Above all, however, Steve points to a God in heaven who is the perfect father, friend, and comforter. If we follow the path of this book to Him, we find the power and strength to heal, hope and live the life pain has robbed from us. When we discover the acceptance of our Heavenly Father - not simply conceptually but viscerally - we discover a strength, courage and proper perspective that without Him it is impossible to know.

Pastor Dave Akerman
Practising Psychotherapist, Oxon

FOREWORD

It always amazes us when someone is able to be at the forefront of pioneering for many decades and yet without surrendering to the constraints of tradition, conformity and man-made religion. Steve Hepden is such a person, one who has known what it is to be fully dependent on the fathering of God. It is this very dependency that keeps him close to the cutting edge of what Father, Son and Spirit are doing on the earth. We have watched Steve walk through some phenomenal highs, but also seen him when his only option has been to crawl forwards on his knees, through considerable challenges and tests; yet he has shown none of the usual resentments, frustrations or bitter anger that often creep in during trials and tribulations. This is rare and remarkable, but Steve is so secure in his sonship that he is able to refuse to wear the ugly robes of rejection. His life has not been one of ease - not by any stretch of the imagination - but it *is* a life that has been lived so powerfully under the revelation of adoption by the Father that you can learn from him. In doing so you will be able to mature and grow older *gracefully*, not broken.

Have you ever felt that your life is going around and around in a cycle of one disappointment or disaster after another, or from one pattern of poor decisions to the next? Have you ever had the feeling that your own behaviours have been jeopardising or sabotaging your life, faith and relationships in ever decreasing circles of pain and hurt? Are you restless, always striving to achieve a goal that never seems to be attainable? Life doesn't have to be like that! As Steve makes clear early on in this precious book, 'you have stayed long enough at this mountain' (quoting God's words to Moses). The joyful truth is that you *can* be on a meaningful journey from one degree of glory to another, step by step moving forwards, in a secure relationship with your loving Heavenly Father. This book will help you to move on from anywhere that you have become stuck - into healing, freedom and the abundant blessings that God has for you on the path of true sonship that is ahead of you.

Steve has been a very significant father to us, always displaying great wisdom and kindness. God trusts him with secrets, and he understands liberation and freedom more than almost anyone else I know. He is unceasingly funny; the Holy Spirit clearly delights in being with Steve - as Steve clearly does in the Spirit! Whenever Steve walks into a room there is always a sense of Holy Spirit freedom and joy, and one never knows what is going to happen next. He is completely yielded to whatever and however the Spirit of God wants to move. This is uncommon, and it is beautiful.

Truly Steve is a rare breed, a Prophet-Pastor, someone who speaks bold, heavenly truths - yet with the gentle tone of a kindly shepherd. In *The Orphan Heart* he presents us with choices, in the direct-yet-gentle ways that are so characteristic of the man. He asks, 'Do you want to be in a performance-based life with God (always restless, always striving) or do you want an experiential-based life with God (with a good, safe and secure relationship with Him)?' This very personal question is at the heart of this wonderful book and, as you allow Steve to take you by the hand and walk you through the reasons why you might have chosen one answer over the other in the past, you'll find his gentle shepherding, nudging you towards the grace and the rest of God

Whatever your reason was for picking up *The Orphan Heart*, please know that when you begin to turn its pages and start to dive into the stories inside, you are about to go on an incredible journey, in the company of a remarkable man. The insights, teaching and personal testimony that you will read in this book are more than mere head-knowledge information to be skimmed. These are transformative Scriptural truths and principles that, if you're willing to absorb them, will turn your life around - they might save your relationships and perhaps even your life! We encourage you to work through each chapter of this book carefully and prayerfully, allowing the Holy Spirit to transform you from the inside out, as new layers of revelation bring to the surface thoughts, emotions and learned behaviours that have been kept hidden deep down.

This book is theologically rich and absolutely packed with superb Bible teaching and the sage-like wisdom that only comes from navigating decades of leadership in the church, as well as a life lived in the fires of trials and pain. Indeed, this is a book that ministry leaders will refer to again and again as they seek to shepherd their flocks with grace and wisdom - and the insights in Chapter 18, 'Orphan Leaders' should be a must-read for all who seek to pastor in Jesus' church.

Steve has a wonderful ability to make well-known Bible passages - such as the Temptation of Christ - come alive in ways that will make you gasp in delight. When Steve teaches from Scripture he uncovers precious hidden treasures in the verses, one after another. It's like sitting down at a familiar restaurant, only to discover that there is much more on the menu than you ever realised - and the chef is bringing out new dishes all the time!

Perhaps the main course in this banquet of Bible scholarship is the story of the Prodigal Son, or as Steve rightly calls it, the story of the 'Pursuing Father'. Despite being perhaps the best-known of Jesus's parables, you will be amazed at the way Steve retells, explains, and dives deeply into all the nuances that the Lord revealed to him. Over two riveting chapters we explore the story from multiple angles and points of view, gaining revelation about our inheritance, our home, our wrong beliefs, and how we always manage to get things completely wrong whilst simultaneously being seemingly powerless to put things right again!

Just like the Prodigal Son, all our own efforts are meaningless and never get us anywhere - we just end up making things worse! However, as we dine out with Steve on this parable, we discover the most important thing that we can learn from this story - who our loving, pursuing, gracious Father is, and how He makes things right. As Steve says, 'God's outrageous grace, which includes His unconditional love, is a tool to undermine and demolish our performance mentality and our striving to be perfect... give up trying to meet conditions that aren't there.'

Rich though it is in Bible study and insights, *The Orphan Heart* is not simply a theology book. This is a deeply personal story of family turmoil, told with honesty, transparency, and without any hint of bitterness. Steve tells his own story with a vulnerability that is rare in today's culture, and yet is completely a reflection of the man that he is - open, authentic, real and tender.

Dear reader, in your life you may have had all kinds of horrible experiences with parents, leaders, and those who should have been looking after you, but please know that Steve is someone you can trust. He has a pastoral heart and compassion for the individual unlike many in these days. He and his beautiful wife Chris have been wonderful friends and mentors to us over many years. As we set out into pioneering prophetic ministry they watched over us with kind, grace-filled eyes, allowing us the freedom to make our own wrong turns and mistakes, the mistakes that we had to learn through in order to qualify for next level adventures in the Kingdom. Their encouragement to us has always been a 'go for it', and they have always stood alongside Jesus in believing in us, cheering us on without a hint of jealousy or competition. When we have needed a 'course adjustment',

Steve has always given wise counsel with a smile and a wink, his warm humour allowing him to correct us without us even realising we are being corrected!

It is such a blessing to have leaders like Steve and Chris Hepden in the body of Christ. Their immense legacy, which continues to bear so much fruit, cannot be measured in this earthly lifetime but is for sure being recorded in the books of Heaven's library. As we consider the Hepdens with smiles on our faces, we recall the many times that we sat around their kitchen table, chatting for days on end. We always come away feeling refreshed, heard and loved. The truth in this book is lived, learned and, if you apply it, it will be like dynamite to you.

Enjoy your freedom!

David and Emma Stark
Leaders, Global Prophetic Alliance and Power Church, Glasgow

PREFACE

For a long time, I have wanted to write about the story of my life, particularly regarding the secrets and lies which hounded our family for many years and sowed the seeds that fashioned my orphan heart and mindset. I've therefore designed this book around the narrative of my own story, in order to help give a clear understanding of the orphan heart. I've been careful to include a foundation of appropriate theology and biblical illustrations, interspersed with anecdotal experiences. I hope that what I've written will resonate with many people, as well as give understanding to leaders and counsellors.

My parents died many years ago, and out of respect for them, I have waited for a period of time before writing this, as I loved them and always will.

Please be aware that it is not my intention to be self-indulgent when you read some of the early chapters that refer to my family history. My purpose in sharing what has happened to me is to explain how I have been changed through the Father's unconditional love and amazing grace, because His mercy rewrote my life.

The story of the Father's love fills me with passion because His love is unfailing. One of the names of God is Abba, and this is a name that Jesus used probably more than we realise. As the author Brennan Manning has stated 'Abba - the name that scandalised both the theology and public opinion in Israel - the name Jesus was given for God. We have that name too.' Out of the approximately 300 names of God in the Bible, it is this one that has probably affected me the most, as it reveals how close and cherishing He wants to be to His creation.

At the time of writing, our world has found itself in the middle of the worst pandemic for generations. Covid 19 has meant that the phrase 'social distancing' had become law for a period of time in the UK. For many months we were told, among other things, not to meet, embrace, hug or touch our loved ones. As a result, there has been a huge rise in social issues including mental health, depression, and loneliness. We all need closeness; an awkward chat wearing a mask at a distance is not enough.

It seems that many Christians may have missed something with regard to their relationship with Father God. You will see later that it took me years to realise that, although I loved Jesus and followed Him, I knew very little about His Father's love, and because of my orphan heart it was a struggle. I now understand that as we see Jesus, we can see the Father, and through that, we can enter into the deeper relationship He offers. The cry of Jesus in Gethsemane was a cry to the Father using the term 'Abba,' something which indicates closeness and intimacy, Mark 14:36.

I feel that it is important to explain the difference between an 'orphan heart' and the 'orphan spirit,' as these are easily mixed up and this could lead to confusion. I define an orphan spirit as demonic oppression, in which the enemy sees an opening and takes advantage of the orphan condition affecting the person. The orphan heart, however, is the wounded heart, which is an integral part of the person and is not something demonic to be cast out, but is a heart that needs healing, transforming and renewing.

When I mention the word 'son,' I use it in a generic or all-encompassing sense rather than as a reference to the specific gender. We are all sons, and we are all part of the bride. These areas will be explained further - from both my own experience and from a biblical perspective.

The book has turned out to be a little longer than I expected and there was a temptation to cull certain parts of it. However, in the end, I decided that it would be important to leave it as I had written it for you, because I really want you to see the whole picture which includes my history, anecdotes, theology and the various revelations that I had recently received that are associated with them.

As you read, it is important to remember:

- A child with parents can still have an orphan heart.
- Your past is not your future.
- You are not a prisoner of your past; you are not under a life sentence.

Of course there are still battles, but what sustains me is that foundationally I know that I am adopted into sonship and that my God is Abba Father.

Special Acknowledgement

There are certain occasions in our lives when the right person comes at the right time. Barbara Todd, a friend of many years, is one of them. She has been an editor par excellence, and a doyen of all things regarding the English language. She has been a considerable help regarding grammar and sentence structure, all of which have led to a smoother and better read of the narrative. I am truly grateful to her for doing a fantastic job, and I know it would have been a struggle to complete the book without her.

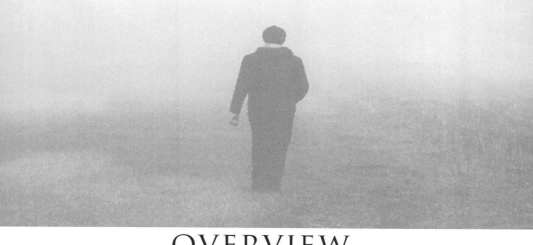

OVERVIEW

*'I have to go away, but I will not leave you orphans [fatherless],
I will come to you,'* (John 14:18).

There is a theme which runs throughout the Bible that can be described as a love story between God as Father and humankind. It has been said that God is in search of humanity for love and relationship; God is in pursuit of us! It is enthralling that God has it in His heart to pursue us: He wants to be where we are and wants us to be where He is. That is why the scriptures consistently talk about Him coming down to where we are, to be at home with us. God's desire is to inaugurate family, with Him as Father, so that He can commune and communicate with His creation and us with Him.

The design of the enemy has always been to stop that in any way possible through subtlety, trickery and deception, or by using any conceivable situation, personal or otherwise, to bring division and augment the belief that humanity can manage on their own without the need to depend on God. However, separation from God meant fatherlessness, and Satan and his powers have always been adept at reinforcing the disconnection of the orphan heart by any conceivable means, whether internal or external.

The Beginning

'*Then God planted a garden in Eden, in the East. He put the Man He had just made in it,*' (Genesis 2:8; 15-17). The garden of God was His paradise which He had made for the man and the woman to tend and care for. It was the place where God could commune with His family. '*Then the man and his wife heard the sound of the Lord God as he was walking in the garden in the cool of the day,*' (Genesis 3:8). This refers to the time when Adam and Eve had just disobeyed God, and as they heard the sound of God, they hid. They knew that it was God, which implies that they had heard, seen and been with Him before. God had placed them in glorious surroundings and provided for them in a kind, considerate and generous way. It was magnificent; they were His pleasure, and God was their friend, as well as their Father. Eden is about family, and at the heart of the family is relationship. This was God as Father living with His son and daughter in the garden, which is a demonstration of Heaven on Earth, a wonderful place of peace, with abundance and divine fulfilment.

God's desire has always been to come down amongst His creation and form a close personal relationship with them. This is not them taking an initiative to find God, but God intentionally coming to them consistently. The purpose of God is to be with His creation, not expect them to work to reach Him. We talk about going to heaven one day: He talks about Heaven on Earth now. God wants to be with us where we are, whether it is the Garden of Eden, the Tabernacle, the Temple, in the person of Jesus, in the presence of the Holy Spirit, or finally the New Jerusalem, which will come down to Earth from Heaven (Revelation 21:2). What God intended when He first created the world is fulfilled in the renewed heaven and earth (Revelation 21–22).

Scripture says that, '*He has set eternity in our hearts,*' (Ecclesiastes 3:11), which means in this context that God has put within each one of us a desire to seek Him, to be close to Him. When He came to be with Adam and Eve, it was the cool of the day, which is literally 'in the wind of the day,' They heard the sound of the Lord as He walked towards them, and they knew that He had come to walk and talk with them. The word walk means walking for pleasure, or even strolling! The Hebrew word for 'sound,' is 'ruach,' and can mean wind, breath, or the Spirit of God. They recognised God because He came in human form, and was surrounded by a whirlwind of His Spirit. It was a glorious foretaste of incarnation. What an illustration of the Trinity! God's ruach is the source of life, and Job understood this truth, *'the Spirit of God has made me; the breath [ruach] of the Almighty gives me life,'* (Job 33:4). We also see God's care for the man and woman because He came in the cool of the day, and it was not because it was more pleasant for Him, but more the best time for them. This is God, in His kindness considering His creation. This is this complete harmony, God at home with His creation; this is Heaven coming to Earth! Could it be that the purposes of God were to expand the garden to the whole earth, but what started in such unity and harmony became a place of division.

It is amazing that all religions apart from one, Christianity, began with a man seeking God. The Bible starts with the reality that God was and still is seeking man. This highlights the crucial difference between our faith and every other religion in the world. We start our relationship with Him in His acceptance of us, and in an awareness that we are not orphans, but His sons and daughters. We probably all have in some way tried to gain acceptance from Him, but it has led to a pressure to perform and a life of being a slave to our achievements.

Adam and Eve Leave Home

One day, God came into the garden. Adam and Eve heard Him coming and hid in a fig tree because they realised that they were naked; they were ashamed and afraid. This prompted the first question asked in the Bible, *'the Lord God called to the man, where are you,'* (Genesis 3:9). God knew the answer, but He wanted a response from Adam. Something had changed: they were not where they should be, waiting for God. They had disconnected, because of Satanic interference, which involved temptation and deception. However, God wanted to find them because He did not want to abandon them. They were lost, but God came looking for them. His deep love for them together with His immeasurable grace meant, that He did not come with anger and condemnation, but with compassion and reconciliation. However, they had lost that deep and intimate communion with Him. We may feel lost, we may be hiding and be fearful, but God comes as our loving Heavenly Father to save us from the judgement we deserve and bring reconciliation. As He comes to offer sonship, it gives us an opportunity to recognise and deal with the condition of our hearts, and to receive our inheritance and walk into our destiny with Him as Father.

There is an indissoluble link between Adam and Eve in the Garden of Eden and Jesus in the wilderness, (Matthew 4:1-11). Satan came to undermine their relationships with Father God through temptation. Jesus overcame, but Satan succeeded in bringing division, and Adam and Eve had to leave the garden, (Genesis 1:22-24). Their severed relationship with God left them fatherless. Their irresponsible decision gave God no choice, and in great sorrow, He sent them away from the security they had with Him in the Garden of Eden into exile in the wilderness. They became orphaned: they were separated from His love and all that it represented. By leaving home, they lost closeness and presence. What God wanted then was what He wants now, which is everyone close to Him in an unconditional, loving relationship.

Distance

In the Old Testament, very few were able to approach God. Moses was one of the few, and inside the Tent of Meeting, the Lord would speak to him face to face, as one speaks to a friend, (Exodus 33:11). The Lord said to him, *'come up the mountain to the Lord with the elders and worship at a distance, but only Moses alone is to approach,'* (Exodus 24:1-2). The elders saw God and ate and drank at a distance. What I love is that they did what was natural by eating and drinking in the presence of God, something which is covenant, but at a distance. It was a place of manifest glory, but at a distance, but it cannot have to be like that anymore. We can be as near to God as we want. God at that time was worshipped either in the Tabernacle - the glory of the Lord filled the Tabernacle (Exodus 40:34) or the Temple - the glory of God filled Solomon's temple (2 Chronicles 5:13-14). However, there was a restriction on the people, and to some extent on God Himself, and only a few had a personal relationship with Him.

The fact that many Christians, including leaders, were troubled by difficulties in their relationship with God as Father, was underlined in the renewal of the 1990s which began in Toronto, Canada, and impacted numerous places throughout the world with the message of the Father Heart of God. Despise countless people being challenged and changed then and subsequently, there are still many with an orphan heart mindset, who have not grasped the concept and personally experienced God as Abba Father. They would still default to distance when personal issues and other problems affect them, rather than bring Father God into their situation. Instead of living in the revelation of sonship, they behave more like slaves. You may identify with me in carrying unhealed childhood hurts, in that my father was at home, but emotionally absent. You will see later how this affected me from pre-birth into childhood. I was twenty years into my Christian faith before what had happened to me years ago was actually revealed. There is no doubt that the enemy had some kind of hold on me throughout all those years which to some extent affected me in my relationships, and in future leadership roles. Over the years, counselling, prayer ministry, and common sense have helped me understand my emotions, mindset, and spirituality, all of which led to my healing.

One of the keys to healing has to be the realisation that distance is a fundamental issue in our relationship with Father God. We often behave as though the veil which was rent in the Temple at the death of Jesus is still there. It is not, and we can be as close as we want to be to Abba Father.

The Tent of David - Closeness

David, a man after God's heart (1 Samuel 13:14, Acts 13:22) longed for the Ark of God to be brought back from Jerusalem, and even though this was inspired by God there were some difficulties, but finally, it returned. It was a time of great celebration for most of the nation, and the king's exuberance and joy were infectious, even though to some, including his wife, it was offensive (2 Samuel 6:15-16). At that time, the tabernacle of Moses was at Gibeon; it had all the objects and implements for sacrifice including the Holy of Holies, but the Ark of the presence of God was not there, and without it the Tabernacle was considered empty. It was expected that David would return the Ark to Moses' tabernacle, however, it would seem that David's decision started a revolution with tradition being overturned. Instead of returning the Ark to Moses' tabernacle, David pitched a tent for it in Jerusalem because he wanted it in the place where he knew God desired His dwelling place to be. It was never to return to Moses' tabernacle. Both tabernacles existed simultaneously in Israel, although David's tabernacle only remained for thirty-three years which was the period of his reign after which, Solomon became king and the temple was completed for God's presence to reside in.

The tent David erected was not a solid structure; it was an empty fabric shelter with side curtains that could open. There were no barriers, no veil, or sacrifices except it was home for the Ark. Anyone could enter because all had equal access, there was no exclusivity. After placing the Ark in the tent, David established an order of worship that continued through his reign. Singers and musicians were employed to praise, give thanks and prophesy before the Ark of God, (Psalms 132:7-8, 13-14). Amazingly, it was a twenty-four-hour radical kind of worship, and this lasted continuously for the whole of the reign of David. '*These are the singers, heads of the fathers' houses of the Levites, who lodged in the chambers, and were free from other duties; for they were employed in that work day and night,*' (1 Chronicles 9:33 NKJV). It was a dramatic departure from the established worship. In Moses' tabernacle, the Ark resided in the innermost room, the Holy of Holies, as well as being separated by a veil and certainly off-limits to everyone other than a few priests. It had all of the paraphernalia necessary except for one item which was the most important, the Ark of God.

The prophetic significance of David's tabernacle during this period was remarkable. It must have been quite a shock to the religious leaders and the people that conventional and orthodox religious worship and procedure were being ignored, and that a new and free type of worship was introduced by David. The tent became God's resting place where He was able to receive the people's worship and manifest His glory. Later in the Old Testament, one of the prophets declares that God would again restore the Tabernacle of David (Amos 9:11-12) something which was quoted by James in the council of Jerusalem as he unconditionally welcomed the Gentiles, who were turning to God, into the church (Acts 15:15-18) without having to submit to the Jewish law and its regulations. The external barriers that separated God from the people had gone. It was as though the prophetic word that Amos gave had leapt across the years to the time of Jesus, and James, with wisdom, discerned it.

David pitched a tent, placed the Ark of God in it, and encouraged the people to come and worship without any encumbrances. This event was a prophetic statement to the Jews at that time, for they were able to get close to God instead of having to worship at a distance. It was as though David had glimpsed something of the heart of God in His desire to be close to His creation.

Jesus pitched a tent, *'and the Word became flesh and made his dwelling among us. We have seen his glory, the glory of the one and only Son, who came from the Father, full of grace and truth,'* (John 1:14). The Greek word 'dwelling' means 'He pitched His tent,' or 'tabernacled.' David saw the unveiled presence of God as it would be in the future, as John did when he wrote about wanting the closeness of God revealed to us as it had been to him. Jesus too caused a revolution amongst the people, which included the lawyers and the various religious groups, with the revelation of the presence of God, particularly regarding how He related to His Father and how He introduced Him to the people as Abba. We are aware that in David's tent there was no barrier or veil preventing closeness to God, and one of the dramatic things which happened, just as Jesus died, was that the very large veil separating the people from God was torn from top to bottom giving us full access and closeness.

Distance Continued

After the death of David, things went back to the traditional procedure in the magnificent newly built Solomon's temple. The people were once again prevented from getting close to God, and even though the glory and presence of God were there, so were the restrictions, including the veil. This was about 1000 years before the coming of Jesus, and though Solomon's temple was destroyed by the Babylonians, it was rebuilt and later improved and refurbished. However, nothing changed until Jesus came. Amazingly, though, the very last words of the Old Testament, in the book of Malachi, are prophetic and so still meaningful to us today, '*behold, I will send you Elijah the prophet before the coming of the great and dreadful day of the Lord. And he will turn the hearts of the fathers to the children and the hearts of the children to their fathers, lest I come and strike the earth with a curse,*' (Malachi 4:4-5). This passage is still relevant and challenging.

Distance Challenged

Four thousand years after Genesis, the Word, Jesus, came and as we have seen, this was radical and completely different from the presence of God in the Tabernacle and then the Temple. However, Jesus, as the last Adam (1 Corinthians 15:22-24) came to begin a new Genesis, a new creation, John 1; to proclaim the Kingdom of God and introduce His Father to the people. Adam and Eve were vanquished by the temptation of the enemy, but Jesus overcame him. This made a way for closeness and for us to be part of the family of God. We will see later how this radical gospel was worked out by Jesus.

John 14:18

It was the Festival of Passover and Jesus was with His disciples. He was talking to them and preparing them for the future when He said something about how they could relate to the purposes of God as Father, which is crucial and pivotal for the orphan hearted. *'Jesus said to His disciples, I have to go away, I will not leave you as orphans, I will come to you,'* (John 14:18).

- 'I have to go away' - The disciples found it hard to understand that He had to go away to return.
- 'I will not leave you,' He is not going to abandon you.
- 'I will not leave you as orphans,' He will not leave you fatherless, comfortless, bereaved or forlorn (despondent or cast down). The New Testament Greek word for 'orphan' is 'orphanos,' meaning without a father, or an orphan.
- 'I will come to you' - He will never leave you or forsake you; He will always be there.

We need to be aware that these words are as powerful today as they were two thousand years ago. This promise is our reason for hope. Hope in biblical terms is translated as 'a confident expectation.' However, at that time, there was a sense of foreboding that affected the disciples, as they felt that something was about to happen. They did not understand that He was talking about the resurrection and coming of the Holy Spirit, who would introduce God as Abba Father to humanity, at Pentecost.

A New Relationship

Jesus was certainly not going to leave His friends like this. He wanted them, and ultimately us, to have the same kind of a relationship with His Father that He had, and which we could have through the coming of the Holy Spirit at Pentecost. *'Because you are his sons, God sent the Spirit of his Son into our hearts, the Spirit who calls out, Abba Father,'* (Galatians 4:6). The Holy Spirit reveals the Father to us, as sons and daughters, who speaks into our hearts, 'Abba Father.' The promise was fulfilled (I will come to you) and the Holy Spirit can now draw us close to our Heavenly Father. We can enter into that promise, not as orphans, but as Sons, knowing closeness and intimacy with our loving Father God. We are part of His new creation, indwelt by the Holy Spirit, carrying the life of Jesus and communing with the Father. The reason why the veil or curtain in the Temple in Jerusalem was torn from top to bottom as Jesus died, was not only to give us access to God but to give Him access to us!

From the Garden to the City

There is a clear connection between the Garden of Eden at the beginning, and the City of God at the end. God came to dwell with His two created humans in the Garden of Eden and will dwell with humanity in the New Jerusalem. The New Jerusalem reflects the Garden: The tree of life, the river, the precious stones, built into a city and God with His people, the Bride. It was always meant to be Heaven coming to Earth in glorious unity. Would this mean that the whole world will be the Garden with cities scattered around it? Interestingly, it was Cain who built the first city, (Genesis 4:11). Redemption will finally come to cities.

The fullness of God's purposes will finally be seen in the New Heaven and New Earth. The New Jerusalem will come down from heaven from God prepared as a Bride for her groom, and a voice from Heaven will declare, *'the dwelling place of God is among the people and He will live with them. They will be His people and He will be their God,'* (Revelation 21:1-4). Therefore, the city symbolises the church, the bride. We saw perfection at the beginning for a while, and we will live in perfection at the end. This is our *'blessed hope,'* (Titus 2:13).

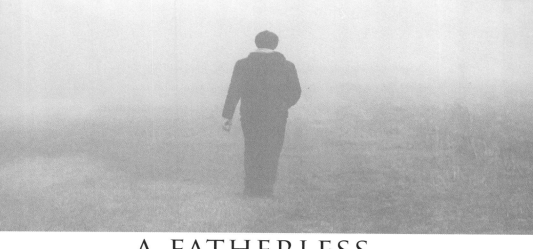

A FATHERLESS
GENERATION

There have been millions of children who, through death, divorce, or abandonment have lived without a father. There are many more whose fathers are physically present, but emotionally absent. If fatherlessness were classified as a disease, it would be a pandemic and treated as an international emergency. A father is not replaceable! We need loving, caring and supporting fathers. Children who grow up without a father may never experience that special sense of security and identity, with the precious feeling of closeness and belonging, which comes from having a father in the home. If that sense of closeness, affection, and love is not there, they may either retreat into self-protection or try to find it elsewhere. There are many mothers, however, who in my opinion are heroes, because of the way that they have nurtured their children despite the many difficulties they themselves have faced.

We saw in the previous chapter, 'Overview,' that the word 'Fatherless' is synonymous with 'Orphan.' You will recall that Jesus said to His disciples, 'I will not leave you as orphans [fatherless].' He was very aware of their position and He made a promise to them, which would meet their need of God's love as a Father. As we will see, in the forthcoming chapters, the revelation and experience of Abba Father is fundamental in the gospel of the Kingdom of God and is still relevant and powerful today. Therefore, the term 'Orphan,' is not only applicable to those who have, for whatever reason, never seen their fathers, but also to those whose fathers were at home but emotionally missing - as though he was not there.

As I write this, it is Father's Day in the UK, and I have read on social media many lovely comments about fathers. I am so touched by this, but I am also very aware of all those people who are not able to celebrate in the same way because a day like this evokes different kinds of memories. There are, of course, many children who are really thankful for their good, caring and loving fathers, with Father's Day being the appropriate and affirming way to express their love to them. Recently, I saw a card which said, 'You're the Dad everyone wishes they had.' There must be so many people who never had a father like this. I do wonder how some people cope with their memories as they rue Father's Day every year.

Family Trauma

The connection between fatherlessness, adolescent anti-social behaviour, and family structure, has been known to create significant social issues with long-term consequences, such as knife and gun crime, leaving people seriously injured or dead. I read an article in a national newspaper about a fourteen-year-old boy who had been knocked off his moped in the middle of the night and stabbed to death in East London, UK.

'The first thing after the first wave of revulsion and pity at a young life wiped out was, what was a kid of that age doing out at night illegally riding a moped. Poverty and racial inequality are comfortable answers always given when something like this happens. What is complained about is a lack of policing in problem areas yet at the same time there is criticism of the police for stopping and searching youngsters as it is described as racist? At least 50% of black children have no dad living at home. The problem is nobody wants to go there, for political reasons. The police do not want to go there, nor, do the social workers, the politicians or the black community itself, which then complains that it is becoming victimised. And so, it is never ever addressed. It seems the root causes cannot be addressed because the authorities are beholden to an ideology that precludes coming to a conclusion that could be construed as 'racist.... As you consider this would you not think: where was Mum? More to the point, where was Dad? If we do not ask these difficult questions, are we not complicit in these harrowing deaths?' (The Sunday Times, 13 January 2019)

There is currently is an epidemic of knife and gun crime that has led to numerous injuries and some deaths - something affecting many cities in the UK. Although the article highlights the dilemma of the Black Community in London, there are plenty of examples of white young men stabbing or shooting others. The issue is beyond race and culture, it is about family; about the absence of fathering, which denies cherishing, affection and intimacy. That is something that all children need.

Here is another illustration of fatherlessness, which, as you will see, is not connected to physical violence. This is because of the emotional and mental abuse and trauma, which is as difficult to handle by the victim as being shot or stabbed:

'By the time I was eight years old, I had already lost three fathers. Each one had abandoned me. Each one wounded me - emotionally and psychologically. At an age when I was supposed to be carefree, brimming with happiness and laughter, I frequently felt a deep sadness, an abiding loneliness. Nothing seemed powerful enough to permanently soothe the agony I felt. A girl abandoned by the first man in her life [her father] entertains powerful feelings of being unworthy or incapable of receiving any man's love. Even when she receives love from another, she is constantly and intensely fearful of losing it,' (unknown source).

The emotional damage caused will always bring consequences and more often will become generational. For example, if the victim becomes a mother herself, it is quite possible that her child will replicate her own experience, in anger, rejection and worthlessness, and the man she loves she will also fear. Even when parents are still alive, together or separated, their children are often affected by this orphan mentality and live accordingly. It is this that undermines their destiny and affects considerably their relationship with God. There is very little choice for the orphan hearted but attempt to make it alone. It is easy to become independent and self-sufficient, which causes him or her to close down, become withdrawn, and distant to preserve some semblance of control. Paradoxically, orphans hunger for affirmation, attention, and affection, which could come from the very people they are pushing away.

Father and Child

There are other ways a father could react to his children:

- Children who are deprived of a father are robbed of physical, emotional, intellectual, and spiritual well-being, which could affect them throughout their lives. Some fathers would find it very difficult to show affection and intimacy; they just do not know how to do it.
- Many children grow up never hearing their fathers say, 'I love you.'
- Instead, they hear high expectations: 'if you work a little harder, you can turn the exam grade B into an A.' 'If you keep practising, maybe next year you'll win first place.' These fathers may mean well, but they convey a message, 'you are not good enough.'
- Under pressure, and with frayed and unravelled emotions, a father's words can become a sword, cutting into the heart of the child, often causing long-term wounds.
- All too often, children feel they have to compete for their father's attention because he is preoccupied with more 'important stuff.'

- Children learn very quickly whether or not parents are willing to listen to them.
- A father's touch is crucial; healthy affection is so important.
- Children who have been on the receiving end of the pain of fatherlessness will mostly have a negative outlook toward God who is 'Father.

Without affirmation, attention and affection a child will not survive in a healthy relationship with their father.

1. Affirmation is not just an action, but the right words said in the right way. Children take literally every word spoken to them. Life and death is in the power of the tongue (Proverbs 18:21) therefore to use cheap words would contribute to undermining the status of the child. If children are used to, either an angry reaction, or the adult resorting to silence to show disapproval, the child will grow up believing that this is the only way to respond to conflict. If the father models a different way with humility, love and care, his children will know that they are loved for who they are not what they do.

2. Attention is about a child just wanting to be with their father, and often for no reason except for being close to them. Sometimes, if the child feels neglected, he or she will begin to demand attention, which will be perceived as bad behaviour. A father may be preoccupied with 'more important stuff,' but he can still listen. The child learns very quickly if he is willing to listen. When they reach adolescence and something important happens and a child needs to make a decision, they will find it difficult to talk if the father has not listened in the past. If he understands that his child needs cherishing and nourishing, he will choose to put aside any distractions so that he can give full attention. Doing that for a short time actually can save a lot of time. Children need to understand that they sometimes have to wait and, that is up to the father to build trust. If for example, he promises full attention in five minutes, he keeps his word.

3. It is possible for the word affection to be lost in the relationship that the child has with their father. It will show the child that there is no feeling of comfort and tenderness to feed on. Whatever is believed and said, the father has a clear ability to nurture the child. To say men do not have feelings or do not nurture is completely wrong and is deceptive. Arms are for hugging, and however small children are, there is a natural and impulsive need to hug and to hold. Even in teenage years, the father's touch is vital as it brings security and emotional stability. Fatherless children have no legacy of affection, sensitivity, or knowing the bonding of touch, and this will lead to dysfunctional attitudes, that will contribute to the development of the orphan heart and mindset.

The 'Elephant'

Could fatherlessness be the 'elephant' in the room?' There is something about human nature, at least in the UK, that with a hugely controversial issue, which is obvious is ignored, and could be construed as denial. This is 'The Elephant in the Room.' Fatherlessness in both society and the church needs to be understood and confronted with care and compassion so that the past, with its unhealed hurts, can be faced and healed.

God and a Fatherless Generation

There are consequences to being fatherless, and as we have seen they can be powerful in damaging lives. However, God is faithful in a faithless world and is a Father to a faithless generation. *'Can a mother forget her nursing child? Can she feel no love for the child she has borne? But even if that were possible, I would not forget you! See, I have written your name on the palms of my hands,'* (Isaiah 49:15-16, NLT). The fatherless can find mercy, for God's love as a Father is tender and unchangeable. In the extremity of his family deprivation, David said, *'when my father and my mother forsake me, then the Lord will take care of me,'* (Psalms 27:10, NKJV). This shouts that God is a God of affirmation, attention and affection, and we are invited to be close to Him. The first person in the Trinity is God the Father and the first phrase of the Nicene Creed (AD325), which is foundational to the church, underlines this: 'I believe in one God, the Father almighty.'

Revivals and renewals come and go and leave great legacies. From the very beginning of the last century, there have been powerful moves of God, such as the revival in Azusa Street, Los Angeles, California, USA in 1906, and from this came the worldwide Pentecostal movement. More recently, there was a renewal in Toronto, Canada, which began in 1994; this will be referred to in more detail later. It was powerful and effective, and enhanced the spiritual foundations of thousands of people globally, but there were still many churches and people groups who had never heard of it, and there were also those who rejected this renewal for various reasons. Maybe it is significant that the last prophecy in the Old Testament focused on turning the hearts of the fathers to the children and of the children to the fathers and came with the threat of a curse if it did not happen, (Malachi 4:5-6). Many people, including myself, give thanks to God for this life-changing experience. However, twenty-seven years on, I feel we are still in a minority. Here is a summary of the facts as I see in terms of fatherlessness:

- There are still many children and adults who have never met their fathers.
- Some children have lived, or are living with their fathers, but have had little or no fathering.
- There are countless children, of course, who have had good fathering.

However, there has been a lack of fathering in the church even though there have been and still are, good fathers. In saying this, there are still too many people who know God as a Father theologically, but not personally in a close relationship. We will see later that Jesus introduced His Father as Abba Father, the personal, loving and caring Father. He wanted everyone to have the same relationship with His Father as He had. God as a Father is more than a theology! No doubt we are thankful for having so much good information and teaching about God being a Father, but our lives are not built on theology; they are built on Jesus Himself, who reveals the Father to us through His Spirit. Is the church limited in its impact on people's lives because it does not see the fatherless as God sees them? Does the church realise that there are as many fatherless people in the church as there are outside of it? People look at the outward appearance, but God looks at the heart (1 Samuel 16:7). What is needed in the church and outside of it are fathers. 'even if you had ten thousand guardians [instructors, teachers] in Christ, you do not have many fathers, for in Christ Jesus I became your father through the gospel,' (1 Corinthians 4:15). The fatherless need to find their true identity, but who can help them do that other than those who have the revelation of God's heart themselves?

Paradox and Pain

We live in a generation of paradoxes, where people no longer have the desire or the ability to cope with difficult situations in which they find themselves. Loneliness is powerful and debilitating. It seems that home can be the most emotionless place to live, and one which can foster withdrawal into an isolation in which people create their own defence mechanisms, such as 'i do not need help,' 'I won't ask for help,' 'I won't admit failure,' or 'I will do it myself.' We learn to bury the hurt and pain related to this, but sometimes it seeps out or overflows in anger. All this may result in stress or emotional and physical problems. Many people then become unable, incapable, or may just refuse to share their feelings with fatherly men and women. No one can escape their history, and at some time, the past will become the present, as its wounds influence the way we think, behave and make decisions.

It is possible that we carry a reflection of what it means to be a father from our own fathers, and much of what we recall can be emotionless, neglectful, controlling and in some cases abusive experiences, which distort our image of God as a loving and caring Heavenly Father. If we have never had a healthy paternal relationship, we won't want to be close to anyone who is a father and a negative outlook of God as Father will develop. What Jesus did when introducing His Father was to show them the image of the Father as He saw it in His relationship with Him. At the cross, distance was dealt with and closeness with Abba Father was made accessible.

Esther - The Orphan Queen

There are two books in the Old Testament which are named after women. One is the Book of Esther who was an orphan yet became a queen. As well as being a dramatic story of hope with her adoption by Mordecai, it is also a narrative of the role Queen Esther had in saving the Jewish people in the Persian Empire from annihilation. Although God is not mentioned in this book, He was working like a Grand Master moving the chess pieces in the drama to fulfil His purpose.

To the orphan hearted this is a story of encouragement and hope.'I pray that God, the source of hope, will fill you completely with joy and peace because you trust in him. Then you will overflow with confident hope through the power of the Holy Spirit,' (Romans 15:13). The Apostle Paul is saying that God is not only the source of hope but the object of hope. Culturally speaking, hope is more of a wish or an optimistic desire with a measure of expectation that something will be fulfilled. There is no guarantee or basis for hope; biblical hope, however, is an optimistic assurance that rests on God's promises, which are undergirded by faith (Hebrews 11:1) which sustains us in the difficulties we face. Hope and promise are infinitely connected. A promise is a covenant or declaration that a person will do exactly as they say. If God has made a promise, the promise will be kept! He has said that, 'I will be a Father to you and you will be my sons and daughters, says the Lord Almighty, (2 Corinthians 6:18). The Psalmist declared that *'He is a Father to the Fatherless,'* (Psalms 68:5). As we see this worked out in the story of Esther, we can be confident that it can be the same in our personal story.

The Characters
Mordecai

Mordecai was among the Jews who went into exile (Esther 2:5-6). He was Esther's cousin, and after both her parents died, he adopted her as his own daughter (Esther 2:7). He became her father because he chose to; he loved her as a natural father would have loved her. Esther consistently asked him for counsel, advice and direction - in fact, she seemed to rely on him totally. There's probably no greater example of a man with such a father's heart adopting a child who is not his. He gave himself purely, as a loving and caring father would to his daughter. As we will see, it was he who encouraged her to speak to the king regarding her people, the Jews, and through that they were saved. Mordecai is a type of the Holy Spirit who gives us the benefit of His wisdom and knowledge and brings us into the Abba Father relationship.

The King Xerxes

Xerxes known as Ahasuerus, ruler over the Kingdom of Persia, was known as a tyrant and an abuser, and some described him as a cruel, self-indulgent womaniser! He was more attracted to Esther than he was to any of the other women in his harem, and showed her favour and approval (Esther 2:17).

Haman

He found favour with the king and was elevated and honoured above all his nobles; he was like a Prime Minister (Esther 3:10). He was proud and arrogant. He became an enemy of Mordecai and when he found out that he was a Jew, he planned to kill not only him but the whole of the Jewish nation.

Esther

- She was an orphan.

According to Scripture, Esther had no parents. She had lost both her father and her mother and was raised by her older cousin, and such was the relationship, that Mordecai became a father to her, and she a daughter to him, (Esther 2:7).

- She was taken captive.

  Esther was taken captive in two ways: When Jerusalem was destroyed by Nebuchadnezzar, she was among the people taken captive. Later when King Xerxes disposed of his wife, Vashti, Esther, with many other suitable young women, was forced to go to the king as a possible replacement, (Esther 2:8). Esther was young and very beautiful and found favour with everyone who saw her.

- She lived in exile.

  Esther and a significant number of the Jewish people lived throughout Persia having been deported from Judah. Although they had been granted freedom to return to their homeland, many of them stayed in exile rather than go back to a devastated Jerusalem.

- She was a sex slave to the King.

  Esther was chosen (taken) along with many others to be prepared for the king, (Esther 2:12-18) because the previous Queen, Vashti, was deposed, (Esther 1:12-22). The young women were taken one by one to sleep with the king and then added to the many other concubines. They were sex slaves with no status, and they were not allowed to be married or ever see the king again, unless he was pleased with them. The king was so captivated by Esther, much more than any of the other women, he immediately made her queen.

- She risked her life as a 'Saviour' of her people.

  Haman wanted to control everyone under his authority and insisted that they bow to him when he approached or passed by. Mordecai refused to do this. Haman was enraged, and when he found out that Mordecai was a Jew he hatched a plan to not only dispose of Mordecai but also to annihilate the whole Jewish nation throughout the Persian Empire, (Esther 3:5-6). Haman persuaded the king to create a law which would lead to the destruction of the Jews. Soon Mordecai found out and felt that the situation was helpless, however, Esther was told it, and in her position as Queen began to help. There was a problem however: she could only see the king if he invited her, and if she approached the king without being summoned, she would be put to death. There was only one exception, and that would be for the king to extend the golden sceptre and spare her life, (Esther 4:11). Mordecai responded in faith and encouragement, saying that if deliverance does not come from you it will come from another, but perhaps you were made queen for such a time as this, (Esther 4:13-14). Esther told Mordecai, '*go and gather together all the Jews of Susa and fast for me. Do not eat or drink for three days, night or day. My maids and I will do the same. And then, though it is against the law, I will go in to see the king. If I must die, I must die*' (Esther 4:16).

In response to Mordecai's plea, Esther was prepared to lay down her life for him and the Jewish people. God was with her, 'it was for such a time as this,' and it was God who destined her for this influential position she had with the king. On the third day she went into the court and the king saw her standing there (Esther 5:1). This was the moment of the life or death decision. Amazingly, the king was so pleased to see her that he offered her half his kingdom before she spoke. Through an astonishing series of events, the king heard the truth, Haman was executed, and Mordecai was given his position. The Jewish people across the Empire were given freedom and protection because the orphan queen was willing to give her life for her people.

Personal Application

This remarkable narrative is a message within a message because there is so much which can be personally applied. Esther's story demonstrates a powerful incentive to believe that God can bring freedom even when things look impossible. God took an orphan to fulfil His purposes even though her whole life was effectively stolen. God used a woman and took her into exile in a foreign nation where she was powerless and somewhat invisible due to gender and culture, and through very difficult circumstances made her the Queen of an Empire where she was able to influence the King to save a nation! God gave her such amazing favour with a despot king who granted her request, something which could have cost her life.

Summary

- An orphan hearted person was used by God to make an impossible situation possible.
- Her cousin, Mordecai, adopted her and became a father to her, and she a loving daughter to him.
- Mordecai's commitment to Esther cam be seen in the way that he counselled and guided her with wisdom, revelation and encouragement. This speaks clearly of the Holy Spirit and the way He will bring us into all truth and reveal Abba Father to us.
- Esther's strength brought her through the abuse of, quite frankly, an environment of sex trafficking at the king's court. Many orphan hearted people have been abused verbally, mentally, emotionally, physically, sexually and spiritually. She refused to let these very difficult circumstances drag her away from the higher purpose in her life.
- Haman, the King's Prime Minister, was the enemy of Mordecai and the Jewish people he conspired to destroy. Did not Jesus say, '*the thief's purpose is to steal and kill and destroy. My purpose is to give them a rich and satisfying life,*' (John 10:10, NLT). So, an orphan hearted person can overcome the wiles of the enemy because God is with them as He was with Esther and Mordecai.
- The words from Mordecai, 'for such a time as this,' were crucial to encourage Esther to move into God's purposes. These words are

as significant now as they were then.

- Esther showed passion and resolve to influence the king to change his mind when she said, '*I will go in before the king, which is against the law to do, and if I perish, I perish,*' (Esther 4:16). We can be as determined as Esther and overcome the orphan heart mindset, which will keep us as slaves when God sees us as sons.

- 'It was the third day' (Esther 5:1) when Esther went to see the king. This term appears many times throughout scripture and is very significant. The third day denotes resurrection and always looks towards the raising of Jesus. We are resurrection people who live in the assurance that death did not hold Him down, but He broke out to bring a new day, a new era, a new society in a Kingdom, which is not of this world. What Esther was doing was looking beyond the realisation that her people could have been destroyed, to the fact that they would be saved, which juxtaposes resurrection. Her people began a new redeemed life; we live in the power of His resurrection today and every day, not as orphans and slaves, but as sons and daughters.

- Esther was in danger when she entered the court of the king. She had to stand and wait for the king to receive her or reject her. Esther knew she could die, but when he held out the golden sceptre, she knew all she had permission to approach and touch the tip of the sceptre, (Esther 5:1-2). Doing this was a way to show her gratitude to the king for his grace and favour, and her reverence and submission to him. The sceptre was a symbol of absolute authority, and as it was extended, it meant that the king had given Esther the right to come forward and petition him. She knew then that the king had shown her favour, (Esther 5:6). Haman was executed for treason.

- The word sceptre is also used to symbolise God's rule and reign, '*your throne, O God, will last for ever and ever; a sceptre of justice will be the sceptre of your kingdom,*' (Psalms 45:6, Hebrews 1:8). The sceptres of earthly kings were tainted by injustice, but the sceptre of the Kingdom of God is one of mercy, grace and justice. It is a sign of the authority and sovereignty of God and His Kingdom. The glorious difference is that we do not have to wait to be called to enter at the whim of a king who may receive us or execute us! As we turn to our King, we come with the confidence that we are already accepted. We have the right to enter God's presence and stay there because Jesus has already paid the price by laying down His life for us. '*So let us come boldly to the throne of our gracious God. There we will receive his mercy, and we will find grace to help us when we need it most,*' (Hebrews 4:16 NLT). '*We can take heart because God is with us, and if God is for us who can be against us,*' (Romans 8:31).

- Esther's God of hope is our God too.

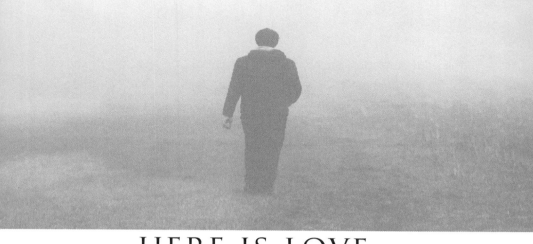

HERE IS LOVE

During one of the darker moments of my life, I had two revelations. Chris and I were in bed talking when she brought up the subject of my family. The first was the consequence of a family feud, which led to Chris being told everything about my early years and my parents' circumstances that had all been deliberately hidden from me. The second revelation was that my Father God really does love me and longs to get closer. That night He did.

The New Testament Greek word for 'revelation' is 'apokalupsis', meaning unveiling or something hidden but now revealed - in other words, the disclosing of a reality that has been concealed. What occurred was that events at the beginning of my life concerning my parents and myself, were deliberately hidden and consequently there were lies and deception for many years. It was one of those moments when the light comes on or the curtains open wide and the sunlight pierces the darkness. It was a time of great surprise with shock, trauma, and for a while profound pain. I will never forget the suddenness of it all, and I am talking about something that happened well over thirty-five years ago. It was so meaningful, so relevant and pertinent to my life, yet it is still so clear that it could have been last night!

The word 'revelation' can be used in a number of ways and I have found two that fit my situation. It is a revealing of truth. *'Then you shall know the truth and the truth will set you free,'* (John 8:32 NIV). Once I had received the truth of my past and what happened to me I was able to take responsibility and pursue healing which led to freedom. The word can also be understood as God revealing who He is to humankind. It was Jesus who said those words and through Him, I came into an experience of the Father's love that I had never had before. You may wonder if that is all - surely you knew that God loved you? Well, of course, He does, we all know that! Yet as much as I thought I did know that in a theological way, the actual experience that evening made me realise the superficiality of my belief. I was brought up in my Christian faith to love Jesus. There was an obvious emphasis on Jesus in the Pentecostal Church in Bristol in the mid-1960s, and I committed my life to Him there. The main focus was that He was 'our Saviour, our Baptiser, our Healer and our coming King.' These are good foundational truths, but there was little emphasis regarding the love of the Father other than the introduction to prayers often being, 'our loving Heavenly Father' or 'Almighty God.' Some of you will recall that. However, it was as though God as a Father was distant.

Of course, we knew wonderful scriptures such as, *'Behold what manner of love has the Father has bestowed or lavished upon us that we might be called the sons or children of God,'* (1 John 3:1 NJKV). However, I had no context in which to apply that, as the scripture was never taught in a way that encouraged us to respond and receive the Father's love. Now, I am clearer as to the meaning of this due to a greater appreciation of the Father's love to me personally, particularly when I apply myself to the text. I am loved, accepted and I feel safe and secure in Him which is amazing! It is summed up in these words, *'he who dwells in the shelter of the Most High will abide in the shadow of the Almighty'* (Psalms 91:1 ESV). This is the closeness of the presence of God. The Hebrew term for 'presence' can be translated 'face.' I would consider, over the years, that we have had only a superficial understanding of the presence of God. Of course, it is talked about and we feel His presence, but when you actually consider the term His face, which is so connected to His presence, I realised that very little was said about how close the Father is.

What this did, looking back now, was leave a gap in my personal and intimate relationship with Father God - something that took me many years to realise. Also, my childhood issues brought their own restrictions. I am now aware that I knew very little about the relationship that Jesus had with His Father, which is such a key in our relationship with both of them. The problem is that we can all say the Father loves us, for this is taken for granted but can we say, 'I know He **really** does love me.' Do we have the kind of personal intimacy that He wants with us? Certainly, for me, that intimacy was not there.

On that eventful evening, I had an amazing and spontaneous encounter with Father God through the Holy Spirit coming and revealing His love to me. It was truly supernatural and looking back I have had some effective healing, which you could not manufacture or even conceive, yet it was real to me and to my wife, Chris, who was next to me watching and helping me go through it. It was this experience that brought light and understanding to my past and impetus to my future. It did not matter that I was one of the leadership team of a large church and I had a growing itinerant ministry. What did matter was what was going on inside me. It was almost a 'eureka' moment, a sort of 'I have got it,' where everything begins to make sense and fall into place. What began was a glorious healing process, which I am sure is not quite finished as I am still flawed and frail. I intend talking more about this key moment in my life in more detail later. Amidst the pain and tears, a deep conviction of the Father's love began and even now as I am writing this I feel quite exhilarated with a joy and peace within and I now know that I cannot do anything to make God love me more, or do anything to make God love me less, so I rest in that. This experience is the focal point of my story and provides the backdrop to the whole area of the orphan heart and the orphan spirit.

A few years ago, two things happened that affected me quite dramatically. One of these was the death of my mother. She was the last of our four parents to die. Chris said, 'we really are orphans now,' which strangely touched me, although I knew my orphan heart had been very much healed many years previously. My father had died twelve years before my mother and after his death, Sybil (my mother) and I developed a deeper relationship, which was good as I had never experienced that before. Although she lived two hundred miles away, I think we saw more of her than at any time since we were married. I recall those days with fondness and joy. All of this helped to bring closure to the distance (I do not mean geographical) I felt when both parents were still alive. Of course they loved me, but so much was missing in our relationship. Some of that was restored through those the times I had with my mother. This area is foundational with regard to the orphan heart and will be considered in a subsequent chapter.

The other point came was when I watched a TV programme about children being sent to Australia after the Second World War. It gave me quite a shock as I realised that, in view of the circumstances my parents were in at the time, it could have been possible for me to be sent there. After the Second World War, the British Government ordered the migration of tens of thousands of its children, severing all connection with family and the past, to various countries of the British Empire. The nation's orphanages were emptied of a generation of children, some as young as four, who were shipped to Australia, Canada, and other Commonwealth countries. Often the children were told that their parents were dead when they were very much alive. When circumstances changed so that it was possible to have their own children back, parents were told they had been adopted. The policy continued until 1967 and in 1986 this horror was finally exposed. Apparently, the aim was to populate the Empire with 'good British stock,' but a serious violation of human rights took place, and the pain and abuse to the children and their families was unimaginable. Culturally speaking, at that time unmarried mothers were shunned, despised and rejected and children born to them were stigmatised.

I was born in an 'unmarried mothers home', and I have no doubt steps were being taken to either get me adopted or ultimately sent to an orphanage. If that had happened, it would have been during this period, and I might well have been sent to another country. Thankfully, that did not happen, and I will describe what did happen in my own life when my father found out that I was born and how my mother suffered. However, what transpired, was that my parents kept me. Amidst all of the traumas of that time, I can look back and see the caring and protecting hand of God on me and I am so thankful, as I could have so easily have been one of those children who was taken and sent away to another country. Both these things affected me quite dramatically, for, as is so often the case in the death of a loved one, memories surfaced, photos of the past appeared and all this, together with family talk, brought more clarity to me.

'I was seized by the power of a great affection' is a commonly used saying these days and for me, this was very much the case. It is as though God himself, as a fantastic loving heavenly Father, has pursued me, got hold of me and lavished His love upon me. He actually cares for me and has feelings of warmth, affection, and care toward me, His child.

The teachings of most religions say that we have to do something; to perform in a certain way to attain acceptance, yet the God of the heaven and earth, our loving Heavenly Father, has come down to where we are in Jesus to bring us to where He is. This is the incarnation, God Himself made flesh to dwell among us so that we might receive His love. I have realised that we talk about going to heaven, yet the scripture is clear about God coming to earth to be with us. Perhaps we need to be more aware that actually God is in search of humanity for love and relationship. He is in pursuit of us! He wants to be amongst us. The heart and core of the message of Jesus was that the Kingdom of God would be established on earth. It is not so much about us wanting to get to heaven - it is more about Him coming to earth. God is passionate about coming to earth. He came into a garden; He dwelt in the Tabernacle and the Temple. He came in the person of Jesus, He released the Holy Spirit and finally, we read at the end of the book of Revelation about the New Jerusalem coming to earth from heaven when there will a garden once more.

Religion insists that we have to find God but work to find Him, which leads to a performance mindset whereby we try so hard, yet never quite reach our goal. However, we need to know that our goal has come down to us! *'And the word became flesh and dwelt or tabernacled among us and we have seen his glory'* (John 1:14 ESV). The Message translation puts it like this: 'The Word became flesh and blood, and moved into the neighbourhood. We saw the glory with our own eyes, the one-of-a-kind glory, like Father, like Son, generous inside and out, true from start to finish.'

Jesus came to make his dwelling place with us in order to show us His Father's love. It took a long time for me to find answers and satisfy my longing for the depth in my relationship with God that eluded me. Yet today I am much closer than ever! I now know it is because the Father wants a loving relationship with us through His Son Jesus and by the power of the Spirit.

The Kingdom of God is founded upon a personal relationship. Jesus said, *'the Kingdom of God is at hand'* (Matthew 4:17 ESV). In other words, it is so very near it can already be seen and felt. This kingdom is revolutionary and radical based on love but it is not empire - founded on power and control. It really is the power of love not the love of power. Yet I know personally that many hurt and wounded people are good at empire but not so good at kingdom because I was one of them an orphan...with parents!

It is important to realise that we are on a journey. It is linear, yet so often we go around in circles when it is actually necessary to go forward, progressing from one stage to another. God said to Moses, *'you have stayed long enough at this mountain'* (Deuteronomy 1:6 ESV). He told him that it was time to move into the fullness of your promised inheritance. I think it is time for both the church and individuals to do just that. Surely we want to go into our 'Promised Land' or our 'Land of Promises.' There is so much more that the Father has for us. I have seen the hand of God on my life right from before the beginning, but in all honesty, the greatest event in my life was when I found God as a loving Father and the Lord Jesus as Saviour and friend. Being free from the orphan curse releases us to fulfil our destiny.

It is possible that you may already have been challenged by your own memories. What should you do with them? It is not difficult to ignore, deny or push them away. The truth is that we never bury our memories dead, they remain alive, deep within us and they certainly do continue to affect us. Barbara Streisand sings in the beautiful song, 'The way We Were,' relating to our memories, 'what's too painful to remember, we simply choose to forget' (Barbara Streisand. *The Way We Were*, Colossiansombia, 1974).

I finally realised that choosing to forget is not expecting the memories to simply disappear never to return and never to affect us again, for refusing to admit the truth and reality of our memories is simply denial. Forgetting is a somewhat deceptive concept because the memories are actually still there but they can be healed through the loving-kindness of the Father in the power of the Spirit.

So, as I tell my story, I invite you to come into it with me and to begin to realise that, as I am utterly loved by Father God, so you are too. It is without doubt, that orphans can know that they are the sons and daughters of their Heavenly Father.

ENCOUNTER

Am I Too Ordinary and Too Distant to Have An Encounter with God?

Waiting at the bus stop in the Bristol City centre was becoming a frustration. I had left school after 'A' levels and started work in the City Valuers Department of the Bristol City Council, UK and the following year would see me studying for my Chartered Surveyors exams. The interesting thing is that I had had no idea there was such an office. I had applied to join the Local Authority, and after acceptance, I was told that I was going to work at the Valuers Department. They were responsible for the purchase of property on behalf of the Council for the various planning schemes and other redevelopments in the city. Actually, it was my father who 'told' me to apply. Little did he suspect the outcome. If he had, he would have shut the door in my face and I never would have met Chris.

Our office department had recently become entangled in local authority bureaucracy as they changed the time of starting and leaving work. Strange really as it was only a few minutes later in the evening but it meant I missed my usual bus! This was very annoying at the time, but on a later bus, I saw someone I had more than noticed over the past few weeks. Not long after I started work in September 1964, I became involved in a certain ritual with my new-found friends. We had a lot in common including any kind of sport.

Most lunch hours, we would go to an empty ground floor office for an hour or so and look at and comment on the young ladies that would pass us from their offices in the commercial part of Bristol to the shopping centre. This was not a regular feature, and probably only happened for a few weeks. One day as we were looking out of the window, something happened to me. I saw her! To me, it was quite an encounter. She might as well have been gliding along the pavement dressed in a shimmering white gown bedecked with precious jewels. Bells went off inside, my heart pounded and no doubt I uttered a comment or two, all above board of course... I won't tell you what the boys said. Oh yes, they noticed my reaction and did not let me forget! I was caught, something happened in my heart right away and the funny thing was I began to see her, again and again, walking through town and I knew she saw me. This went on for a while, but nothing was ever said between us.

The Bus

Missing my usual bus suddenly paled into insignificance for as I was impatiently waiting for the next one, I saw her. Amazingly, there she was, waiting for the same bus as me. It was fantastic. I almost died and went to heaven, and in a state of nervous excitement got on the bus behind her. She went downstairs and I ascended to the smoking room. Remember those buses? Of course, I was inquisitive as to where she got off, and it turned out to be the stop before mine. As she got off and the bus turned the corner to the left, I looked down towards her and she looked up. She noticed me. What was I to do? What could I do?

This went on for, well, it seemed ages but it was probably a few weeks at the most. We did not speak, but only glanced at each other. I did enjoy it when the bus was full, as I made sure I was standing next to where she was sitting and of course leaned into her with the movement of the bus, especially around corners. I became a victim of many jokes at the office and finally, I came up with what I thought was a good plan to take, or at least attempt to take, the relationship further. Discussing it with my friends, I decided to get off the bus at her stop, then walk up behind her and walk with her for a short distance, which would give me enough to give me time to talk to her and ask her out. When I eventually did this, she did not realise that I got off of the bus and was behind her. As she usually did, she looked up, but I was not there. She heard footsteps behind her and looked around. I think that the reason she ran off at speed from me was the shock of seeing me behind her, when I should have been on that bus! Yes, she really ran away from me, leaving me in panic, embarrassment and humiliation. Fortunately, I made a hasty exit along a road to my right. However I had a problem. How was I going to explain this farce to the guys at work the next day? The mockery! The only answer was that could give me hope was to try again. I found out later that Chris regretted running away and wanted contact. So I did, with more than some apprehension approach her again, and this time she did not run away, much to my relief! We talked as we walked and all that I remember is asking her out on a Saturday when I knew I was free. She said no, and would not tell me why. 'What's going on,' I thought, 'I go through all of this to ask her out and she says no!' Eventually, she told me that she was going to church. I was ok about that, but she said she was singing there and she had to wear a hat! She did not want me to see her in the hat. I said, 'I want to come, please.' She could not refuse. Apparently, I said, 'I am sure you'll look lovely in a hat.' Funny really because I think I evangelised myself! But what would the guys say at work? Not a lot because I did not tell them...

I had met a Christian, but not one in the way I had understood. This one actually lived what she believed and talked about God differently and Jesus was real to her, like a friend. As I looked back, I have thought about whether we are we part of a greater strategy, and whether meeting Chris in this unusual way was preplanned? Even today I have no idea. Maybe it is the wrong question as I do have a free will and I chose to follow her, however, all I know is that she, Chris, who became my wife, was soon to introduce me to a spiritual dimension that would blow me away. There's no doubt in my mind that God was behind all of this... He was about to touch an ordinary (well fairly ordinary) young man with His presence. Even today, it still amazes me — that this happened to someone like me. It has to be God's grace and mercy - His favour on my life.

I have found an interesting verse hidden away in the book of Ecclesiastes that says that, 'He, [God] has set eternity in our hearts.' (3:11). This is intriguing, as it might mean that everyone, Christian or not, has an eternal deposit within. It is clear to many that God has deeply rooted the idea of eternity in every human heart. I believe that too, and as we connect with people wherever we are, this eternal influence within us can touch them. We really do have more within us than we think we have. I have no doubt that when I began to draw close to Chris, my spirituality began to come alive as 'eternity' within me stirred. Of course, the accusation came later that, 'you have become a Christian just to get to Chris.' But that was not true for something in my spirit responded to God, and Chris became the channel for that. Did I fall in love with her? What do you think?

At that time I was a great fan of Elvis Presley and had many of his vinyl (it was a long time ago) records including some I could not relate to, which were his gospel recordings. I used to sit or lie on the floor sort of swooning and singing along in my Bristolian Southern American drawl with the left side of my upper lip arched, just like Elvis, well I thought so! I knew most of the words including those of the gospel songs. Of course, I had no idea what they meant, but even then I knew something deep inside was being affected.

Another Encounter!

The meeting I asked to go to with Chris took place in a very large post World War Two housing estate in the south of Bristol; there were masses of people living there with few amenities. I remember walking up to this strange corrugated hut type building and could just hear some singing coming out of the door. What happened next totally spooked me! As we walked along the path and got closer, I realised I knew the words and tune of the song. It was one of the gospel songs that Elvis has sung, which I had listened to many times at home. The song was 'It is no secret what God can do' and I knew the words of the chorus!

'It is no secret what God can do
What he's done for others he'll do for you
With arms wide open he'll pardon you
It is no secret what God can do'
(Stuart Hamblin. *It Is No Secret What God Can Do*, RCA, 1957).

I could hardly believe what was going on. What was happening? Why should they be singing that song? It was more than strange; it was disturbing, yet I felt a measure of comfort, but I did not know what to do...Now, I realise it was another encounter with God, which affected me deeply and I could not explain it. I think I touched something of the Kingdom Of Heaven that night, especially when the speaker talked as though he knew everything about me. I said to Chris as we waited for the bus, 'how did he know all of that that about me, I have never met him.' It was not long though before I saw him again, and as he preached the same thing happened; it was as though I was the only person there! Before long, Chris and I were going out together and two further things happened.

She met my parents and they liked her although things changed, at least with my father, when I became a Christian. For some reason, my mother wanted to show Chris our family photographs. Typical mother and so embarrassing! She found the Christmas print of me with others around the tree in our primary school, where a child was taken from each classroom to sit under the Christmas tree to represent the school. Chris looked at it and said, 'that is me.' So there we were, about six years old, brought together, from different classes to sit under the tree. Was that a coincidence or part of the drama? With Chris, I began to attend a Pentecostal Church with Chris on Sunday evenings.

Confirmation

Going into that strange Pentecostal church building in South Bristol and being impacted even before I got through the door made me think of another strange experience that I had when I was around eleven years old. My friends and I went to confirmation classes at the local Anglican church in South Bristol, St Cuthbert's. Why, I do not know, it just sort of happened, but, regretfully we spent more time out of the class than in due to our ability to disturb everyone and the vicar quite often threw us or me out of the lesson. When threatened that we would be banned from the ceremony, we calmed down. St Cuthbert's was a typical Anglican church, one that had a good past with evangelicalism, but for many years had become very dull. In more recent times St Cuthbert himself has become one of my Celtic heroes and his exploits in and around Lindisfarne on the East coast of England, north of Newcastle were awesome, both during in his life and yes, even after his death. Many were healed praying at his grave, for the presence of God there was both heavy and effective.

Some Sunday evenings I had more fun counting the woodworm holes in the pew in front, than anything else the service could offer. It was pretty dire, but we stuck it out. I often wondered why; now I know. The evening arrived when we were to be confirmed. Even after all these years, I remember the event so well. Looking back it was another of those encounters when God comes and reveals his presence. I have had a number of these throughout my life, I think from birth and into my early years, as we will see later, and this was another one and oh my, what a shock it was... I do not recall very much except kneeling at the altar rail at the front of the church waiting for the Bishop to come down the line. Suddenly it was my turn, and I looked up to see a shock of white hair under a funny hat and large hands that were placed on my head whilst prayers were said, as I was welcomed into the Anglican Church through confirmation. As the Bishop laid his hands upon my head, I felt something course powerfully through my body. It was like an intense electric shock coming through his hands. It stunned me, shook me and impacted me. 'What was that?' I thought, 'what is going on?' It was such an amazing encounter that I can still almost feel it today. I now understand much more about that time. I know that I felt the power of the Holy Spirit through the Bishop. Perhaps it was the Kingdom of God coming to me! I think the event showed me that God's hand was on my life and great things, which I had no idea of then, were going to happen in the future. I went to the local library the very next day and decided to read a book that has directed my life ever since. Why borrow a Bible from the library when surely there was one at home? I did not wait to ask, I just did it on impulse and I think my parents just thought I was having a strange moment that would probably pass quickly. It did not and although I immersed myself into my teenage years, I never forgot that moment of encounter and never will.

Could it be that God was interested in me? It felt like it, as the God of Heaven and Earth, He cared enough to consider me and show me His presence in such a dramatic way.

'It is as if a great drama is being enacted. History is the theatre, the world is the stage, and the church members in every land are the actors. God himself has written the play, and he directs and produces it. Act by act, scene by scene, the story continues to unfold,' John Stott, *The Message of Ephesians*. (IVP, 1979, pg 123-124).

That is just about where I feel I was, somewhere in this drama, not yet a Christian, but definitely in the play! Does God care that much? Does God care about me that much? My experience says a resounding yes.

Encountered and Impacted by God

For some reason, I thought it would be really nice if I went to church with Chris and attended the Mount of Olives Pentecostal Church on Blackboy Hill in Bristol. We went there on many Sunday evenings and I began to get used to the way the services went. The singing was hearty and there was an occasional 'Hallelujah.' I began to think seriously about my own spiritual health and through many talks with Chris, I knew I wanted to follow Jesus for the rest of my life. I remember one Sunday evening in 1965, an appeal was made to those who wanted to become Christians. A public confession was necessary. I think I went through a lot of torment because something deep inside was urging me to give my life over to Jesus. I knew I needed to be cleansed inside but it was a battle.

A Son?

Then the evening came, it was 28 March 1965, and I made the decision to follow Jesus. I actually put up my hand when the appeal was made and amazingly the same feeling of the previous encounters came to me again. It was so powerful, coursing through my body and I knew something life-changing had happened. I now know it was a clear manifestation of the presence of God. The Pastor, Robert Fairnie, saw my raised hand and said, 'young man come out to the front.' Not only did I freeze but also my feet turned into lead. I could not move and it seemed ages before I was able to. Probably it was thirty seconds but that seemed an age. Finally, I moved out and that public response settled something regarding the future of my life. The Pastor took me to another room, talked to me, opened the Bible and read, *'But as many as received him, to them gave he power or the right to become the sons of God, even to them that believe on his name,'* (John 1:12). This became a key scripture to me as I repented, believed and received power to be a son or child of God. I remember going home and lying on my bed and thinking, 'what has happened to me?' Yet deep inside I knew. I did not know then how to explain it, but I knew that I knew, and this became a sustaining factor when my father threatened to throw me out of the home for being a Christian.

However something was not explained, something was missing, something that years later I found out about. It revolves around the word 'son.' It was as though there was a block. I responded to Jesus as my Saviour and Lord and began a relationship with him as my friend. Later I could say with passion 'I love him,' yet I was not aware of what being a son meant. If I had the right to be a son, it would mean I had the right to know the Father of the Son. Yet at that time God seemed distant as the Pentecostal Church emphasised knowing Jesus as Saviour and Lord and the Holy Spirit as Baptiser, yet nothing was said about God being a Father, the Father's love or the Father heart. It just was not talked about. It was many years later that I realised I could have as close a relationship with Him as Jesus had. That happened when the family secrets about me unravelled and I had that wonderful healing revelation. There was another reason why God as a Father seemed far away and that was to do with the role of my parents in the way they brought me up. In many ways, they were distant to me. There was no doubt they loved me but they very rarely showed it in affection, intimacy, and closeness. It was only in the last few years that I experienced something of that with my mother. My father had died years previously, and Sybil (my mother) and I became closer than we'd ever been before.

Kissed

Somewhere around the middle of the Bible is a fantastic love story probably written by Solomon and known as his Song of Songs. There are some challenging interpretations of the text, including the depth of a personal and intimate relationship that a man can have with a woman. However, there is another interpretation and to me, it has a very special meaning. The first line of the second verse of chapter 1 has deeply impacted me, as it underlines the longing in my own heart for a close and meaningful relationship with Father God. It is a dramatic and impulsive statement, which is enough to shatter the religious illusion that you cannot get close to Almighty God. *'Let him kiss me with the kisses of his mouth, for your love is more delightful than wine,'* (Song of Songs 1:2). Go beyond the physical, the erotica, to a kiss of spiritual intimacy, which emanates from the heart of God, who in Himself is hungering after a deeper walk with His children. This kiss is an expression of intimacy, a direct and personal expression of love. This is the cry of the bride with a heart burning with desire. The bride's expression is one of longing for intimacy, for she is not satisfied with a relationship from a distance. She desires close contact. Kissing is close, face-to-face relationship. This is the kiss of spiritual union, complete spiritual union, and a union of God's Spirit to our spirit. It is the evolution of the believer from a place of need to a place of satisfaction. This is not something for only a few moments or even hours but should be continual and consistent; it is direct communication and communion as we abide with God - a divine kiss, an awakening of the heart with His power and love. The Rabbis talk about the kiss as God kissing us with His word.

That is what I longed for, but it is what I missed for many years.

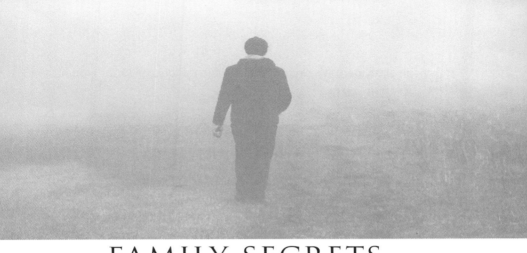

FAMILY SECRETS

Funeral

Some months before my mother died, I had a feeling that I would be speaking at her funeral. I wanted to honour her, particularly regarding those early years of my life when she went through some very difficult circumstances, and to draw a line under some events that were never spoken of in the family. As I began to talk at the funeral, I said that there were two things I had never understood - one of them was the actual date of their wedding anniversary. Usually, wedding anniversaries are celebrated, my parents' never was. I recall Chris asking about it at times, but Sybil, my mother, always managed to change the subject, so I never actually knew how long they had been married. Secondly, I had always wondered why I had duplicate, and much smaller birth certificate, which had none of the usual details on it. I remember very clearly seeing this certificate a few times, but I was always given an excuse about the original being lost. Again I never asked about it. Of course, every parent is different in the way they handle what they think their child may or may not need to know. Some perhaps would, for whatever reason, feel it better not to talk about the past if it is embarrassing or too painful. I now know my parents had many secrets and many of those secrets revolved around me. All the details of my early years, and those of my parent's circumstances were deliberately kept hidden.

Family Feud

They probably still would be hidden if it was not for a family feud that occurred in the mid 1980s, when a cousin who was very much part of the problem decided vindictively to tell Chris the family secret. My cousin's motives were not good, to say the least, although there is no doubt in my mind that God turned it into something good and began a process of healing in me that has been very effective. Chris, though, was placed in a massive dilemma. She knew she had to tell me, but was not sure how or when to do so. The problem was that it could bring division between my parents and I. The whole relationship might explode and be so damaging; there were consequences to be considered. Chris wisely waited - actually for quite a while. Then one evening, as we were chatting in bed she told me all she knew. I believe I had two revelations that night. Of course, I had no prior knowledge of what Chris was going to say, so I was very shocked and traumatised by it, but it turned out to be an amazing God moment. In the release of pain, there was also a mixture of anger and sadness. I wondered why they had never told me but had hidden it from me for so many years. It was a close moment for Chris and me, as she held me through my tears and pain. Finally, a deep sense of healing came as I began to perceive God's love. It was a love that seemed, at the time, to be so tangible. I do not know how long it was for, but I still remember it, as if it were last night! It was so amazing, and it was like a new chapter in my life was beginning. It changed me and inspired me to tell others. That revelation of what happened to me was necessary to open me to the revelation of the closeness and healing of God's love; one revelation was necessary to bring me to the other.

Confrontation

I realised later that Chris and I were the only ones who hadn't known in our family - the whole family knew. Even my cousins were aware of it and we were very close, but I had always been kept in the dark. However much later one of my lovely cousins filled in many of the gaps for me. She was a fantastic help and without her, this book could never have been written. Part of my shock was because of how deliberately hidden the whole thing had been. We decided to visit my parents and tell them what had happened. It was not easy, but they did need to know. We talked and they listened. There was not much, if any, outward response from them. In fact, I cannot remember them saying anything. I am convinced that my father kept his anger, particularly towards the cousin who had told Chris, hidden. Nothing was ever said about it again until after my father had died, when surprisingly my mother gave me the missing birth certificate. She had had it all the time and I reckon she had always wanted to give it to me. I saw that it had recorded her married name to her first husband. I think that all that was typical of how my father handled things, and my mother had to just go along with him. We talked about it a little to Sybil then, and there is no doubt that she was relieved that she still had a relationship with us. That relationship actually deepened and I was thrilled. Through it all, it was certainly the grace and love of God that sustained Chris and I. Forgiveness is so releasing and healing, and I was able to begin the quest for further revelation of the depth of the Father's love.

Early Years

I was around three years old when my parents got married. They had known each other in their school days and had been friends. My mother had previously married another man in Bristol, and seemingly he did well in business. This must have been during the Second World War, because it was not long before he was sent to Africa with the 8th Army. Of course, she did not see much of him then, but seemingly she lived with her mother in law at that time. My own father, who was in the army, was sent to Northern Ireland as it was essential that there was a military presence there in case the UK was invaded through Ireland. He used to come home to Bristol regularly on the train via Heysham, which is close to where we live now. In fact, I sometimes hear the trains, particularly in the night if the wind is blowing in the right direction and I often think of my father travelling down to Bristol. In those days, he would meet and socialise with a group of young men and women and Sybil, my mother, was part of that group. I was told that I was conceived in a park. Interestingly enough, I know that park very well as when I was growing up I would play football and meet friends there. It was not far away from where we lived and is called 'Victory Park.' The irony is not lost; me, being conceived in a park called **Victory**! The consequences of the pregnancy were extremely difficult. I do not know much about it, but, it seems that my father was not told that Sybil was pregnant and did not even know I had been born. Somehow he found out and went to the Unmarried Mothers Home afterwards. He gave Sybil an ultimatum, 'either we get married or I will take the boy and bring him up on my own.' All a bit harsh, but Jim was an angry man and I cannot imagine what he would have been like after finding out that I had been born. It was certainly clear that the threat to my mother would have been intimidating and controlling. He said he would take me away, if necessary, through the courts.

As previously discussed, it is possible that I could have been taken away and perhaps even sent overseas, to somewhere such as Australia, as many 'orphans' were. I also have wondered who told my father that I had been born. It seems that my mother did not tell him, but he found out much later. I dread to think about the consequences of that at the time, because of his anger. What I think about today, after all of these years, is how shocked and traumatised my mother must have been when presented with such a dilemma. She was already married to someone else, and I found out from a family member that her first husband would have willingly taken me in and brought me up as his own. This, however, would have enflamed the situation further with my real father. My mother was living with her mother-in-law at that time, but when she became pregnant with me she was told to leave. I was born in an Unmarried Mothers Home, but we ended up living with her sisters in south Bristol. My real father joined us sometime later.

Shame

The Unmarried Mothers Homes were known as **Houses of Shame**. At the time I was born, single parenthood was a scandal. The homes were not quite prisons, but more refuges for single mothers. What mattered to the authorities was that my mother was not married to the father of her child. What made matters worse was being married to another man and then separated rather than divorced. Some mothers were treated like criminals and told they were entitled to no financial or material help, and if they left the home, they would be arrested and have their babies taken for away adoption. Motherhood was certainly revered in marriage, but it was reviled outside of it. The marriage certificate became the dividing line between what was seen as 'good' and 'not good.' Without this certificate, women were stigmatised and made to feel ashamed and guilty for their 'transgressions.' Pregnant women were told that they needed to hide and were sent off to mother and baby homes as soon as possible. They needed to be sent as far away from home in order to avoid the neighbours finding out the 'family secrets,' and of course to protect the family's social standing, their good name, and respectability. They were, therefore, effectively banished and sent into exile. It is no wonder that both mother and child were deeply affected emotionally, mentally and without a doubt spiritually by all this. There was nothing good to be seen in the mother, which in turn would have affected the newborn. Yet so many of these mothers never gave up their children; they never stopped loving them even though some of these children were torn away from them and given to another family. The whole situation is so tragic. The horror of the way the mothers were treated in those days is overwhelming. How could society and those in power have treated these women like this? Nobody knew of the far-reaching consequences that would have affected those children, and their own children, in later years and many of them became part of a dysfunctional generation. My mother decided to divorce her first husband and marry my actual father. It was a period of great pressure and torment for her, as it took two years for her to get a divorce. Nobody can tell me where I was then, although some photos from that time indicate that I had remained with my mother. This must have been a desperate and lonely time for her, full of guilt and shame. It was amazing that she was able to survive with my father. I am so thankful that my mother held on to me through it all. I do not think I can describe the pain, the hurt, the isolation and abandonment she must have felt. This was wartime, and in that context, many difficult societal issues sadly happened. It was a time when many children were born to unmarried mothers. I used to play with a little boy who lived just down the road and he was the product of a union between an American GI (soldier) and a Bristolian girl. Suddenly in mid-1944, the Americans left and the invasion of Europe began. I still do not know whether my little friend ever saw his father again. Sadly, this is so often one of the many bi-products of war.

I am an Only Child

Being an only child produced many challenges, even more so as my mother had at least three miscarriages after me. I now know that she felt that God had judged her for the way she had conceived me. Chris and I talked to her once about that, and I know that in the years after the death of my father as we saw Sybil consistently, fear and perceived judgement faded as we bonded so well, and nothing could ever convince me that I would not see my siblings in eternity one day. There is no doubt that the Second World War brought turmoil to twentieth-century life and that, as a result, society changed forever. People today would not feel the same about these things as they did then, of course. I mentioned my situation to a family friend just before Sybil's funeral and she said, 'so?' That just about sums it up, for these things no longer shock and horrify people today, but are normal and acceptable.

Anger

My father was not happy that I became a Christian when I was nineteen years old, as it was not what he had planned for me - he did not get on with God at all! Sometimes he went berserk and it was usually at night. I recall him in his rage trying to force me to give up this rubbish (actually the language was much worse). For quite a while he had difficulty in even talking with Chris, as he blamed her and her parents. The whole thing was obsessive, and his controlling behaviour nearly destroyed our family. My faith was strong, and eventually he told me to leave home as he did not want a son who was a Christian living there. I began to prepare to move out, but before leaving home, I went to see my father's parents. My grandparents were brilliant and told me to take no notice of him, but to come and live with them! I do not know whether they then had a word with him or whether it was my mother who tried to put some common sense into him, but things settled down finally, and I did not need to leave in the end. In 1968, Chris and I got married and my father kicked off about that as well, and very angrily threatened not to be part of it, but at the last minute, he decided to attend. April 1 is always a bit of a strange day in the UK, and it was on that date in 1981 that I left my job to go into full time ministry in our dynamically growing church in Bristol. I had been a Chartered Surveyor specialising in the valuation of property and in my father's eyes that was the best job ever. When we told him, you would have thought we had announced the end of the world. It did, indeed become somewhat apocalyptic, and in his anger, he stormed out of the house, got very drunk, then phoned very late at night and threatened me. Through prayer, God sustained both Chris and I during this traumatic period. As far as I am aware, my father never accepted that I had become a church minister, even to the extent that when I was preaching abroad, he would lie and tell people I was away with my surveying job!

Love

Years later, at the Toronto Airport Christian Fellowship where there was such a move of the Spirit revealing the Father's love, much hurt and pain were released and I received a powerful healing with regard to the issues with my father. The orphan hearted will use any means to get their own way and are usually motivated by anger. I know that my parents loved me, but it was incredibly rare that they demonstrated it. I cannot remember them ever saying, 'I love you' or showing me any affection, such as a kiss or cuddle. I suppose it must have happened when I was really small, but I have no reColossianslection of that. The only memory I have of my father showing his care to me was when as a teenager, I was playing football for the school, and someone kicked the ball and it hit me in the stomach. I went down on the ground desperately struggling to breathe. It was a wet morning, the pitch full of water, and I lay there groaning. Suddenly, I felt myself being lifted up. It was my father who had come to watch me. He ran across the very muddy pitch taking no notice of the match as it went on, and held me as I recovered. That memory only came back to me in the last couple of years. We never bury memories dead, just deep, and to me, it was a sign that he had cared, and for him to rush onto the pitch, while the match was still in progress, said a lot. I will not forget it, but my cry is why did not that sense of love, care and intimacy happen continuously? At least, however, I have one good memory regarding how my father looked after me, and I had be delighted if more were to surface.

I have often wondered how all of this affected me from before my birth on into my early years. Now I know this was major contributing factor in the way I developed into adulthood. I think it was foundational. I have no doubt at all that the events and circumstances in my life, revolving around my family deeply affected me emotionally, mentally, and spiritually even in the womb, as I would have been wounded by the shock and trauma, the anger and grief and the guilt and condemnation of it all. That my married mother became pregnant by another man could have blown the family apart. As a result of it all, I grew up with my own deep pain, which affected my personality and character and the way I lived and behaved.

We will explore the many principles that I have found through my personal experience, relating to the orphan heart, in the coming chapters. As I began to understand what was going on in my own life, I received an impetus to seek healing through the Father's love. Throughout all of this, I loved my parents and still do, even though they are now gone. There is no doubt, though, that I have been sustained by the grace and love of my Heavenly Father, and I have found deep healing in my own orphan heart, including release from the oppressive orphan spirit. I know too, *'that God causes all things to work together for good to those who love Him, to those who are called according to His purpose,'* (Romans 8:28). He works to bring the good out of every situation, however bad, and I have experienced that with great joy! It is amazing to me how the details of God's purposes have worked out in me meeting Chris and in her introducing me to the love of God. We have a wonderful God, who intimately knows us, and in His glorious purposes for me, even changed the actual time that I left the office so that I would miss my usual bus and would have to catch the next one - the one that Chris was on. You could not make it up!

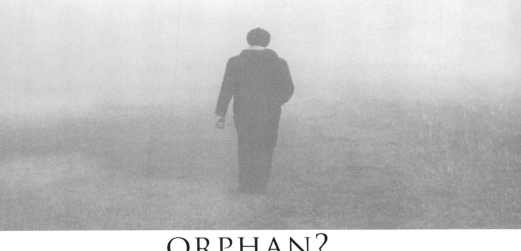

ORPHAN?

It must have been close to the mid 1980s when a good friend, Ian Andrews, was invited to our church, Bristol Christian Fellowship in the UK, to teach and mentor on the subject of 'Healing.' This was well over thirty years ago but, remarkably, what has stuck with me, is that he taught, and then prayed with people, about the 'Orphan Spirit.' Basically, it was a time of deliverance, and many responded, which was great. However, this term was, at that time, virtually unknown to us, and we did not really pick it up until a few years later. Ian's teaching became to me something of a key, which connected back to the evening when Chris had told me about my past. There is no doubt in my mind that something was seeded into me that day when Ian spoke, and it was not very long before the eventful evening took place, when Chris told me about my family history and I had a revelation of the Father's love. I can now look back at it with a measure of understanding of what happened and why my life was totally turned upside down, actually, turned the right way up in my relationship with God. It seems that I was left with many questions about the way I lived, my behaviour, my character, and my personality. What sort of person was I? How did this orphan issue affect me in my relationship with God as a loving Heavenly Father? Why was it, for example, that my insecurity and anger were so apparent at the same time as my spirituality was growing particularly in a pastoral and prophetic way? How was I affected by what had happened to my mother and father in their pain and wounds? What sort of legacy had I received from them, and what was my spiritual destiny? How could I have been affected by the orphan heart whilst my parents were still alive? I am sure there are many more questions, and you probably have your own. There are answers, too, which revolve around the caring, loving and grace of our Heavenly Father who longs to heal and free us so that we can know a glorious closeness to Him as sons and daughters, without the sense of striving or performance which only lead to condemnation.

The challenge that confronts us can be summed up as:

- Do we want to be in a purpose-driven performance-based life with God, or in an experiential-based presence life with God - with a good, safe and secure relationship with Him as a loving Heavenly Father?
- This will lead into one of two ways. Either we will continue to live in a restlessness, striving to achieve or we can live by, and in, the grace of God, through which we can enter into His rest and live in it in every area of our lives.

Definitions

Most definitions of orphan begin and end with the idea of having no parents, however, one can have two parents and still bear deep orphan wounds. Emotional abandonment, in the form of critical parents, neglectful parents, or just very immature ones, can leave a child having to strive to supply his or her own needs. Life in an orphanage is one of deprivation and competition, but sometimes life in a family can echo these same familiar themes.

I believe that the term 'orphan' can be applied in two ways:
The first is a '**conscious**' awareness of being an orphan, and living in an institution due to the child losing both parents often through death. There

are also further reasons for loss, however, including being deprived of one or both parents because they are unknown or because they have permanently abandoned the child. In addition to this, there can be desertion, separation, abuse, mental illness of one of the parents, or the situation in which a parent or both parents are unable to cope with the child. I only know a few adults who were orphaned as children. At one time, most of them would have ended up in a residential institution devoted to the care of orphans. There is, of course, no substitute for a home with loving and caring parents, and some have found that with foster parents. In the UK, at least, things have gradually changed, and those imposing large orphanages have virtually disappeared, as smaller family units have taken place and adoption or fostering have become more prevalent.

The second is just as real, but can be defined as '**unconscious**', and it applies to parents that are still alive and living with the child. The child may not physically or legally be an orphan, but exhibits the same tendencies. An orphan, child or adult, might feel cut off from their father and mother when there is, or has been, a lack of the key area of nurturing. Care of the child is a fundamental issue, and if this is undermined or missing it will cause dysfunction. The adult will experience the same pain by feeling insecure and cut off. I have met so many people whose parents did not actually die or even abandon them as children, yet as adults, they still exhibit the many tendencies of being orphaned. Typically, there has been a deprivation of consistent and genuine exposure to the love, affection, warmth, and care that contributes to healthy social connection. This has to include the crucial area of touch, something that contributes to nervous system development, as well as trust in others and a sense of self-worth. Touch-deprived children are more susceptible to paranoia, insecurity, and distrustfulness, which can become embedded as they become adults. In this situation, the parents of course, are still with the child but, paradoxically, in terms of affection, they are distant. Some fathers may be physically present in the home, but are emotionally absent. It is as though they are unable to help, and in some cases, are unmindful of their child. This leaves a relational gap, which can be perceived as loss to the child. As much as there are different definitions, there is very little difference in the outworking and consequences of them. I was adversely affected by both my mother and father, in different ways, and this led to a disconnection, out of which the orphan heart developed. I became an orphan in my heart, although, in practical terms, I was not actually an orphan.

Mother Wounds

It is hard to imagine what my mother went through regarding her relationships during the Second World War. I remember her telling me that in the worst time of bombing they either hid under a table or, after her mother had died, superstitiously stayed in the same room where the coffin was kept in their small terraced house until burial.

In addition, there was her marriage to her first husband, who was in the army and was sent to North Africa straight after the wedding, so would not have been seen again for many months. Helpfully, my mother lived with her husband's mother, but then the problems were exacerbated, because my mother became pregnant by another man - the man who was my actual father. There is no doubt that the circumstances exposed deep shock and trauma, as not only was she thrown out of her home by her mother-in-law, but the father of the child was not told that she was pregnant. My mother was on her own, although it seems that she was taken in by her sisters, but her isolation continued when I was born in an Unmarried Mothers Home. My father still did not know, but was finally told by a relation and came and angrily confronted her with threats of taking me away from her. I say all of this because of the effect it had on my mother and of course me in the womb. As much as my mother was wounded throughout that time, it is clear that I would have been wounded too.

Think of the time when Mary, who was pregnant with Jesus visited her cousin. At their first greeting at the door of the house, the baby inside

Elizabeth leapt in her womb. Not only was Elizabeth filled with the Spirit, but so too was her baby, John, when he was born, (Luke 1:15, 41). Surely this indicates that a baby, even whilst still in the mother's womb, can be affected by its mother's feelings and emotions including the various circumstances that life brings. As explained previously, the wounds that my mother received through the shock and trauma of the situation, would have certainly affected me.

The term trauma is important from a biblical point of view. It is mentioned in the story of the Good Samaritan, (Luke 10:34) when he went to the terribly beaten man at the side of the road and bandaged his wounds. The Greek word that is used here is 'trauma,' which can be translated wound. Trauma can be defined as a deeply distressing and disturbing experience, and extreme stress overwhelms a person's ability to cope emotionally and mentally. This would explain how the man would have probably felt whilst he was at the side of the road. I am convinced that when you consider the sum of all of the circumstances that affected my mother, she would have felt the same too, and I wonder how much this affected me. There is no doubt that it contributed considerably to my orphan heart, and when you add to that the wounds I received from my father, the picture becomes clearer.

Father Wounds

My father was an angry man and he would wound people through his angry reactions. He frequently exhibited quite extreme anger leading to rage; he seethed, he bubbled, boiled, simmered and fermented with anger. Sometimes it was contained, just about, but sometimes it was like a volcanic eruption had happened. It is certainly true that, *'life and death is in the power of the tongue'* (Proverbs 18:21). Words spoken in anger or rage cut deeply into a person affecting the very core of their being. There is no doubt I suffered from the effects of this anger from my father, and there were times when I became an angry person myself, and although it manifested differently in my life, it was still anger. I am thankful that I have recognised it and have been able to do something about it. As we will see later, anger is a key component of the orphan problem. I would say that my father expressed his negative emotions much more than my mother, for she was more passive, maybe because of his control. Passivity locks in emotions, and as much as my mother loved me very much, it was so difficult for her to show it. I do think that she lived under the control and domination of my father, and it took time for her to recover, to some extent anyway, from her pregnancy with me and from its subsequent consequences. I do think that they grew to love each other as the years went on, but it is obvious in my case, that my orphan heart came from both my parents and their wounds.

Did My Parents Love Me?

Of course, they did, but they did not express it outwardly. My father was a provider and that was clear, but he had no ability to show affection and intimacy. My mother showed some affection, but was more passive. Again the intimacy was missing. I know she deeply loved me because she kept me when she was under pretty extreme pressure to give me up, but I have no memory of them saying to me, personally, 'I love you.' I am sure they did love me, but it was never expressed orally or by intimacy, affection, and touch. All of this created gaps in my heart. The loss needed to be compensated, and it was, but not by something I wanted. It opened me to a propensity towards the orphan heart, which began with the process of a different belief system. Sometimes it becomes clear that the parents do not love their child at all. What the child would receive is rejection, and that in itself would lead to an orphan heart.

In the context of '**Orphan**,' I want to divide its meaning and for your consideration I will use the terms '**Orphan Heart**' and '**Orphan Spirit**.' There has been some confusion regarding this, particularly when some would intermingle the terms, and you are left wondering whether they mean the same. Obviously, there is a connection, and an overlap but there is also a difference.

What is the Orphan Heart?

When writing about the heart, it is necessary to bring some definition, because there is a mystery about what it really is, and of course we all have our thoughts about how to best explain it. Understanding the heart biblically and from a spiritual context is different to, and goes further than, the biological and scientific definition. It occurs over one thousand times in the Bible and can be described as a person's centre or core, whether physical, emotional, mentally or spiritual. It occupies the most important part of a person's system. It is the source of life and used as a symbol for love, describing the seat of our emotions and our primary faculty of thought, affection and will. It is clear that the wounds received through the unintentional or intentional actions of parents can cause deep wounds in the heart. The emotional state of the heart will affect the rest of the person. If the heart is the source of life in biblical terms, could it be that the human spirit has a place in its centre or is, at least very much connected to it? The human spirit is that part of our being, enabled by God to know, to commune with and to worship Him. It is where we connect with God. 'We worship God in spirit and truth or reality' (John 4:24 NIV). The human spirit communicates life and receives the life of God through His Spirit. '*God breathed into man the breath of life and he became a living being*' (Genesis 2:7 NIV).

The point of this, is that if the heart is wounded to the point that it becomes affected   by orphan tendencies, we need to be aware that this could have a great bearing on how we respond to God through our human spirits, as it might result in a difficulty in giving and receiving God's love. This is a spiritual condition in which some Christians maintain that they do know God as their Heavenly Father, but within them there is a conflict and contradiction that undermines their belief system. The struggle is in comprehending that God actually loves them, and, on most occasions, this struggle is due to unhealed hurts and wounds. Simply speaking, we can be described as being comprised of body, soul and spirit, but these areas are not separate from each other - each affects the other, for everything is connected. The orphan heart is a stronghold with a mental attitude and belief system that will rule us, undermine our destiny and deny us of our true inheritance! This structure is built from within the heart, originating from deep hurts and wounds, that in turn affect it, by forming a network of negative beliefs that will control the way a person thinks, acts and behaves. This stronghold can be described as a fortified place, which protects and defends itself against attack. In the context of orphan, the heart becomes affected to the point that it desires to control every area of life in a negative and destructive way. The orphan heart is a learned behaviour which becomes entrenched internally with a specific pattern or mind-set. The source of this is deep wounding, and some say that it most commonly originates from the father, although it would be wrong to discount the mother. These wounds release negative and painful emotions that begin to create a belief system which ultimately undermines, or can even separate, the child from the sense of identity, security, and purpose that parents have a responsibility to instil. All this has consequences that can affect our character and personality in a detrimental way. Things will change, but for the worse. The heart of the issue has to be the issue of the heart! This is the key, and it is the wounded heart that needs healing. This is not deliverance; you cannot cast this out, but what you can do is allow your Heavenly Father to begin a process of healing.

As we will see the demonic can and will affect the orphan heart with its oppressive and afflicting power. But God can heal our hearts through a personal experience of His love as a Father and the revelation of our identity of sonship.

What is the Orphan Spirit?

I consider the orphan spirit to be a demonic power that will oppress us. Oppression in a biblical sense, means a person under another's control, power or rule, being exploited in a deceptive manner. The person would be 'pressed' down or afflicted by the enemy and can be affected in thoughts, behaviour, and spirituality. This is not full control, but only an influence, sometimes strong, in a specific area of a person's life. It is crucial to look at this subject with seriousness, because it is clear both biblically, and through experience, that we are not immune to demonic power affecting us. Of course, we need to be sensitive when considering this and we need to continually remember that our God is bigger than the enemy! However, it is important to live in reality with discernment, being open to any involvement that the enemy might have, and being aware that we are able to deal with him in the power and name of Jesus.

As Christians, we live in a paradox. We are in this 'evil' age, but we have been greatly affected by the age to come. '*Jesus gave himself for our sins to rescue us from the present evil or oppressive age, according to the will of our God and Father*,' (Galatians 1:4 NIV). This present world has been corrupted under the authority of Satan, and his demonic powers have been loosed to afflict and harass humanity. However, Jesus brought the message of the Kingdom of God to turn people's lives around and to set them free from the enemy's power. '*And you know that God anointed Jesus of Nazareth with the Holy Spirit and with power. Then Jesus went around doing good and healing all who were oppressed by the devil, for God was with him*' (Acts 10:38 NLT). What Jesus has done through His life, death, and resurrection, we have received as we make Him Lord of our lives. '*We have tasted the heavenly gift, have shared in the Holy Spirit, have tasted the goodness of the word of God and the power of the age to come*' (Hebrews 6:4-5 NIV). What an amazing experience we have! This coming new age, when Jesus comes back to this earth, to renew everything and finally deal with Satan, will succeed the age we now live in. However we have experienced the age to come through Jesus, so it means that we are already living in an overlap of the new age with the existing age - the future event of the new age is to us a present reality!

That is why Jesus said to John the Baptist's disciples when they asked Him if He was the one, *'go back and tell John what you have seen and heard. At that very time, Jesus cured many who had diseases, sicknesses, and evil spirits, and gave sight to many who were blind'* (Luke 7:21-22 NIV). Demonic powers need a place to express themselves. If there is an opening for them, they will invade. The issue is not possession it is yielding. *'Whoever has no rule over his own spirit is like a city broken down without walls'* (Proverbs 25:28). Demons will invade if they are given a right or an opportunity. They will not possess the 'city' - us, or even the 'town hall' - our spirits, but they could be in some of the streets of the city causing havoc. They need to be evicted and the walls built up. We are very strongly advised to, *'not give the enemy a foothold'* (Ephesians 3:27). This is more than an influence, for it is probable that the text could refer to a room in a house, which means that the tenant cannot own the whole house, as it is legally owned by someone else. Giving a foothold could also mean surrendering something and allowing it to be taken over.

As we are aware, many people were, as children, deprived of love from their parents, which caused a wound, and it is possible that, ultimately, a demonic power could take advantage of this and affect that person. Even from an early age, this deprivation could create a sense of rejection that results in anger and resentment etc., and it is this that can give the enemy rights, with an opportunity to take ground in a person's life. People affected by this demonic spirit find it hard to respond to the Father Heart of God, as it is so difficult for them to understand this concept when they haven't received love from their natural fathers and mothers. A clear sign that the Kingdom of God is among us is the deliverance from demonic powers. *'If I drive out demons by the Spirit of God, then the kingdom of God has come upon you'* (Matthew 12:28). The Kingdom of God could not be established without the power and authority to cast out demons. The people in Jesus' time had no problem in understanding and accepting the realm of the supernatural, including the demonic. What was different, was that they were amazed that someone had the authority and power to cast demons out! Deliverance was prevalent in Jesus' own ministry. In those days, the existence of demons was assumed and Jesus spent much of his time freeing people from their influence. There are both general and specific examples and descriptions of Jesus setting demonised people, free (Matthew. 8:16, Mark. 1:21). This gives us, as disciples of Jesus, a mandate to do the same. Orphan can be a type of demonic spirit that invades and afflicts a person's mind, causing a sense of abandonment, loneliness, alienation, and isolation. This can result from any form of abuse and experience of rejection in their lives. A person operating out of an orphan spirit compensates for these feelings of insecurity by being performance-driven, competitive, and independent. They struggle with self-worth and find it difficult to maintain healthy relationships. We often live with dysfunction for such a long time that we do not realise that we are struggling with these issues. Demonic powers are no respecters of persons; they will manifest their malevolence wherever and to whomsoever they can.

Power and Ownership

If you buy a house that needs renovation, you cannotdo anything about the repairs until you actually own it. Ownership is vital. Until the house is legally yours, you cannotbring restoration. When the transfer of ownership is complete, you have the remit to do the work. When we come to Christ, a change of ownership takes place, and it is then, that the restoration to the house can take place. Of course, we need to discern and understand what the demonic powers are and how they affect us and as we take responsibility change can take place.

Remember

We need to be aware that some problems, pressures, or afflictions in our lives may not be sourced in demonic power, but in some areas they may well be. It is clear that the very core of our life, our heart, can be affected by the orphan condition and will require a process of healing and transformation. The orphan heart is not something you can cast out, for it is more of an ungodly belief system that has been motivated by attitudes of the flesh (sin) that have developed over many years. It becomes part of our personality and character, and we need is to have a personal experience of the love of our Heavenly Father, with the revelation of who we are in Him, so that we can enter into our destiny as sons and daughters and transformation can take place. However, if there is a sense of the demonic present, and we discern and deal with it, there is no doubt this will enable us to see more clearly with regard to our response to the orphan heart and the love of our Heavenly Father.

The Biblical Definition of Orphan

The meaning of orphan does reveal keys which give us understanding as to how we can relate to our Heavenly Father. When He was talking to the disciples about leaving, Jesus said, 'I will not leave you as orphans, but I will come to you.'

The New Testament Greek word is 'orphanos' and is very close to the English word we use, 'orphan.' It means fatherless. There is a connection here to being powerless, bereaved, comfortless and restless and even to feeling desolation. There was no way that Jesus was going to leave His friends in any of those conditions. He wanted them, and ultimately us, to have the same kind of a relationship with His Father as He had, and, as we will see later, also through the giving to us of the Holy Spirit, who is the one that reveals the Father to us as sons and daughters. Some translations substitute comfortless for orphan, which is interesting because Jesus said that He would send the Holy Spirit, whom He called the Comforter, to us. '*And I will pray to the Father, and he shall give you another Comforter, the Spirit of Truth that He may abide with you forever*' (John 14:16 KJV). A great sense of comfort from God comes from the Holy Spirit, who is **the** Comforter, and He will be, to us, everything He was to Jesus. In addition, the Holy Spirit introduces us to 'Abba' Father. '*Because you are his sons, God sent the Spirit of his Son into our hearts, the Spirit who calls out, Abba, Father*' (Galatians

4:6 NIV). This is the feeling of intimacy, affection, love, and confidence in our Heavenly Father.

Old Testament

In the Old Testament, the term orphan relates to those deprived of parents. *'Do not take advantage of a widow or an orphan. If you do and they cry out to me, I will certainly hear their cry,'* (Exodus 22:22-23 NIV). This is the first of many times that the word orphan is used in the Old Testament. *'We have become orphans and fatherless, our mothers like widows,'* (Lamentations 5:3 NKJV). The father was the main means of economic support for the family unit at this time. His absence left his wife and children in a particularly vulnerable condition. The orphan and the widow were known as the epitome of the poor and deprived in that society. God, in His compassion, was known as 'the helper of the fatherless,' (Psalm 10:14 NIV). He is the Father to the fatherless. The prophets expressed God's heart for the need to protect and provide for the totally dependent, and a prime example is the orphan, (Isaiah 1:23, 10:2; Jeremiah 5:28; Ezekiel 22:7 and Malachi 3:5 NIV). The people's lack of response became an indictment on the nation of Israel because it seems that their poverty prevailed as these were ignored. The prophet Hosea said to God, 'in you the fatherless find compassion' (Hosea 14:3 NIV), and *'even if my father and mother abandon me, the Lord will hold me close,'* (Psalms 27:10 NIV). God's heart response is to gather the orphan into Himself. This is amazing because there is a thread in the Old Testament that indicates that we should worship at a distance. I am so pleased that the veil in the Holy of Holies in the Temple, in Jerusalem, was torn from top to bottom when Jesus died, giving God access to us and also allowing us to become close to Him.

There are three areas to consider:

1. In all of the scriptures mentioned above, the word 'fatherless' is translated in the Greek version (Septuagint) of the Old Testament as

the word 'orphanos.' It is the same Greek word that we find in the New Testament, as used by Jesus. This is a key connection.

2. There is also a mandate for justice led by our compassionate Heavenly Father. 'He has told you, O man, what is good; and what does the Lord require of you, but to do justice, and to love kindness, and to walk humbly with your God,' (Micah 6:8 ESV). We need to take note of the way God responds to us in our orphan condition and of how He longs for us to come close. The issue is one of justice and righteousness, and God wants to set us free from this iniquitous orphan oppression.

3. The final prophecy of the Old Testament in (Malachi 4:5-6), is key to both the relationship that Jesus had with His Father and also to that which He has with us, leading us to how we can be restored to Him. It is this prophecy that leads into the New Covenant. All this clearly shows us how crucial the Father Heart of God is: it gives me hope in my relationship with Abba Father, as I know that He wants us to be as close as possible to Him, and that is amazing! The prophecy is powerfully expressed and very challenging, 'I will send the prophet Elijah to you before that great and dreadful day of the Lord comes. He will turn the hearts of the parents to their children, and the hearts of the children to their parents; or else I will come and strike the land with a curse.'

New Testament

There are only two clear references to orphans in the New Testament: Firstly, *'religion that God our Father accepts as pure and faultless is this: to look after orphans and widows in their distress and to keep oneself from being polluted by the world,'* (James 1:27 NIV). This emphasises Old Testament teaching and is the essence of a true relationship with the Father of the fatherless, leading to our imitating Him, as we genuinely and sincerely care for the orphan - both those who have lost their parents and the many more who feel lost in their relationship with their father or mother or both.

Secondly, at the Last Supper, Jesus stated that He would not leave his disciples as orphans but would come to them in the presence of His Spirit, (John 14:18). We now know that, even in today's world, the word orphan has the same meaning - that is fatherless. We are also aware that we live in a fatherless generation, in which so many children are bereft and comfortless. It is possible that the emotional, physical and spiritual ills of society can be traced back to humans feeling alienated from God because of their fathers - in many cases their biological fathers. There are so many men in our prisons who have acted out lives of violence and rebellion because their earthly fathers abandoned them. There are churches filled with pastors and leaders who are driven to succeed and have no hesitation in using people, leading to a further destruction of relationships. This is, more often than not, due to their need for a father's affirmation - something that cannot be met or filled by any ministry success or performance. This orphan heart is so often motivated by the orphan spirit, and causes someone to live in such a way that they do not have a safe and secure place close to the Heart of their Heavenly Father. They are distant, and therefore do not have a place of affection, intimacy, affirmation comfort or belonging. They will also manifest loneliness, which breeds an independence that leads to isolation. All of this can result in a sense of striving, competition and a drive to achieve by performance, in order to have to earn everything in life and even in their relationship with God. It may also create a sense of anxiety, fear, stress and frustration in others.

CONSEQUENCES - PART 1

The Spiritual Impact

The orphan heart develops out of a spiritual source and is very much affected by sets of circumstances that will considerably impact in a negative way, not only in a Christian's life but, also in those who are not followers of Jesus. The orphan heart refers to a condition, which affects both male and female, young and old, mostly in their relationship with their parents, particularly with their father, which leads to difficulties in their relationship with God as Father. The effects of these relationships will produce dysfunctional responses and reactions, which can seriously undermine the person in their family, society and their relationship to God. Some Christians outwardly profess to know God as Father, but experience an internal contradiction to that belief. Deep down they struggle to understand that God loves them, and this will lead to them harbouring negative feelings and reactions, which would be connected to the unhealed hurts from painful past experiences. There will not only be a difficulty in believing that their parents love them, but also problems around whether God loves and accepts them. Circumstances like this create a mindset which pressures the orphan hearted to have to work to earn favour with God. This includes thinking we are not worthy to be God's children and cannot ask Him for anything, but if we do ask Him, we may well feel ashamed in asking God for good things. A person may go to church, do all the right things, and still feel orphaned, for being a Christian does not automatically mean feeling secure, loved, and accepted as a son or daughter of our loving Heavenly Father.

In order to simplify things, I want to summarise the consequences of being orphan hearted, and then later in this chapter, as well as the next, describe some of the specific issues of the orphan heart, which need further clarification. In my own life, a lot of these areas were not recognised, but as I opened up to my Heavenly Father revelation came, and I can remember thinking how clearly I then saw things. Bear in mind though, I am not saying every person has every condition mentioned, but some of you will have some of them:

- An orphan has no home, no place of security, no place of belonging, or no place of rest. They will also find difficulty in putting down roots in a church and might change churches frequently.
- The orphan hearted person has no sense of identity, and therefore will lack a personal perspective of destiny, which would undermine their godly inheritance.
- There may have been little or even no source of emotional, mental, physical, and spiritual provision.
- Discipline would have been lacking, other than the wrong sort of discipline, which could have been abusive.
- An orphan hearted person would be afraid to trust, or to receive love, and would not be able to give or unconditionally express love because of a fear of rejection.
- A son or daughter accepts and believes that the Father accepts them as they are. An orphan hearted person strives to please the Father to gain acceptance.
- Before being able to accept others or feel accepted, they must have confirmation that they are doing the right thing in order to gain acceptance.
- There is often a need for approval, affirmation or recognition,

which means performing, fighting, or competing for everything to gain approval. The reaction is to look after 'me' and then compete to be the best.

- There are certain roots related to rejection that will afflict the orphan hearted: fear of rejection (self-protection), self-rejection, and rebellion (very much linked to anger and control).
- Other important areas to consider are shame, unworthiness, fear, bitterness, and loneliness. This includes feelings of abandonment, even when someone has not been literally abandoned.
- There will be a susceptibility to abuse, either verbal, mental, sexual or spiritual.
- They might feel a lack of confidence, which comes out of insecurity.
- There may be an inability to empathise with others.
- There is often an urge to always look for something bigger or better
- The orphan hearted will tend to have a feeling-based faith, meaning, 'if it feels good or feels right, then I will follow it.'
- They are prone to giving and/or taking offence.
- There can be an attitude of, 'no one is going to tell me what to do,' or sometimes they seem unteachable with an attitude of, 'I know that already!'
- They will have a survival mentality.
- They would not be truly comfortable in the presence of mature people, who have a father's heart, yet paradoxically will tend to gravitate towards them.
- The orphan's heart shuts down when the person does not feel loved and accepted by their parents, or other close people, including those who are in some sort of authority over them. This will start in the formative years of their life.
- When a child starts to close down, it is because they do not know what else to do. A child is still learning and forming their understanding of the world around them.
- If a child believes they are not loved or feels rejection from their parents, they will struggle with love given by God, their Heavenly

Father, as they grow and develop. The more they feel rejected, the harder it is for them to forgive others or themselves.

In considering the above points, I have found there are certain root words, which need further definition to help understand the consequences of the orphan heart. The orphan can be affected by some or even all of these words, and because of their importance, it is necessary to continue their explanation in the following chapter. Some of these words are usually construed in positive terms, but in this context, it is necessary to bring definition from the 'orphan' perspective. For example, the word 'home' would to the orphan hearted be the opposite of what many of us would know and love, and they would subtly interpret home in a negative light. We are all different in character and personality, so bear in mind that we are all affected, but to different extents. This requires sensitivity and discernment rather than a reaction to what we are reading, because we may think we are affected by all of these or conversely none of them. However, we are affected by some, and therefore it is necessary to take responsibility personally and be open to the way the Holy Spirit reveals the specifics to us. At one time I had no idea of the orphan roots in my life, but the time came when I began a journey, where I recognised some of these specific areas and took responsibility to work with the Holy Spirit in the process of healing. I now understand that hurting people hurt people, and in the light of this it would be helpful to consider the following root words:

Loss

The scripture highlights the important issue of loss to the orphan hearted. *'My people have been lost sheep. Their shepherds have allowed them to go astray. They have wandered around in the mountains. They have roamed from one mountain and hill to another. They have forgotten their resting place,'* (Jeremiah 50:6 NET). Who are the shepherds? Biblically speaking they may well be our leaders, our pastors, those who have responsibility for us before God in our churches. However, could it be that we have narrowed the definition, and neglected a biblical principle about family? If the word means to take care, to feed, to guide, to train, to watch, to tend, to guard, and to nurture, cannot it mean that our parents, close family, friends, teachers, etc., come into that context?

The firstborn son of Adam and Eve was Cain. He was an angry man, who wanted to build his kingdom, and not only wanted things his own way, he also wanted God to submit to his demands. He was such an angry man, that he ultimately killed his brother. God banished him, and what He said is so typical of orphan hearted people. *'From now on you will be a **homeless wanderer** or **restless wanderer** on the earth,'* (Genesis 4:12). This is loss in its most devastating form. As well as this, Cain realised he would be hidden from God's presence as well as his own family, meaning he was fatherless. Cain was destined to wander throughout the earth, for there was nowhere for him to belong. Being homeless, restless, and fatherless is just about the core of the orphan condition. It is as though you are in a place where you think no one else has ever been, or will never see, alienated, separated, isolated, and alone. Loss shapes who we become. Loss is a key part of the root of deprivation, which is being without something you once had, or something that has been taken away. It leaves a feeling of grief and impoverishment. Loss relates to the value that was placed on what you once had. Yet, how can you value nurture, love, and intimacy, which has been either taken away or never had? Would it not exceedingly enhance the orphan feeling? The orphan hearted need to recognise and then cope with loss. Even if they are not aware of loss in their own lives, the ability is still there to manipulate and control others, or situations, to attempt to fill the void within them. Because much has been taken away, the ensuing deprivation feeds the feeling of separation. All that is left is a grieving process, which never seems to finish. This can become one of the greatest hindrances to people receiving their healing, and then being able to walk in love, intimacy, and healthy relationships. Look at this as an adult and consider how you would manage. Then ask yourself how a child would manage with this kind of loss. They would not, and could only cope by deliberately denying their pain, or even in some cases dissociating, which in its simplicity means hiding the pain deep within for another day.

Loss has consequences for the orphan hearted:

- There will be deep emotional pain; shock and trauma. How do we cope?
- There will be changes forced upon us in everyday life. How do we come to terms with them?
- Our sense of identity will be severely challenged, because the person we once were is not there. How do we manage relationships in the context of loss? There may be withdrawal, avoidance, and losing touch. Then we will have the provocation of reconnecting or making new relationships, and words like trust will harass us.
- What do we do with our dysfunctional and undermined belief systems? Making sense or understanding the issue will be very difficult. Our basic core assumptions will have cracks appearing in them. Finding meaning and moving on is easier said than done.

Home

Many people whether they are young or old, male or female, live their lives as if they do not have a home. Many have lamented, 'I never feel I belong anywhere.' They feel cut off from all of the benefits of what home is and brings. Parents may be present, but in reality one or both are absent. The orphan hearted often goes from home to home, living as if they do not have a home. They will struggle with getting close to people and wander in the restlessness of not being able to settle in a strong relationship - it means that going from one place to another, such as church to church, from job to job, and from one relationship to another, which becomes regretfully, easier than staying and working things through. It is as though you are on the outside looking in. They live like spiritual orphans feeling that they do not have a safe and secure place in the Father's heart, where He protects, affirms, and provides for them, as well as expressing His love so that they know they belong. For home is the established place of love, care, comfort, nurture, warmth, tenderness, protection, safety, security, honour, affirmation, and acceptance. God has made His home among mankind, therefore we can make our home with Him. This is not hiding in life waiting for Him to return to take us to Heaven for Heaven has come to earth. God is amongst His people; incarnation is so real! It is not just God is providing us a home, it is that **God is home!** It means that we live in the here and now, where God is and we need to know that He is with us. God as our Father, is calling for a homecoming in these days. You may have been introduced to the Father, but you cannotreceive His love. However, scripture is very clear in that we are legally His sons and daughters, but there are still many that live their lives as though they do not have a home, and so receiving His love becomes very difficult. Yet, we have an ability in Christ to deal with this; to understand, acknowledge and take responsibility, and to make the right choices and decisions.

Love

Can you remember your father telling you that he loved you? I cannot. Chris and I vowed, that we would never be passive in our love for our two daughters through our actions and our words. There is a desperation to be loved by the orphan hearted, and they will attempt to manipulate others to give that love. The need for love within the orphan hearted is so great, that almost anything goes, including grooming, which would make them easy prey for the perverted. The need to love and to be loved is an integral part of our being, and fulfilment brings satisfaction, but frustration will bring a host of negative feelings and reactions.

Love is a somewhat strange and difficult word to those with the orphan heart, because it is love that is our core foundation, and even though the desire to love is there, the manifestation of that love is missing. How can someone who has not received parental love respond to God in receiving and giving love? If love and nurture are rarely expressed in a family, and there is a deep and longing desire for that, what can be done? We understand that *'God so loved the world that He gave His only son,'* (John 3:16), in order to bring us into fulfilment in relationship with our Heavenly Father. This love was the ultimate sacrifice of all time, made on our behalf, for you and me. It is an amazing love, and instead of being orphan hearted we can live as sons and daughters, as we open our lives to Him. The scripture is transparently clear about this love being the beginning, end, and everything in between of the Christian faith. It is the heart of the greatest commandment, *'Jesus replied, love the Lord your God with all your heart and with all your soul and with all your mind. This is the first and greatest commandment and the second is like it: love your neighbour as yourself. All the Law and the Prophets hang on these two commandments,'* (Matthew 22:37-40). It is important to consider the immensity of these words, for everything a Christian is connected to these commandments. We are made to love like this, however, the orphan hearted will grieve as they lack the capacity to do that. They will try other means, but sadly nothing else works, and the deception and pain will grow. This commandment is the first and greatest of all, in order of importance and greatest in excellence. God desires that we love everyone, and He is to be loved to our greatest extent, which means absolutely and utterly with everything we are and have. As we love Him, our affections will then be directed toward His creation in a right and proper way. To love Him with all the heart is to fix our affections totally and completely on Him, more strongly than on anything else. That in itself will release a love, not only for others but also love for ourselves. This is love towards God, love towards your neighbour, and love towards yourself, walking as Jesus walked. It is revolutionary for every culture, and in its own right will bring peace, release, fulfilment and healing. These three imperatives are crucial, but in many cases it is important to emphasise the third point. How can you say you love God and your neighbour, if you do not love yourself? The testimony of many, including me, is that we can change in these aspects of love, and through them come into a strong, safe and secure relationship with our Heavenly Father.

In saying this, we need to be aware, that the orphan heart will affect us as to how we see God. Is He a loving Heavenly Father or a Master? What do we do with unconditional love, when we have been brought up with the perception, that everything has conditions and often harsh ones? To consider you have a duty to earn God's favour is not understanding God's grace or His love. We need to be aware that love is an act of will, for we choose to love because we want to. Therefore, there has to be first an intention and then an action. Do I have to love? Do I want to love? Any person who is not comfortable with love shows they are not healed. Orphan hearted people have an ability to hide the truth of how bad they are hurting inside. The way to break through is to be filled with a sense of the Father's love for them personally in Jesus, which then enables them to grow into mature sons and daughters, who serve God out of knowledge of His undeserved grace, instead of trying to earn the Father's love through performance.

Identity

Two questions will help us define identity:

- Who am I (Who are you)?
- Do I matter (Do you matter)?

We need to understand that the orphan hearted will look at these questions from a negative perspective. As Christians, the key to personal identity is our relationship with God as a loving Heavenly Father, however with the orphan heart, we can attain to be godly, but still be dysfunctional. This will cause an undermining and distortion of how we see things, how we see others, and our response to God will be brought down to a level where we think continually about ourselves, bringing perpetual conflict. Our identity is our sense of self, of who we are, and we carry that wherever we go. The way we perceive ourselves, our actions, thoughts and our interactions with others are very much influenced by this. It is our sense of who we are, which has the thread of orphan through it, and this will affect every area in our lives. What will be seen will not be the real person we long to be, and we may even not realise it, because the easy way will be to protect ourselves by walls, masks, passivity, and even our reactive emotions. In response to that, the question, 'who am I' will be exceedingly difficult to answer, because there will have a problem in recognising who you are. This will quickly connect to the second question, and the answer will be obvious to you, 'I do not matter.' However, that is not the way God or others see you, and confusion will get the upper hand. Identity relates to our basic values that dictate the choices we make, such as relationships and careers. These choices reflect who we are and what we value. Many simply internalise the values of their parents or dominant cultures, which can include the pursuit of materialism, power, and appearance. Yet these values are not aligned with a person's authenticity and will soon create an unfulfilled, and unreal life, when the goal is to live and be a genuine person. Like you, I know it is not difficult to be somewhat dysfunctional as well as pursuing godliness.

Identity is acquired particularly from parents but would include other family members, peers, and other role models such as teachers. Children come to define themselves in terms of how they think their parents see them. If their parents see them as worthless, they will come to define themselves as worthless. Without parents to help shape the child's sense of self, the orphan hearted will grow into adulthood with a pronounced need to answer the core question, 'who am I,' and struggle with it. Parents establish true identity and purpose and without that, the orphan hearted will wander throughout life in search of true identity. They look for someone who has their perceived qualities of a father or mother and then try to emulate them. How we choose to live and function is a product of how we view ourselves, and how we view ourselves as an orphan, or as a true son or daughter of Father God is a matter of identity. And it is not just part of our identity, but the core of it, the foundation upon which, all the other facets of our identity are built. Get this right and what is built will be right.

Belonging

It is very important that the definition of belonging is understood in the context of the orphan heart. Synonyms such as closeness, familiarity, inseparability, intimacy, and nearness give such clarity, particularly when the antonym is distance. Belonging in itself is a fundamental human need, just like the need for food, shelter, and survival. It is a word that the orphan hearted would continually struggle with. A typical response is, 'I never feel like I belong anywhere,' as they find it easier to withdraw, separate and live in isolation, often amidst people. The truth is more like this, 'if you do not have any roots you feel you do not belong.' However, in our relationship with God, we can live as though we belong, rooted in Him, which gives the impetus to make secure relationships with others. Roland Evans has wisely and aptly said, 'The deepest dream of human longing is to belong, to find a place of unconditional acceptance where we can be at home.' Is not this what God would have us to be, quenching the thirst to belong, to know acceptance and to rest at home in Him?

The reason why people are so strongly motivated to have relationships is because of a fundamental need to belong. People need to feel closely connected to others, and that caring, affectionate bonds coming from close relationships are a major part of human behaviour. Personal connections that give acceptance, attention, and support are so important in this. This is not just a simple acquaintance; it is so much more leading to close and intimate relationships with emotional depth. This is something that is a massive challenge to the orphan hearted, as they come to a place where they need to accept the need to belong and to have stable and long-term relationships. A desire for closeness and bonding results in the creation of family and social structures, which in themselves will attract others to relate, giving them nurture and support on an on-going basis. The need for love and belonging includes the range of intimacy between and among people, which encompasses caring, compassion, empathy, a sense of having a place in the world, being part of a community, feeling accepted and approved.

This is exactly what the orphan longs for. It is there for them.

The song by John Denver, 'Take Me Home, Country Roads, (RCA Victor, 1971)' touched millions of people in the 70s and 80s.' His father was in the United States Airforce, which meant considerable travelling and living in numerous locations in the USA and around the world. In his early years, John Denver had a hard time making relationships, since he did not ever live very long in one place, so he became shy, introverted and lonely, mainly because there was lack of nurture, affection, and intimacy with his father. He was magnificently talented but it would seem that he had orphan heart tendencies and the song could be interpreted in that way by the many that would identify with him. The first two words of the song underline his desire about home, 'Almost heaven.' It goes on, to where he sings 'Country Roads, take me home to the place where I belong.' A loss of belonging with an absent father creates great pain, meaning the orphan hearted feel lost in life; they experience isolation, loneliness, and a lack of identity all of which would make them feel that they do not belong, and would undermine their relationship with God. Their plight certainly identifies with the words of the song.

Acceptance

Acceptance in every relationship is absolutely fundamental, and that is a huge challenge to the orphan hearted. Naturally, people can and do survive without being connected to others, however many typically exhibit abnormal development, displaying a host of dysfunctional behaviours. Inclusion brings approval and exclusion brings abandonment. The word acceptance gives a feeling of worth and value. It also means self-acceptance, adequacy, and validity. All of this will be a positive influence on behaviour and attitude; it is feeling welcome and being received as adequate or valid and knowing favour from others. So being accepted will lead to a sense of worth and value and appreciation, which has a positive influence on behaviour and attitude in and to life. We all want to be liked, but the orphan hearted have an intense need to be liked - to love and be loved. When either of these basic needs is threatened, self-esteem is too, and this, in turn, affects the view of how worthwhile living is. To the orphan hearted this is bittersweet, because they see so many people in good relationships, and long for that, but they do not feel accepted themselves. It needs to be underlined that acceptance starts with God. His invitation is to a place of unconditional acceptance in a unique, God fashioned identity. Is not that why Jesus said, *'the greatest commandment is to love God with all your heart, all your soul and with all your mind and then love your neighbour and yourself?'* (Matthew 22:37-38).

The orphan heart is affected by feelings of worthlessness, rejection, and sadness and this is especially true of those who have been abused or abandoned by a parent. They receive a message that their lives are unimportant and their contribution to the family is neither wanted or needed. In other words, they view themselves as undesirable to those who are supposed to love them, which produces profound sorrow and even depression, and leads to a sense of a lack of value and significance. In this context the effects of the following are important:

Fear of Rejection

People are wired to seek love and acceptance, but the orphan hearted may have had an almost habitual regime of being shamed, blamed, and criticised, and would have learned that the world is not a safe place. This will lead to a self-protection with barriers being put up and the wearing of masks to cover up reality.

Fear of Being Accepted

Being accepted and liked will be such a challenge to the orphan hearted, and they self-protect to prevent anyone from getting too close to them, something which is easier because there is no trust that any sense of connection or acceptance will last. It is not difficult to succumb to fear and pull away at the first sign of disagreement. The orphan hearted will find it easier to do this as it is better to play it safe by using distance as a defence against possible future pain. Many spiritual orphans in their fear of acceptance, feel the need to prove their worth and in doing that may well:

- Seek to hide their limitations
- Perceive the strengths of others as competition
- Secretly take satisfaction in the weaknesses of others
- Seek attention inappropriately
- Expend an amount of energy on the 'impression syndrome'
- Tend to become perfectionists to prove their worth, and so will work hard for a reward of recognition and affirmation. If work can become their identity, it will give a sense of worth, however, take them out of their job and identity and value will be stripped away
- Deny the shame, which has closed down and hidden past hurts leaving the person living in unreality

CONSEQUENCES – PART 2

Trust

The orphan hearted knows all too well about trust, but mostly from a negative point of view. Trust can take years to develop, but it can be destroyed in an instant, and then it will take an age to be restored. People who have issues with trust have often had significant negative experiences in the past with family, friends, individuals, organisations, and even churches that they initially trusted. Children of divorced parents and those from abusive households are more likely to have trust issues in future relationships. Placing confidence and dependance in someone is the binding for the deepest, and strongest, relationships. Take away trust, and fear will take its place. The orphan hearted will understand the pain regarding the loss of confident trust which has often been destroyed in childhood.

While trust issues sometimes develop from negative communication experienced during early childhood, social rejection during adolescence or traumatic experiences during adulthood can also lead to trust issues. A person with trust issues will have negative beliefs, and will find themselves creating social barriers, making pronouncements, inner vows and thinking undermining thoughts, such as: 'I can never let my guard down,' 'If I open up

I will only get hurt again,' or 'everybody is out to get me.' They will do or say anything to avoid pain with the rejection associated with it. A belief system marred by violations of trust will significantly burden an individual both mentally and physically. Anxiety and stress will become a daily challenge. For those who do attempt to start a friendship, uncertainty or insecurity about whether a person feels the same, may result in pulling back, hence increasing the psychological distance. It is this self-protective behaviour, that reduces the risk of being hurt and let down. The problem is, there is no love without trust. Trust is not only born out of emotional ties with others, which include the security and confidence in them, based on the feelings generated by mutual interaction, but also on knowledge and evidence. A child or adult will trust with their head and with their heart. Both are so important in growth and maturity, particularly when mixed with faith. That is faith in the person and faith in the belief that the relationship can work.

To the orphan hearted, a loss of trust happens when those who were supposed to love and care for them, abandon and desert them. They will, after that, be determined never to allow themselves to be hurt again by those they were close to. Fear of trusting others will begin to develop, because of the past hurts, and this will include those in any measure of authority, where they have been previously wounded. The orphan hearted will want to reject any sense of order, because of the fear of control, and this will include their relationship with God, as they will see Him as a taskmaster and a tyrant rather than a loving, caring and intimate Heavenly Father.

Security

Responding in a positive way to trust, will create security, which is both a feeling and a reality, leading to becoming safe. A response in a negative way will feed the orphan heart, and lead to the continuance of dysfunction in attitude and behaviour. There are certain areas that will affect the orphan position in being secure, which will need to be honestly considered:

Do not Let the Past Define Your Future

The past is for learning lessons, dealing with issues; the present is for experience, and moving forward; the future is for dreams and destiny. Insecurity increases when the past continues through the present to become the future because people have not resolved their past fears or failures. Many orphan hearted people enter new relationships with a self-defeating, cynical, pessimistic expectation of loss. Biased by their predictions, they see only what they expect to see and react as they have in the past. They may even continue to choose the same kinds of partners, because of the familiarity those relationships offer.

Insecurity

The orphan hearted person will struggle with insecurity. They feel that they are unworthy, but their actions and words often indicate the opposite meaning. Fear of abandonment is a common driver of insecurity for many people who are mostly interdependent for existence and comfort, but the orphan hearted will have a problem with this as they are often motivated by unresolved hurts.

Lacking Confidence

When you are insecure, it changes the choices you make and alters what you might choose to do, which will often result in you having little confidence. This means that self-doubt leading to a sense of holding back will be prevalent, including the pressure of not trying different things or even other relationships, because of fear of failure.

Rejection

Simply, rejection is an inability to give or receive love - something which the orphan hearted relate to, but they also may find it difficult to define whether the rejection is real or perceived. If they are clearly aware that they are rejected, then any hint or suspicion of that from other people will destabilise them. It can become a vicious circle leading to further distancing from others, and confirmation to themselves that nobody cares. Their perception will affect negatively their sense of social acceptance, group inclusion and their fundamental feeling of belonging. Of course, everyone knows that is not true, except for the hurting person. It is probable that it will get to the stage where the orphan hearted will come to expect rejection, and also, out of fear of further rejection, will push away and withdraw from friends and others close to them. This will lead to isolating themselves further, which in turn will expose feelings of loneliness, worthlessness, and helplessness. Some have known rejection from those who are close to them, who have authority and influence, such as a father, or mother, a pastor, a spiritual leader, a boss, a teacher, a husband, a wife, a boyfriend or a girlfriend. Depending on the personality and character, there will be a reaction - for some a withdrawing, for others the showing of a rebellious, reactive and angry attitude.

The need to belong is prevalent to the orphan hearted, and rejection carries with it the power to destabilise and disconnect, which will only feed the orphan heart and create further pain. In certain difficult circumstances, rejection will produce a sudden surge of anger and aggression, both within the person and also expressed at others. Anger is synonymous with the orphan heart, whether emotionally or through demonic oppression. The orphan hearted has a strong sensitivity to rejection as well as a deep desire for acceptable social contact. The personal conflict comes because they long for closeness with others, yet what motivates them is a fear that makes it is easy for things to go wrong because there is no trust or realisation that people are not perfect. It leads to a distorted idea that, if things become too difficult, the best way is to back off quickly and reject them. This is not the way to make relationships, as it will lead to shame and grief, and if mixed with previous hurts, could make the person react in trying some way to take their pain of rejection out on another person, often through some type of emotional abuse, or even internalising it, which will damage self-esteem even further. If rejection is one of the most common emotional wounds in life, with the fear of rejection close behind, the orphan hearted has an immense challenge on their hands. For these strong negative emotions, if allowed, will create a vicious circle, prompting behaviour that no one wants, by withdrawing from people, or even attempting to abandon them, rather than taking a risk by reaching out. What remains continual and constant, is that it always hurts, and usually more than we expect. Bringing all of this to a loving, caring and willing Heavenly Father, who has such an ability to heal, however deeply wounded with rejection the orphan hearted is, has to be the way forward. I refer you to my book, 'Rejection Hurts' for a more detailed explanation.

Abandonment

Abandonment is a powerful and destructive word with long-lasting consequences, defined as desertion, to utterly forsake, to leave completely, to give up or withdraw from. Abandonment will nurture the orphan heart. It is considered that abandonment is a wound that never heals, as well as something an abandoned child never forgets. The instinct of the orphan hearted, when suffering a sense of abandonment, is to go it alone in an attitude of independence by withdrawing physically and emotionally from others. Abandonment has its source in childhood and can have lasting effects into adulthood. Whether real or perceived, it occurs when parents do not provide the emotional environment necessary for healthy development. Often abandonment will occur when:

- Children cannot live up to the unrealistic expectations of their parents.
- Children are held responsible for the actions and feelings of their parents.
- Children are continually shown disapproval, which undermines

their identity with very personal comments like, 'you're worthless,' 'you're useless,' or 'you'll never get anywhere in life.'

It is crucial for a child that boundaries are put in place, as abandonment will bring confusion and lack of definition, and will lead to a belief in their inadequacy. This will cause shame, which means a child will feel that they have done something wrong when they haven't, but what has happened is that the parents have abdicated their responsibility for them. Children are not adults and are helpless with little understanding, so they will take these issues personally and interpret that they are no longer loved. An adult is different and will make decisions, and become self-reliant, with a sense of independence. Abandonment will feed the lack of belonging that the orphan hearted have and they will feel no sense of belonging in the family of God, which will erode further what self-esteem there is. Children of God embrace interdependence, as they relate well together, which brings security, not low self-esteem, or any anxiety about the future. An abandoned child will have problems accomplishing strong and lasting bonds with others and therefore will have attachment issues in later life. The orphan hearted will consciously or unconsciously bond to abandonment, and will allow strong roots to be established, which will impair their desire and ability to move into their Heavenly Father's promise of sonship.

Control

Control has its place in the engine room of the orphan heart. Simply, it is power over another and can be manifest in different ways such as dominance, intimidation, and manipulation:

- Dominance is to assert authority or superiority over someone else or in dealing with an issue. Not only are people required to pay attention, but also to submit to the person's wishes whatever they are.
- Intimidation is an aggressive act to make another feel timid or

fearful; even filled with fear by bullying them into compliance. This could be to force or coerce, with threats or threatening behaviour. Intimidation can also be called coercive control, which is the ability to persuade someone unwilling to do something using threats of even force.

- Manipulation is a clever, skilful, artful or insidious and sly way to make another agree with something or to serve one's purpose to that person's advantage. It is a stealthy use of emotion to exploit a person in a deceptive manner, to make them feel bad about themselves, or guilty, or even ashamed, and often they are not aware of what is happening to them.

Anger plays an important part in these three areas. It can be used to create fear, whether in a loud manner, or in a quiet way, that will be recognised to gain the power that the orphan hearted desires.

Control is food and drink to the orphan hearted, because they have a subconscious selfish motivation that says, 'do anything you can to get your own way, to get people to love you, and submit to you.' They will feel safer and more superior because they are in charge, and in that no one can control them. The fear they have, is that they have to keep others under their power so that they will never leave them. This gives the orphan hearted the impetus to feel in control of their own lives, as well as the lives of others. Ultimately, they have to be challenged with the truth because it is knowing the truth, Jesus, that sets a person free, (John 8:32). Desiring control in this manner is to live a lie. It is building a house on sand and believing it will stand strong. A house built in that way never will, for destruction will inevitably happen. Only building upon the rock, Jesus, will bring the safety and security that is longed for.

Loneliness

Loneliness is a fruit of the orphan heart, which mainly grows out of childhood wounds due to an absence of love and affection, which lead to a feeling of separation and isolation, causing a person to feel empty and unwanted. It is not necessarily about being literally alone, for a person can be surrounded by people and still experience a deep and penetrating loneliness. There may well be craving for human contact, but the orphan state of mind makes it much more difficult to form good and strong bonds with others, therefore exposing a deficiency in social interaction. Humans are social beings and are wired with a natural need to connect with others. The orphan hearted having experienced or perceived rejection, is not motivated to make relationships with new friends. It is the fear of being hurt again, that would make them shy away in the belief that they have no chance of being fulfilled in a new relationship. Loneliness is not solitude, for most people need time out from others, particularly if they are somewhat introverted, as they seem to be more comfortable in conversing with as few people as possible. However, those who are lonely want to interact with others, but find they find they cannot, and struggle to find a way to do so. They will take the other alternative and back away, as the realisation of the difficulty of not being able to mix with others gets stronger. It the orphan hearted has no one to confide in, they will give way to negative reactions such as self-criticism, a lack of self-worth, or self-confidence with an underlying shyness, that can lead to depression. They will always think it is someone else's fault and never their own. Loneliness is not cured by making more and more friends, but by being able to trust those friends to the extent, that revealing something about themselves, gives them a sense of purpose, and achievement, so much so, that they can even begin to feel good, accepted and certainly less lonely.

God Himself will never have a problem with loneliness because He is three persons, Father, Son, and Holy Spirit, who are in a complete and perfect communion with one another. They are indeed inseparable and epitomise such a depth of relationship. Amazingly, we are made in that image and likeness, (Genesis 1:27), and can share in that communion with our whole being, and an intimate relationship, knowing completeness in body, soul, and spirit. We were made for this and it becomes a core challenge to the orphan hearted person because they have great difficulty in perceiving that kind of relationship. Adam and Eve did have that relationship with God to the extent that He walked in the garden with them in the fulness of who He is, and probably day by day (Genesis 3:9). That was until they chose to leave home, thinking there was something better that God was concealing. There was not, and they lost everything. However, God has provided a way to return through His son Jesus, for He would never leave us alone without being able to commune with Him. Regretfully the firstborn son of Adam and Eve was in great conflict, and there is no doubt that something of the loss, the hurt, and pain from his parents had transferred to him. Cain was an angry man, who tried to control and manipulate God by selfishly attempting to get his own way. It did not work, and after taking no notice of God's warning, killed his brother Abel, (Genesis 4:6-7). God had no choice, but to banish Cain with these words, *'you will be a restless or homeless wanderer on this earth,'* (Genesis 4:6-7; 10-12). This is the perfect example of the orphan hearted, which is underscored by rejection, as it feeds into the deep personal hurt. No matter how attractive life looks on the outside, the orphan hearted cannot escape the disturbing feeling of loneliness on the inside. This will drive the person to seek peace and contentment, feeling that there must be something better or different, but it is almost always without success, as they continue to search for someone to accept them, or somewhere to belong.

Many years ago the issue of loneliness provoked a powerful and penetrating, yet poignant song, which became a classic. In the centre of Liverpool there is a bronze sculpture of the subject, Eleanor Rigby, sat on a seat in a square for all to see, and take in the challenge of belonging:

> 'All the lonely people
> Where do they all come from?
> All the lonely people
> Where do they all belong?'
> (The Beatles, *Eleanor Rigby*, Parlophone, 1966).

Our home is in God alone, we belong with Him, and in Him, and this includes the orphan hearted, for there is no reality outside of Him, only emptiness.

Fear and Shame

These areas are keys in the core of the orphan heart. They do not just hang around waiting to turn up, they deliberately break into a life, sticking like Superglue, and they know how and when to manifest, and cause as much destruction as they can. They intrude at the worst possible moments and are often embedded in the brokenness of people. They are leading components in separating people from a relationship with God, and others, as well as themselves. The first time these words are mentioned early in Genesis, is concerning Adam and Eve leaving home, and becoming orphan hearted, something which affects many lives today.

Genesis 2:25: '*the man and his wife were both naked, and they felt no shame*'

Genesis 3:7-10: Their eyes were opened and they realised they were naked, so they hid from God and took leaves from a fig tree to cover themselves. When God questioned them, Adam said, 'I was afraid because I was naked, so I hid.' Since then humankind has continued to hide, whether from God, each other, or themselves.

There are two principles here: Firstly, where something is mentioned for the first time in the scripture, there is often a key to their interpretation in further situations in the future. To the orphan hearted, today, fear and shame will be prevalent in their lives in various ways, and, as can be seen with Adam and Eve, contribute to their isolation, and their separation from their Heavenly Father. Secondly, fear and shame are often hidden in lives, maybe through denial, or even a person not realising they are there, yet can still contribute in driving the orphan hearted away from God, as happened with Adam and Eve.

Fear

Fear is a powerful and primitive human emotion, which alerts us to the presence of danger. It cannot take much to trigger the fear response in most people's lives. We become afraid when we encounter things and situations that we do not understand, cannot control, and/or cause harm to us. It is also a natural emotion and a survival mechanism. Traumatised people, often orphan hearted, have conditioned fears. These are formed when they have a negative experience and are afraid of something similar happening again. Rational decisions are very difficult to make when afraid, leaving fear to become tormenting, and making a person feel hopeless. Being fearful will keep the orphan hearted from accomplishing their goals because they are too afraid to try. The challenge to them is the great difficulty of surrendering their lives to Father God, even while knowing that He invites them to a secure place in His love, care, and nurture. They will attempt to hide, and try working it out for themselves, covering up with whatever modern fig leaves they can find, because they have a wrong fear of God. Being unsure of their place in the human family will undermine their place in the family of God. Sons and daughters of God have nothing to fear, because they are already secure in their Father's love, and know their place in His family. They know how to trust in their Heavenly Father's faithfulness whatever happens, but the orphan hearted do not know how to trust, as they were not nurtured in that context as children.
Fear is delineated in two ways in the scripture:

Firstly, *'there is no fear in love, perfect love drives out fear, because fear has to do with punishment'* (1 John 4:18 NIV). God is not a judge to execute punishment on us, He is just, righteous and merciful with grace and forgiveness.

Secondly, 'the fear of the Lord is the beginning of wisdom,' (Proverbs 9:10). This is a sense of Divine majesty incorporating awe and reverence being joined in love, which creates a closeness to our Heavenly Father in trust, and a desire to serve and worship Him. This is a different, but right kind of fear.

Shame

Shame is an intense and painful feeling that makes a person believe that they are flawed and unworthy of love, value, and worth. It will impact the emotional and mental health of a person, which may lead to dysfunctional behaviour. The initial reaction to shame is to hide and run away, and the term 'dying of shame' has relevance due to the fact a person does not want to be seen by anyone, and certainly not in a way that would influence others to judge them. Maybe 'dying of shame' is more than just a throw-away expression, perhaps something does happen that may affect the person deep within the human spirit. It has been recognised that shame is connected to a person's early years, and if children are not shown love, they internalise a message, that says there is something wrong with them, which leaves them confessing, 'it must be my fault.' Shame is part of the foundation of the orphan heart, and was very much there at the beginning when Adam and Eve disobeyed God, Their eyes were opened, and they felt shame at their nakedness, where there had been none before. They scrambled to cover themselves, being seemingly more concerned and ashamed with their nakedness than with their disobedience to God's command. In its deception, shame directed them away from the truth into a selfish and personal reaction. It is clear that events in childhood, that are abusive and damaging, will produce shame, which will undermine self-esteem, destabilise self-awareness, and bring a child to blame themselves when they wonder what they have done wrong. On the whole, they have done nothing wrong; it is rather the wrong done to them, yet they still feel responsible for what had happened. It is important, therefore, to differentiate guilt from shame, for confusing guilt with shame will cause problems, because people so often will feel guilty even when they have done nothing wrong. Guilt is the feeling that a person has when they have done something wrong, but shame tells a person they are wrong, and it becomes deceptive and toxic as it releases a false condemnation as they internalise it. Guilt says, 'you made a mistake,' shame says, 'you are a mistake.' This empowers shame to feed the orphan heart and will help to produce an ungodly belief system, being a stronghold in the mind, that will need to be transformed by restoration and renewal. In an attempt to cover up shame, the orphan hearted will often react in an oversensitive manner, attempt to justify their actions by going into denial, and even endeavour to blame others. The challenge is to be vulnerable in opening up to others, and in showing them what they are really like, and to experience that others can still love, and accept them in their most exposed state. The remedy to dissolve shame is to acknowledge, embrace, and experience the love of our Heavenly Father. God's love will cover shame, and meet the desire of the orphan hearted to be free from it. What Jesus did was love, and accept the people with compassion and mercy, and today nothing changes, it is still a redemptive love, and will bring reconciliation, and harmony with Father God and to others.

Anger

There is no doubt that anger has a strong connection to the orphan hearted, which can give ground for an oppressive and afflicting demonic spirit of anger to manifest. It is a root issue we must not neglect, not only because of its consequences, but it is one of the hardest emotions to handle. Anger becomes a major factor in so many issues. Even when the person seems afraid or depressed, often anger is underneath. It is a powerful emotion, which can be constructive or destructive. It can be harnessed and channelled with integrity, or allowed to wreak havoc. Anger does not go away, even in childhood, as it highlights what is going on inside the person, particularly when emotional pain is mixed with the frustration of not being loved and accepted. The orphan hearted can be in so much pain, that the anger at various times can explode producing fear and intimidation. At other times it may be more passive, seething or smouldering away, building up resentment, and even bitter root judgment. It becomes very difficult to handle for a child, and it seems clear that anger that is carried in the heart towards the past, makes a person less capable of loving or being loved in the present. Anger can be intense to the degree of yelling or shouting at someone, with a fervid reaction seeking revenge and punishment, or can be at the other extreme, with the silent treatment of rage and fury, simmering just under the surface. Remember it was Cain, who was **very** angry because he did not get his own way, who attempted to manipulate and control God, (Genesis 4:4-8). In his anger, from the consequence of his orphan heart and rejection, he murdered his brother.

Anger is a necessary human passion, which can be handled in a right and proper way. The Message translates it so clearly, *'Go ahead and be angry. You do well to be angry - but do not use your anger as fuel for revenge. And do not stay angry. Do not go to bed angry. Do not give the Devil that kind of foothold in your life,'* (Ephesians 4:26-27). Anger is a necessary part of life and common to all, however, it is not to be denied, rather recognised, understood, accepted, and controlled in the right manner. It is important to understand that the Bible cannot say, do not be angry, but be angry and do not sin! It recognises the true sense of anger. A sense of indignation at a perceived unfair, or wrong treatment, fuelled by injustice, fits in this category. The danger comes when the orphan hearted think that every issue and circumstance, that has affected them gives them a right to be angry, and this becomes an excuse for them to say that their anger is justified. This wrong attitude will only prevent the orphan hearted from solving their problems, for anger is not a solution to frustration, but a reaction to it. Being hateful or desiring revenge is only a small step beyond anger, and Jesus even compares the power of anger to murder, (Matthew 5:21-22).

There are certain facts about anger, that are important to be considered by the orphan hearted person:

- Anger is universal
- Everyone gets angry

- No one escapes anger
- We will react according to the degree and depth of hurt, that we have inside of us
- Certain things will trigger the reaction and it is necessary to find what is underneath, that is festering enough to react.
- Anger can be very self-protective being used to cover painful places within.

Anger is excessively controlling and will be used by the orphan hearted in many ways to dominate, intimidate, and manipulate to protect themselves, or get their own way. No human being was created to control or be controlled, but many of us have been affected, or affect others, by control with impulsive or reactive anger, my father being a clear example. Anger can be used to redirect the strong emotions, by refocusing and inflicting the pain elsewhere, either into the person's own body, so that self-inflicted wounds numbs the deeper issue temporarily, or by shifting blame to others. It is always perceived to be the fault of someone else, because of which they will put others at a distance, or even push them away, when what the orphan hearted really wants and needs, is the exact opposite. Often their anger is not proportionate to the situation, but usually greater than it, because the anger has been stored deep within from past and previous damaging experiences. This will not only lead to a response to any recent problem, but also mixed in with this will be a reaction, that comes out of previous hurt, because it has never been dealt with. If anger is repressed, it may surface as depression, as the orphan hearted has a learned behaviour which recognises that their feelings are so negative that they will make sure those feelings are hiding beneath a so-called acceptable, pleasant, and often religious mask, hoping they will disappear. They never do, and will ultimately make the situation that much worse. As well as this, the manifestation of anger with the orphan hearted will be made so much more difficult if the enemy gets a foothold into the person. This will ultimately open a door to the demonic and access will be given to an orphan spirit to oppress, and afflict the person, which may expose issues leading to uncontrollable anger and fits of rage.

Summary

It is quite clear, therefore, that the orphan hearted have many issues that can seriously negatively affect them, as to how they feel about themselves, and how they foster relationships with others. However, things can change dramatically when they can get to the place where they understand, and then take responsibility for their actions. The longing in their hearts is for genuine and secure relationships, that can be built into something strong, and it is then that healing, and maybe deliverance too, can take place. First and foremost, they need to see that they have a spiritual problem, and that their Loving Heavenly Father is who He says He is. He is the healer and also the Father who wants to draw close to forge unbreakable relationships to bring them into freedom, so that their past does not have to define their future. Then the orphan hearted will have confidence that they belong, even to the extent in which they will be secure enough to trust others, because of their deep and strong relationship with God.

WHERE DO YOU LIVE?

Pursuit

A necessary truth in our walk with God, and something that is often a revelation to the orphan hearted, is the fact that He desires to have a close relationship with us. This may seem obvious, and is, of course, foundational, but I believe it has been somewhat understated, thus affecting us in the way that we respond to God as a Father. It is not just us opening ourselves to Him, but realising that He has always been there for us. I remember so clearly God calling me to come into His Kingdom through Jesus, and I did so through repentance and faith, finding Jesus as my Saviour and Lord. I was undoubtedly aware of the closeness of Jesus in my life. I was overwhelmed by His love, and I began to love Him, but I somehow was not aware of His relationship with His Father, or the Father's desire to have a relationship with me. I needed to understand that closeness means two things: intimacy and responsibility. God holds us close but makes special demands on us. However, many want closeness but nothing else, and our orphan attitude will attempt to undermine both.

A while back, I woke up early with these words on my mind, 'faith is a relationship.' I had been influenced by something I had read, and if faith is a relationship, closeness must be a key. For the closer I get, the more confidence I have in Him; the closer I get, the more the trust that I have in Him grows, which leaves me able to trust in who He is, and trust in what He says. This is trust without reservation. The orphan hearted would agree that there is a longing in our generation for a father, but I would also say there is a Father longing to give this generation closeness and intimacy. So many Christians struggle with this because of the orphan tendencies in their hearts. Orphan and closeness are quite the opposite of each other. The orphan hearted, because of being fatherless, feel that they have no definition, therefore they struggle with identity. It is this that keeps them apart and separate, and it cannot take much to default to keep at a distance.

We can sum up what to look for in our relationship with God in three ways:

- To find affirmation in and from Him
- To know intimacy with Him
- To hear and know His voice

This becomes a place of security and safety where we can feel at home with our God. Our self-image, self-awareness, and self-acceptance become strong because, as we can soak in His love, we can receive the words of acceptance, value, and worth that He speaks into us. We become friends with our Heavenly Father, and there is a closeness and togetherness, affection and attachment because He has made it possible for us to have a close relationship with Him.

Distance

We see that in the Old Testament, very few were allowed to get close to God. It was not like that at the very beginning, because Heaven came down to earth as God entered into His rest, as He walked and communed with His human creation. In this context, it is clear that Heaven and Earth are made for one another. However, we will see later how the man and the woman ultimately orphaned themselves, as they decided to go their own way without their Heavenly Father. So many Christians struggle with this because of the orphan tendencies in their hearts, which keeps them apart and separate. Moses was one of those who were close to God, and God said to him, *'come up the mountain to the Lord with the elders and worship at a distance, but only Moses alone is to approach,'* (Exodus 24:1-2). They saw God and ate and drank, but at a distance. What I love, is that they did what was natural by eating and drinking, which is what Jesus introduced at the last supper, (Matthew 26:26-29) however, it was at a distance. It was a place of manifest glory, but at a distance. Today, things have changed; we can get as near to God as we want, as there are no barriers, and this in itself can present a challenge to the orphan hearted, for many of them feel more comfortable at a distance.

It was in the wilderness that God gave the pattern for worshipping Him to Moses. The Tabernacle became the focus of the encampment in the wilderness, with the tribes positioned in a certain order around it. This, ultimately, became the framework for Solomon's Temple, and later Temples, until AD70, when the Temple in Jerusalem was destroyed by the Roman army. The Temples were designed and built in a similar way to the Tabernacle in the Wilderness, except that they were made of stone. The Tabernacle was designed to provide God with a dwelling place of rest, where everything was made and fashioned in a certain order (Exodus 25:8). In simple terms, there was an outer court, an inner court, the Holy Place and within that, the Holy of Holies. God's presence was visible. It could be seen from the outside, from a distance, looking like a cloud of fire, but only the High Priest could see it on the inside (Numbers 9:15-16). The High Priest could only enter at the times ordained by God and was told that if he went in at any other time, he would die, (Leviticus 16:1-2). There was a very detailed procedure that the High Priest had to follow in order to be able to enter into the presence of God. The Day of Atonement was essential, Hebrews 9:7-8 for it was designated for the purpose of redemption through blood, which put the whole of the people of Israel in relationship with God.

It was a solemn undertaking. No one else was allowed into the Holy of Holies, and the ceremony only took place once a year. The whole area was surrounded by a curtain wall and gate; there was a door into the Holy Place, and a veil into the Holy of Holies. Only the High Priest could pass through the veil; everyone else had to keep their distance. The purpose of the veil was to conceal; it acted as a barrier. It prevented access to God, for the way into God's presence was not open. The veil shut God in and shut humanity out, which concealed the glory of God. We know that the Tabernacle was a type, a symbol, and a foreshadowing of the eternal redemption of Christ who shed His blood to finally give us constant access to our loving Heavenly Father. The reason why the veil or curtain in the Temple in Jerusalem was torn from top to bottom as Jesus died, was not only to give us access to God, but to give Him access to us! This is closeness and God made the way. We can now get near to God in His holiness because He is such a loving Father who longs to draw us to Himself.

From the Garden of Eden, where God consistently walked with Adam and Eve until the coming of Jesus, there was very little personal access to God. There were certain individuals highlighted in scripture that were close to God, however, they were the few, and certainly not the many. After the birth of the third child, Seth, of Adam and Eve, there was a time when men began to call on the name of the Lord, Genesis 4:26. One of them, Enoch walked with God, and ultimately and amazingly God took him to Himself before he died, (Genesis 5:22-24). Others walked with God and entered into a covenant with Him, including Noah, (Genesis 6:9) and Isaac (Genesis 48:15). The cry of a later prophet to the people was to '*walk humbly with your God*,' (Micah, 6:8). Throughout the Old Testament, the prophets walked with God, heard His voice and communicated to the people in various ways, sometimes miraculously, but were quite alone.

Presence

The privilege we have in our relationship with God is that He has made it possible for us to live day by day with continued awareness of His presence. God being distant is not the problem, for that is more due to our personal response to Him, and the orphan hearted would identify with that. The word presence is key to being close to God, and there are those in the Old Testament that understood this because it became a reality to them in their relationship with God. The original Hebrew scriptures often speak of God's presence in human history, and the most common term for presence is the word 'panim,' which is also translated face. Presence and face are synonymous in the Old Testament, meaning that face describes exactly the nature of presence. This would, therefore, indicate that God's intention in a relationship is to get not only close but face to face with His creation; it implies a close and personal encounter with God. The thread through the Hebrew scriptures, that highlights what closeness and present meant, tended to fade as the prophets were raised up. This is probably because of their message, which was often tinged with judgement, although they certainly knew God in a personal way. As the Old Testament concludes, there is a gap of around 400 years, and although some were crying out for the Messiah to come and deal with the oppressor in Israel, however, when He did actually arrive, He was not recognised. Yet Jesus brought with Him the Kingdom of God, declaring that it was at hand, which is very near, and He also called His disciples His friends, and so, accepting all, became close even to the poor, the oppressed, and the sinners.

Moses

Moses knew God face to face, and at the end of his life, there is a compelling testimony to him knowing God in this most amazing way, (Deuteronomy 34:10-12). God even considered him as His friend, '*the Lord would speak to Moses face to face, as a man speaks to a friend,*' (Exodus 33:11). It all began in the wilderness when a burning bush that was not consumed caught his attention, (Exodus 3:1-3). He was tending a flock of sheep on the 'far side' of the desert, and it is apparent that orphan hearted people understand that, but what takes time to realise, is that God was already there waiting for an encounter. Moses was at Horeb, which is called the mountain of God. Being in the wilderness has its advantages if we are prepared to make the right choice. It was a very dramatic time with a scrubby, thorny old bush blazing away when suddenly a voice spoke out of it. Fire indicates the presence of God, and Moses was drawn to this, and this fire was the reality of the manifest presence of God. The fire occupied the bush and did not consume it, but instead revealed God's continuous presence. It became the start of Moses being used for God's purpose to set a nation free. God chooses the despised, foolish and weak to be His servants. In doing this, He confounds the mighty, demonstrates His power, and reveals who He is, (1 Corinthians 1:27-28). *'God gave favour from within the bush, from His dwelling place, His place of rest,'* (Deuteronomy 33:16). It is the last place where you would expect God to be, but that was where He dwelt in His rest. This is totally outside of our perception, conception, boundaries, and traditions, but is not this what God wants, as we tussle with our orphan issues, to refine and empower us to walk more completely in our destiny?

Job

To many, the book of Job is a challenge, however, it is littered with gems that inspire, and give confidence that God is with us, as He was with Job. *'Oh, for the days when I was in my prime when God's intimate friendship blessed my house,'* (Job 29:4 NIV). Another translation says, 'I was in the prime of life, God All-Powerful was my closest friend,' Contemporary English Version. Most of you will be aware of what Job went through, but we do need to harmonise this with the fact that God conversed freely with him, as one bosom-friend to another. God came into Job's tent as a friend and was not afraid to acquaint him with His plans. It was as though God's intimate friendship rested upon Job's tent. God was with him through the turmoil of loss, etc, and it is important for the orphan hearted not to mistake silence and stillness for immobility. God was there working out His purpose for the bigger picture. It certainly puts a different perspective on things.

Abraham

Abraham had a remarkable relationship with God. God's call grew into something more than a servant to master relationship; it was like that of a son to a father (Genesis 12:1) which led to Abraham being called God's friend (Isaiah 41:8). Even in the New Testament, where James talks about Abraham's faith, he writes that Abraham was God's friend, (James 2:23). The term friend leans to intimacy, and conveys a sense of closeness, trust, and sharing, meaning an agreement to walk together. Bear in mind that this is more than being mutual, as it seems quite clear it was God's initiative. This is not just God asking for loyalty and dependability, but amazingly God saying that He will be loyal and dependable to His friend Abraham. And, it is not just left there, for God goes further by changing his name from Abram, 'Exalted Father,' to Abraham, 'Father of Many,' (Genesis 17:3-5). The part of the extended name, 'ha,' means breath, so could it be that God put part of who He is into Abraham? It is clear that God took friendship with Abraham very seriously, even to the point of confiding in Abraham regarding what He was about to do in Sodom and Gomorrah, (Genesis 18:17-19). This can be food and drink to the orphan hearted person, for to consider our loving Heavenly Father in this way has to be the path to healing and release.

Jacob

Jacob had a powerful and spontaneous experience with God, that he neither planned nor expected. Jacob was alone, and a man wrestled with him till daybreak, (Genesis 32:24-29). What God wanted was for Jacob to have nothing except utter reliance on someone stronger than he was. So God touched the socket of Jacob's hip, and he was unable to stand alone, for his strength had gone. The only place for Jacob to look for strength was in someone else. Perhaps being disabled, in one way or another, can sometimes be part of God's plan, so that in our weakness God's strength is made perfect. The orphan hearted should pay attention, and learn to let go, by holding on to God alone. The quality of sonship is also highlighted here, for as Jacob softened and wept, he asked for God's favour, which was granted, (Hosea 12:4). It is as though Jacob had a new start, as God gave him a new name - Israel, meaning a Prince of God. Jacob names the place Peniel, not just because of the presence of God, but he said, 'I have seen God face to face, yet my life has been preserved.' Even with a man like Jacob, God wanted to get as close as face to face with him. This must be an impetus for the orphan hearted - that once again God takes initiative to get close to become a friend.

The Priestly Blessing

There is a wonderful blessing that God wanted to give to His people, and it so compliments the fact of Him wanting a close relationship with them. Even though God's consideration was to bless the nation Israel, corporately and individually, on a consistent and continual basis, it also sums up the heart of God regarding His desire for closeness to all who respond to Him. This certainly includes the orphan hearted who find it difficult to get close to God, for the prayer shows very clearly, that He has provided a way to the reality of the relationship they can have with Him.

'The Lord said to Moses, speak to Aaron and his sons, this is how you are to bless the Israelites, say to them: The Lord bless you and keep you; The Lord make his face to shine upon you and be gracious to you; The Lord lift up his countenance upon you, and give you peace. So they shall put my name on the Israelites, and I will bless them,' (Numbers 6:24-27).

It is a prayer that is founded in the grace of our loving Heavenly Father. This invocation of blessing will enrich and empower our lives with favour, peace, and boundless abundance. It is a declaration that we can speak over one another, releasing the richness of 'shalom' to include good health, security, inner harmony, wellness, material prosperity, and long life. It is God giving us His personal consideration, and He pays particular attention to the individual to make possible the achievement of wholeness and peace. The face of God is His gift of grace to those who respond to Him. The shining face of God indicates that He looks upon His people with pleasure and favour. God is so personal that He turns His face towards us, and pays attention to us as individuals, whoever we are. There is no rejection or discrimination.

God At Home

As we have seen in the Old Testament, some had a strong relationship with God, however very few had what Adam and Eve had. They knew the presence of God in a wonderful way, which was something that God had originally intended for everyone on the earth. When God finished His work of creation and saw that it was good, He rested on the seventh day, (Genesis 1:31; 2:2-3). God's rest did not come out of weariness, but out of the fact that He had completed His work satisfactorily. Rest, in this context, means satisfaction, refreshment, and peace. This rest (Hebrew 'nuach') gives an ability to handle stress and busyness and helps to operate from a place of strength instead of a place of restlessness. What God wanted, was for His created humanity to share in His rest, because it is so linked to His presence. *'My presence will go with you, and I will give you rest,'* (Exodus 33:14). He was saying I will personally go with you, and give you my rest. This was the common expression for possession of the Promised Land, the inheritance of the Children of Israel. This gives safety, security, and peace in a place of wellbeing and shalom. The concept of rest is a beautiful thing, for we meet God as our Father, who desires to be with us, and He certainly does not expect us to perform to attain acceptance! It was in God's heart to be at rest with His creation, and so He came down to the garden where Adam and Eve were so that they could be with Him. Psalm 23 highlights rest from the context of the Lord being our shepherd, particularly verse 2, 'He leads me beside still waters or waters of rest.' Tragically, when Adam and Eve left Him, the access they had to the rest of God was lost, and what became manifest by God's declaration to their firstborn son Cain was a restless wandering. Rest became restlessness and settling became wandering. This is the essence of the orphan heart.

Adam and Eve certainly became aware that God had purposed in His heart to be with them. '*Then the man and his wife heard the sound of the Lord God as he was walking in the garden in the cool of the day,*' (Genesis 3:8). It is probable that God communed with them often by walking in the garden. When they heard the sound of God in the cool breeze of the evening, they knew that He had come to walk, talk, and commune with them. The word walk means walking for pleasure. The man and the woman lived in a deeply spiritual relationship and close communication with God. They recognised Him because He came in human form. It was a glorious foretaste of incarnation. It would have thrilled them that God came down from Heaven because He wanted to be with them in the beauty of the garden. God placed them there in glorious surroundings and provided for them in such a kind, considerate and generous way. It was magnificent, for they were His pleasure - God was their friend as well as their Father. Amazingly, they walked with God. I wonder what they talked about...The essence of scripture is that, 'He has set eternity in our hearts, (Ecclesiastes 3:11).' God has put within each one of us a desire to commune and to be close to Him. When He came, it was the cool of the day, which is literally 'in the wind of the day,' They heard the sound of the Lord as He walked towards them (Genesis 3:8). The word 'sound' is 'wind,' a Hebrew word we might recognise, 'ruach.' It can also mean breath or the Spirit of God. It was as though God came in human form surrounded by a whirlwind of life. God's ruach is the source of life. Job understood this truth, 'the Spirit of God has made me; the breath [ruach] of the Almighty gives me life,' (Job 33:4). We also see God's care for the man and woman because He came in the cool of the day, and that was not because it was more pleasant for Him, but more the best time for them. This is God, in His kindness, first and foremost considering His creation. Is not this complete harmony with Him walking and talking with His creation? This is God at home; this is Heaven coming to Earth.

It is amazing that all religions apart from one, Christianity, began with a man seeking after God. The Bible starts with the reality that God was and is seeking after man. This highlights the crucial difference between our faith and every other religion in the world. It is this that has touched me deeply in the sense of being a son. We have had our priorities the wrong way round. First and foremost, our loving Heavenly Father has pursued us! It is out of that that we seek Him. We do not have to do anything to be accepted. We start our walk with Him in His acceptance, and this begins an awareness that we are not orphans, but sons and daughters.

Adam And Eve Leave Home

One day, God came into the garden. Adam and Eve heard Him coming and hid from Him because they were naked and afraid. This prompted the first question asked in the Bible. 'The Lord God called to the man, where are you?' Clearly, God knew the answer, but He wanted a response from Adam. Something had happened because they were not there waiting for God. They had disconnected, but God wanted to find them and not to leave them to their fear and shame to abandon them. They were lost, but God had come to find them. His deep love for them together with His immeasurable grace, meant that He did not come with anger and condemnation, but with compassion and restoration. However, they had lost that deep and intimate communion with Him. We may feel lost, we may be hiding and be fearful, but He comes as our loving Heavenly Father to save us from the judgement we deserve and bring reconciliation. As He comes to offer sonship, it gives us an opportunity to recognise and deal with our orphan heart, and to receive our inheritance and walk into our destiny in Him. Adam and Eve lost so much, which included the concept of rest [nuach] and the presence of the Spirit of God [ruach]. Their irresponsible decision gave God no choice, as, in great sorrow, He sent them away from the security of home, Himself, into the wilderness. They became orphan hearted, because they were separated from His love and all that it represented. By leaving home, they lost that closeness and presence. By default, they became orphan hearted, as so many are today. What God wanted, and still wants, is not just a few, but everyone coming close to Him in relationship as our loving Heavenly

Father.

How different it is now, as it is not just a few, but all that can come close in their relationship with Father God, Therefore, I can accept myself, because God accepts me, and I can come with a boldness and confidence to not just a loving God, but to my loving God, who opens His heart to receive me. I know my identity and destiny are defined by God, and I am on a wonderful and challenging journey with Him, not as an employee or a slave, but as a son with a servant heart, and a wonderful inheritance. Surely sonship then is our highest calling, which means that, as His Sons and Daughters, we have the closest place with Him, which is more than we could ever imagine. God did not abandon Adam and Eve, but in His mercy, He made provision for them, which became such a prophetic sign for us today. In Genesis 3:21, 'God made them garments of skin to cover them.' He sacrificed animals and clothed Adam and Eve with their skins showing that redemption comes through the shedding of blood and that one day the Lamb of God will be slain to bring us back to that relationship, that we were made for. This would happen through Jesus, the last Adam, (1 Corinthians 15:45-49) and all that was lost will be restored, so that the orphan hearted will come into sonship through the divine exchange of the cross.

Where Do You Live?

The message of Jesus was to bring Heaven to Earth, with the declaration and manifestation of the Kingdom of God. Heaven and Earth are made for each other, but they have been separated for too long. In Genesis 1 and 2, God came down to Earth to be at home with His creation, and what He desired was to be at home with His sons and daughters. Sadly, Adam and Eve separated themselves from Him, and in doing so lost their close relationship, and opened a door to the orphan heart, which took preeminence in their lives.

John 1 is the New Genesis, the New Creation, where God incarnate in Jesus came to live and make His home among us. As God did in the beginning,

Jesus did again, '*the Word became flesh and blood, and moved, or pitched His tent, in our neighbourhood. We saw the glory with our own eyes, the one-of-a-kind glory, like Father, like Son,*' (John 1:14 Message). This was illustrated when Jacob dreamed of a stairway or ladder from Earth to Heaven with angels ascending and descending, (Genesis 28:10-22). He realised that this was the gate to Heaven and called the place Bethel, meaning the house of God. Jacob's life was changed forever, particularly when he returned to Bethel, (Genesis 35), where God gave him a new and very important name, Israel. At the beginning of His ministry, Jesus made an obvious reference to Jacob's dream and said that He was the ladder or stairway in the New Creation between Heaven and Earth (John 1:51). The death of Jesus broke open the veil of separation between God and humanity in the temple; the resurrection of Jesus underlines the fact that Jesus dwells with us, and the release of the Holy Spirit to the church at Pentecost means He dwells within us. For all of us, including the orphan hearted, it means that this is the revelation of God's continual and manifest presence with us and in us, as His sons and daughters.

All of this leads to a strange question that two of John the Baptist's disciples had for Jesus. He was passing by and John said, 'look the Lamb of God.' They began to follow Jesus who turned around and asked them what they wanted. They said, 'where are you staying,' and Jesus replied, 'come and see,' (or come and discover for yourselves), (John 1:35-39). The original Greek word for staying is 'menai,' meaning where you live, or dwell or abide. When John's disciples asked that question, it was so natural, and Jesus replied naturally. Abide means living - to rest and to be at home. They asked a question, and He said, 'come and see.' It is so down to earth. Did it mean that, as they got to know Him, they would find out where he lived? Was there a geographical place? A hotel, or Peter's home, or with His mum and family? He did not rent; He had no mortgage; He had nothing. Jesus did respond to someone who wanted to follow Him with quite a challenge, by saying, '*foxes have dens and birds have nests, but the Son of Man has no place to lay his head,*' (Matthew 8:20).

They just wanted to be with Him; they had a desire to be with Him. They must have felt quite a need to get close. Abide is also used in a deeper way when Jesus declares that He is the 'True Vine.' He said, *'abide [menai] in me, and I in you. As the branch cannot bear fruit by itself, unless it abides in the vine, neither can you, unless you abide in me,'* (John 15:4). The Passion Translation says, 'live your life intimately joined to mine.' Intimacy means, closely acquainted, cherished, deep-seated, faithful, constantly devoted, and inseparable. This is closeness. If we mix our life with another, it does mean we can see into them, and they can see into us. With intimacy with the Father, we will feel known. It is not focusing on what we are not, but on who we are. Intimacy is described as '**in-to-me-see**.' How can anyone 'see into' you and who you are - your fears, dreams, hopes, and desires - unless you know who you are, and are willing to allow someone in? Cannot God want to do that with us? God knows us better than anyone can, therefore He can make us feel known in a way that no one on earth is able, and in this we experience intimacy.

Jesus and the Father

To know, understand and get close to the Father, we need to know Jesus, because He came to reveal the Father. Jesus answered, I am the way and the truth and the life. No one comes to the Father except through me. If you really know me, you will know my Father as well. From now on, you do know him and have seen him. Anyone who has seen me has seen the Father. Do not you believe that I am in the Father and that the Father is in me,' (John 14:6-10). The answer to us being close to the Father is to see how close Jesus was to Him. John 1:18 brings some clarity, 'No man has seen God at any time; the only begotten Son, who is in the bosom of the Father, he has declared him,' (King James 2000). Bosom is a word that is not often used but is such a key. It is the front of a person's chest, and is thought of as the centre of human feelings. The Jewish custom for eating was not to sit as we would, but to recline on couches. Tables were provided, and around them were placed cushions capable of containing three or more persons. On these the guests reclined, leaning on their left side with their feet extended from the table, in such a way that the head of one naturally reclined on the bosom of another. To recline near to someone in this manner denoted intimacy, which is what was meant by lying 'in the bosom' of another. Another translation of John 1:18 says, 'no one has ever seen God, but the one and only Son, who is himself God, and is in closest relationship with the Father, has made him known.' Remember that John, the writer of this gospel, the one whom Jesus loved, was leaning on Jesus' bosom, (John 13:23). It is where a close friend with a special bond could sit beside another, placing his head on the chest as a sign of intimacy, mutual love, friendship, and understanding. Bosom relates to the heart, and to love, to unity and intimate presence, meaning the closest of intimacy. Remember too that the heart, in biblical literature, has a wider meaning and application than just feelings. It is the entire interior life of the person, including the feelings, heart and will, being the seat of deep affection. Jesus in the bosom of the Father is in eternal intimate communion between the Father and the Son, a relationship of love in its purest form. Therefore, Jesus represents God the Father to us in every way possible, because He lives in, and through, His heart or bosom. Jesus has a knowledge of the Father, which no one else could ever possess, that makes Him qualified above all to make Him known. Jesus underlined His unity and oneness with His Father particularly in the Gospel of John, *'I and my Father are one,'* (John 10:30), *'He who loves me will be loved by the Father,'* (John 14:21). Jesus replied, *'Loving me empowers you to obey my word. And my Father will love you so deeply that we will come to you and make you our dwelling place,'* (John 14:23 TPT). The initiative taken in that oneness is to come and dwell with us. Jesus was never alone, for His Father was continually with Him (John 16:32). What Jesus achieved in His life, death and resurrection has opened the door [Himself] for us to commune closely with the Father. Because of our relationship with Jesus as friend, Saviour, and Lord, we come into the same relationship with the Father that Jesus had when He walked this Earth. As He is within, and therefore secure in, His Father, so are we, being in Him as He is in us. *'Our lives are hidden with Christ in God,'*

(Colossians 3:3). Therefore when we sense and begin to know the depth of love God has for us, then we embrace Him.

This is called home because God is home...

This is not Heaven and home in eternity far away from Earth, this is being at home with God, in the here and now! God has made his home amongst humankind, therefore we can make our home with Him. This is not waiting for His return to take us to Heaven. Heaven has come to earth now! Home is where we hear affirmation and receive love and acceptance from God. God is calling for a homecoming in these days. Jesus came from the Father's Heart and He wants us to rest there in the family dwelling - at home. The promise of rest still remains and applies to us, as well to those to whom it was first made - the Children of Israel, who were about to enter into the Land of Promise. It was the place of faith and obedience. The promise is appropriate to all people of God in every generation, and right now we are dwelling in our Promised Land, with Christ within the Father's love. *'Whoever dwells in the shelter of the Most High will rest in the shadow or protection of the Almighty,'* (Psalms 91:1). It is sitting in the secret place, being at home with God; abiding where He abides.

Psalms 27:5 talks about the secret of His tabernacle where He will hide me, which is the most private part of His dwelling. This is the place where He would withdraw to be alone, where no one would dare to intrude. Nothing can adequately describe this expression of friendship, security, and protection. It is not just His dwelling place, but His personal and secret apartment within that dwelling place! This is not a visitation, which is great, but a habitation, which is fantastic. This is constant communion. It is not being a guest, but being a family, with all of its privileges. Psalms 31:20 leads us further, 'in the shelter or secret place of your presence you hide them.' The literal translation is, 'the secret of your face.' Hidden from public view, from the view of our enemies, into the very place where He dwells. It is the place of His desire for us.

There is no doubt that the Lord wants us as close to Him as possible, however, our sense of orphan would hinder closeness. Those with that inclination would struggle, but sons and daughters would thrive. If resting meant that God could enjoy His creation, I would want to give Him that opportunity and also take the opportunity that He gives to me to come close. Orphan hearted people need to know that they have an ability in Christ to deal with their plight. They can understand, acknowledge and take responsibility, and can make the right choices and decisions. Some may have been introduced to the Father, but still cannot receive His love. Some may still live their lives as if they do not have a home, and for them it would be difficult to receive the Father's love. However, they can be changed within by a new way of thinking, by being transformed, through the Holy Spirit, by the renewal of the mind.

Summary

It is foundational for the orphan hearted person to consider where they feel their place in Christ is. Both creation in Genesis 1-2, and the new creation in John 1, underline the fact that God came down to where humanity was.

First of all, God came to be with Adam and Eve in the garden, in a close and intimate way, to make His place of rest and home with them. Heaven came to earth, but sadly Adam and Eve made a choice to walk away from that relationship and left home in fear and shame after being banned from the garden, which severely damaged the close relationship they had with God. They became orphans because they had left the loving heart of Father God. This affected their firstborn son, Cain, who after murdering his brother out of anger, came under a curse and was driven from the land. His cry to God was, '*Today you are driving me from the land, and I will be hidden from your presence or face; I will be a restless or homeless wanderer on the earth, and whoever finds me will kill me,*' (Genesis 4:14). It became that grim, but God, in His wisdom prepared a way back. Some became close to God, they were the glorious exceptions, but the majority were distant from Him.

Secondly, God became incarnate in Jesus bringing in the New Covenant - a New Creation, in which Heaven and Earth came together in a new and powerful way. They are made for each other but had been separated for too long. No more though, and this became the rallying cry for the ministry of Jesus, as He declared that the Kingdom of God was as close as being face to face with Him. He came down to be at home with His creation, dwelling amongst us, dwelling with us, and dwelling within us. His life, death, and resurrection did away once and for all with 'distance,' and dealt with the curse of the orphan heart, by revealing sonship to us.

The plan of God to redeem humanity, and to bring it back to Himself, has been accomplished and completed. This includes opening the way for the orphan hearted to come into sonship. There is no work, effort, or any sort of performance necessary. What is needed though, is for the orphan hearted to make a choice, and that choice needs to be intentional! It has been shown what has been in the heart of God since the beginning is to be at home on earth with His creation. The Old Testament showed that it has been only the few that have known a closeness with God, but the rest were only worshipping at a distance. However, when Jesus came, things changed and He became the way to the Father. It is now possible for the orphan hearted to come to the Father through Jesus, and to know healing and to walk in freedom from the orphan curse.

It is not difficult for the orphan hearted person to look at this and at the same time agree with it, because, as they know the need to take it on board, it is easier to move on without doing anything. Even feeling the challenge of being confronted with the truth is acceptable, as long as nothing is done. As long as nothing happens, anything is possible, so passivity and apathy reign when what is actually needed is passion. We need to remember that circumstances do not define who we are, it is how we respond that matters. However, the mind does need renewal, and therefore a personal response is not only necessary but essential. It is intention that needs to be activated. Taking a conscious, purposeful, deliberate and wilful decision to accomplish the desired goal has to be the way forward. If the orphan hearted person is intentional concerning their healing and freedom, the way they think, feel, hope and believe, the desire will begin to change, and transformation by the renewal of the mind will be achieved. Therefore, begin to open your lives and trust your Father God and you will find the freedom that Jesus has already obtained.

THE FATHER HEART
OF GOD

Why Father?

You may find it surprising to know that there are over 300 names of God in scripture. Jesus used many of them to describe himself, and even taught on some of them. He frequently shocked and offended the religious, and other leaders of the day, with some of the comments that He made about the names of God, and how He applied them to Himself. Jesus told the Pharisees that He had met Abraham, 'before Abraham was, I am,' and it is no wonder that they picked up stones to kill Him, (John 8:58-59). Yet, He was identifying with the eternal name that God gave Moses, 'I am that I am,' (Exodus 3:14) which underlined His continued and unchanging existence. However remarkable we think that is, there was another name that Jesus used that particularly disturbed and surprised the common people, and shocked and offended the religious leaders: Father.

Jesus kept on and on talking about the Father, and emphasising the revelation of Him to the individual, something which no one had ever done before. Of all the different ways in which Jesus referred to God, Father was the one He most commonly used. The Jews, very much aware of the chasm between a holy God and sinful human beings, would never have addressed

God as Father. However, not only did Jesus astonish His contemporaries by referring to God as His Father, He also went further by encouraging His followers to use the term as well. Some people often wrongly assume that the Old Testament scriptures refer many times to God as a Father, but where they do, it is generally in reference to God in a formal way, as in a Father to His people or to nations, not as a Father to individuals. In the Old Testament, the intimate name of Father was not used to address God in prayer. This personal term is mentioned approximately only fifteen times throughout the Old Testament, but, in contrast, when we read the Gospels we can see that Jesus used the word far more than anyone else in the Bible. It was undoubtedly His favourite way to address God, and this is particularly evident in the book of John, where it is used over 100 times, and in the Synoptic Gospels, where it appears about sixty-five times. In addition, the Pauline letters describe God as Father over forty times, and in the rest of the New Testament, the word is used over thirty-five times. The most frequent word for father in the New Testament was the word 'pater.' The other word used - abba, (Aramaic), is only found three times, and when it is spoken, it is always connected to pater, as 'abba Father.' Because of the importance of these two words, not only to the orphan hearted person but to all of us, a further chapter will be devoted to their understanding and definition. It cannot take much to realise that a revolution, which challenged the religious culture of the day, was in progress, as Jesus introduced His Father as a personal, loving and intimate God who, in His tenderness, compassion, and grace, desires to have the same relationship with us as He has with Jesus.

What does God as a Father mean?

God the Father is the first person of the Trinity. The doctrine of the Trinity was established by the various ecumenical councils that took place in the early church, the Council of Nicaea, AD325, being the first at which theological issues were discussed, defined and agreed. One of the key areas considered there was the definition of the nature of God, which led to the Trinity being affirmed as the Father, Son, and Holy Spirit - three co-equal and co-eternal persons, having the same nature and attributes. Each personality is distinct from the others, yet capable of individual action. In the Old Testament, there is an amazing Messianic passage in which Jesus is referred to in terms which would normally have only been used to describe God Himself, *'for to us a child is born, to us a son is given, and the government will be on his shoulders. And he will be called Wonderful Counsellor, Mighty God, Everlasting Father, Prince of Peace,'* (Isaiah 9:6). When terms like this are used, including, **'Everlasting Father,'** all that can be done is to wonder and worship God knowing that He has made a place for us with Him. Although considered to be a divine mystery beyond human understanding, the role of the Father is made clear. It is inspiring to consider how the name Father is such a key, and so foundational in our relationship with God. Remember that God is Spirit, not 'a' Spirit (John 4:24) but He is also a living, personal being that we can have a close relationship with. He is not confined to a human body, He is not a man, but is called Father. God the Son came to Earth in human form, (John 1:14), but God the Father did not. Jesus is unique as Emmanuel, 'God with us,' (Isaiah 7:14, Matthew 1:23).

The initiative Jesus took gave all of us, including the orphan hearted, permission to approach God as Father. He said to His disciples, *'when you pray, say, our Father,'* (Luke 11:1-2). The Father is the beginning of love, as well as the source of all things. The Trinity started with God the Father and we are His children, whom He made in His image, (Genesis 1:27). The term Father does not stand for any sense of a higher position than the Son or Spirit; they are of the same substance, nature, and existence; they have so many unique infinite qualities and yet are the same. The Fatherhood of God is the very essence of the Godhead and the gospel, for *'God so loved the world...,'* (John 3:16). God, the Father is the Father of humanity and has even given us the right and power to be sons of God. But those who embraced him and took hold (faith) of his name were given authority to become the children of God, (John 1:12 TPT). As we will see later, the Father's desire is to adopt us as sons and daughters. He creates, He originates, He is a nourisher and a protector, for everything comes from Him, starts from Him, proceeds from Him, and in Genesis 1 and 2 He establishes and generates a family, with a household where the man and the woman, made in His image, were secure in His love to the point where they walked together in the garden communing and communicating with their God (Genesis 3:8). God the Father is the best example that there has ever been for all earthly fathers. He is righteous, just, fair, with tenderness and a wealth of grace undergirded by love. Who can be more kind, caring and also have our best interests at heart than God our Father? There is no one. Jesus urged us to think of God as our loving Father, and went a step further by calling him abba, which shows us how intimate our relationship with Him is. We were designed for sonship, not to be orphans, and the realisation of this was frustrated by sin, but we now know we can be restored to a full relationship with our loving Heavenly Father

Jesus' relationship with the Father

When we read the Gospels, we can clearly see the kind of relationship that Jesus had with His Father. He talked about His Father all of the time, something that was revolutionary to the people, but an offence to the religious leaders of the day. No one knew God like that. They could know Him at a distance, but it was virtually impossible to get close to Him, because no one would ever say His name, let alone even think of having an intimate relationship with Him. Jesus had a rich, close, and intimate relationship, one of face-to-face communing and communication, with His Father. The Father's love for Jesus gave Him a confidence and security which in turn affected the way Jesus talked to the people about His relationship with Him. It also brought out the sense of obedience of a Son in response to the love of His Heavenly Father. What is apparent, from Jesus' conversations with His disciples, was the union Jesus had with the Father, and this is highlighted by how passionate, direct and specific He was. Scriptures such as, '*I and the Father are one*,' (John 10:30). '*I am in the Father and the Father is in me*,' (John 14:11) are good examples of this. However, what was so challenging for this time was that Jesus took this very much further by involving the people in His relationship with His Father. One key time, when Jesus was praying about being united with the Father, He included everyone, not just His disciples, in this, which introduced a complete cultural turnaround with regard to how they could respond to God. '*So that they may be one as we are one,*' (John 17:11) '*may they also be in us so that the world may believe that you have sent me,*' (John 17:21) '*I in them and you in me,*' (John 17:23). Jesus opened a door for us to be in union with Him and His Father in quite a different and dramatic way. He has presented us with the revelation of God as Father, and the fact that we can have access to Him.

The Old Testament knew Him as God, but through Jesus, we can know Him as both God and Father. The Apostle Paul underlined that fact, '*for us there is but one God, the Father, from whom all things came and for whom we live; and there is but one Lord, Jesus Christ, through whom all things came and through whom we live,*' (1 Corinthians 8:6). It is also necessary to consider that, if we are in Christ, we must be in the same relationship with the Father as He was, for being one in Christ means being one with the Father. The facts are there, but how does that affect the orphan hearted, and what should they do about it?

Father of Lies

The very first lie ever told, was by Satan in the Garden of Eden. He told this lie to Eve, in a cunning and seductive manner, to deceive her, and to draw her and Adam away from God (Genesis 3:1-3). He was the author and inventor of the lie and of all falsehood, which came into God's world to pollute humanity. In rebellion, Satan turned against God and then turned his murderous heart to Adam and Eve to undermine their relationship with God. This led to separation and becoming orphan hearted, as well as their being subject to death because they believed the lie Satan spoke into them regarding their relationship with God. The curse came through to Cain, the firstborn son, who later murdered his brother in anger. The religious leaders of the day continually criticised Jesus.

On one occasion, there was a powerful confrontation as they accused Jesus of being from Satan. He responded by telling them that they were liars, and declared that they, not He, were of the Devil. Jesus said, '*you belong to your father, the devil, and you would want to carry out your father's desire. He was a murderer from the beginning....He is a liar and the father of lies,*' (John 8:44). As they refused to hear the truth, it was obvious to Jesus that they were under the influence of the devil, and therefore could be called his children. Jesus used the term 'father,' because the devil was the author, the source of lies.

Orphan hearted people have been lied to!

The lie from Satan is that you are not enough, and God is not enough to make you enough, so you need something from someone else to make you enough. You respond to the lie through enticement and seduction, by opening up your life, but you never find 'enough,' because it is not there. You try to find the power to succeed and gain value and worth, but what you find is something that drives you, however that will never work, because God never works that way. You freeze into immobility because you think you cannot go back. Satan operates by twisting and contradicting God's truth so that people's relationship with God is undermined, which leads to separation. Finite, frail, feeble and fallen humanity is susceptible to these lies. Satan said to the woman, 'you will not die,' She and Adam did die; they were spiritually murdered, and we have inherited death in our spirit, soul, and body. Fatherlessness means orphan; they lost their relationship with their Heavenly Father and lived out of their orphan hearts. We know that, because of all that Jesus is and did in His life, death, and resurrection, we can come to Him and know restoration by receiving the love of Father God as sons and daughters. This means that Jesus has already made the way for us to leave behind the orphan way and come into what is rightfully ours - sonship!

Living with the orphan heart is real, but is a deception, that has brought separation, which means we live at a distance from God. There is a Spirit of truth [reality], but there is also a spirit of error, (1 John 4:6). When Jesus said, '*I am the truth*,' (John 14:6) He was underlining that He was is the source of truth. Jesus is the complete representation of everything that can be presented to humanity, and because of this, the orphan hearted person has the ability in the authority of Jesus to release themselves from the lie and deception of the enemy.

The Heart of the Father

Some understanding, however limited, is necessary to realise that God has a heart, and through His heart, identifies with a flawed, frail and failed humanity, because He loves us, and wants a deep and close relationship with us. To the orphan hearted, this may constitute a challenge, but if they can get hold of the fact that, despite their very difficult situation, God desires to get close to them, to bring lasting change through a transforming miracle. This is possible, for, however, anyone feels, no one is left out of the grace of God.

God is not **a** spirit, but He **is** Spirit, '*God is spirit, and his worshipers must worship in spirit and in truth [reality]*,' (John 4:24) meaning we connect with Him from our spirits. He does not have a body and is therefore not restricted to a human dimension, but infinite, not limited by time or space. However, He is a living and personal being, who wants a personal relationship with His created family, and will pursue us to that end. Because He is Spirit, He is omnipresent, which means He is present everywhere at the same time. He is also very much active on earth, which includes His constant presence with us in every situation.

At the core and source of God's being, which is His heart, He feels, thinks and acts like a Father, because, from before the beginning, He has been, and will be, a Father to us in His purpose and desire, no matter what has happened.

Biblically speaking, the human heart is the innermost centre, being mind, emotion and, will, thus covering all personality functions, making the heart the gateway to the whole being. The word heart, Gk kardia, is not only the centre of all physical life, but includes all spiritual life, therefore loving God begins in the heart, and, as the scripture says, *'love God with all of your heart,'* (Mark 12:30).

After God had removed Saul from his kingship, He appointed David, and something quite surprising happened, which is a key to how God sees us, and it very much includes the orphan hearted. God made a profound statement about Himself, *'He raised up for them David as king, to whom also He gave testimony and said, I have found David the son of Jesse, **a man after my own heart** who will do all My will,'* (1 Samuel 13:14, Acts 13:22). Paul also referred to David as a man after God's own heart, who served God's purpose in his generation before falling asleep, (Acts 13:36). God's heart was set on David, and He took great delight and pleasure in him, saying with passion, *'I have found my servant David,'* (Psalms 89:20). Would we have chosen David? His father and brothers certainly would not, for he was rejected by them.

Despite all of this, there were so many qualities that David had which would have had influenced how God saw him, and even though he was far from perfect, his heart was focused on God with great passion and devotion. David's pursuit of God motivated a desire in him to know God more and more. Here we have a young man who was a poet and psalmist, a warrior who dealt with lions and bears, a musician who revolutionised worship in Israel, a shepherd, a king, a theologian with absolute faith and confidence in God, that made him fearless, yet like the rest of us, he was flawed. No man after God's heart is perfect, for David made serious errors that deeply affected not only himself but his descendants. What is possible, however, is that even a man like David can be a man after God's own heart! Jesus Himself acknowledged that He was the Messiah by saying He was the Son of David, (Matthew 22:41-46).

Through His life, death, and resurrection, Jesus has not only paid the debt of our salvation but amazingly has given us access to the Father. Therefore, could Jesus be the revelation and manifestation of the Father's heart? God the Father shows His heart through Jesus, so as we know Him, we can know the Father. On Earth, God showed Himself as Jesus, so can it not mean that Jesus is the very heart of God? There is another reference in the New Testament that shows us the nature and reality of God's heart and personality. Jesus said, 'Take my yoke upon you and learn from me, for I am gentle and lowly of heart, and you will find rest for your souls,' (Matthew 11:29). This is the Father saying through Jesus that He is gentle and lowly in heart. Lowly means humble, or modest without pride or arrogance. Who would describe God in this way?

We need to realise and understand that He is, for He is good, caring, compassionate and tender, and without a doubt the kindest person in this world. In saying this, it needs to be underlined that, *'we have Christ dwelling in our hearts through faith, so that we can be rooted and grounded in love,'* (Ephesians 3:17 ESV). His love within us can be as firm in our hearts as a tree whose roots are deep and extensive, or as a building constructed with solid and resilient foundations. When I had a revelation of the love of God, it started a process of healing which revealed the Father's heart to me, so as we have Jesus dwelling within us, we also have His heart, the Father's heart.

Heavenly Father or Earthly Father?

When we compare God as Father with our own earthly fathers, our earthly fathers will usually not come out well. What kind of a father did we have? Was he performance-orientated, authoritarian, passive, absent, abusive, angry or aggressive, or did they show a quality of love, care, and want the best for their child? As so much of a child's identity is formed through the father-child relationship, it is important to see how we feel regarding his response to us. It is possible that our view of Father God is shaped by the way our fathers have behaved, such as being emotionally absent, or overly protective, which would make it very difficult to relate to God as being close or affectionate. Jesus was the man He was because of the Father He had, which enabled Him to reveal the heart of abba, being the one who cherishes. Jesus has shown that His Father is not like our earthly fathers. He continually demonstrates His unconditional love to us, and this alone helps us understand how God is. God's love as a Father shows us what our father's love could look like. God is not one who is far away, nor is he eager to punish us for our failures. He is a Father who loves us more than we could ask to be loved. He wants to care for us, share His life with us, and bring us into a union with Him forever. We know with our mind that God loves us, but we need to be convinced in our hearts so that we can respond to His great love. All of this sums up the fact that the way we relate to our Father God is influenced by our relationship with our earthly father. In God's case, the term Father is all-inclusive, and all-embracing and has the glorious attribute of incorporating everything we need from a father. Therefore, the expression of His love towards us embodies every quality of the best father that we could ever conceive of.

My Relationship with My Father

It is well over twenty years since my own father died, and I still think about he responded to me and of the way that God as my Heavenly Father responds to me today. I did have a relationship with my father, but it was mostly on his terms. In his eyes, I needed to buy a certain newspaper, vote a certain way, live not too far away from my parents and have a good, safe and secure job. He was an angry man, and controlling with it, but I loved him, and even when he so lost it and became severely angry, such as when I told him that I was giving up my job to go into the ministry, I never broke the bond that was between us. His dream for me was shattered, as I, a Chartered Surveyor, gave up everything, in his opinion, in order to follow the call and purposes of God. When Chris and I told him and my mother at their house, he seethed like a volcano, stormed out of the house, got very drunk, and phoned me in the middle of the night and threatened me.

He was very distant, yet he loved me, but it was exceedingly rare that he showed it except in a controlling way. There was no affection or intimacy; he was proud of me, but never said; he was loyal to me, and I never knew. There were photos of me from when I was young found in his wallet after he died, and that makes me sad. He was a provider but was selfish and materialistic above all things.

Sadly, all of this fed my orphan heart and made things very difficult for me to accept God as a loving, kind and trustworthy Heavenly Father. It is not an easy issue to overcome, but I have, through His grace and love. In death, there is a separation just like a bond breaking, which I understood, but it was still a loss to me. I never did get what I longed for from my father, and his death meant that I was finally deprived of that love, the love that I needed, but it never happened, although tragically it was there deep within him, yet it was so rare for me to even catch a glimpse of it. I was not angry, bitter, resentful or judgemental in any way, and I often think of my father and mother with a sense of thankfulness, although it is always mixed with some sadness. Things could have been better; My father could have had so much more. My mother did and, in the later years of her life, I saw a response to God, that had been dormant since her childhood.

Does this Compare with the Way God as Father Responds?

Actually no, as Jesus clearly said, '*I will not leave you as orphans [fatherless], I will come to you,*' (John 14:18). My father would never have made me an orphan, but, because he was absent and distant, although very much present, he unwittingly and unintentionally gave me those orphan feelings, which affected the core of my being. Many orphan hearted people would identify with the term bereaved because the lack of demonstrated love and affection would be construed as a loss in their lives; it is as though something has died deep within. This would be the total opposite of the way God as Heavenly Father would be to us.

How God Loves Me

I love God because of who He is, because of what He has done for me, and because of what He has given me. This can be explained in the following responses, which are personal to us:

- God takes initiative with His love.
- He is constant in His love.
- He is consistent in His love.
- He communicates in His love.
- He is unchanging in His love.
- He is unfailing in His love.
- He pursues us with His love.
- He wants to share His life with us in His love.

God is not one who is distant, for He is a Father who loves us more than we could ask to be loved. He has declared that in His love, He wants to be involved in every area of our lives. There is nothing you do that God does not care about. God is the only being in the universe who knows everything about everyone, who loves unconditionally and is dependable and reliable. God reveals Himself in the Bible as a gentle, forgiving Father, intimately involved with every detail of our lives. The Father's love is boundless, bottomless, inexhaustible, steadfast, unflagging, absolute, ceaseless, and persistent. No human love can be compared with this. I have learned that there is no point in my criticising or holding judgement with any sense of bitterness at the way my own father behaved, as all it does, is feed the orphan heart negatively. It cannot seem appropriate to compare my father with my Heavenly Father, but what is good and right, is to learn, understand and accept the way our Father is with us, particularly from the orphan heart perspective, because it can then be the open door for healing and freedom. I know that this is possible, for it has not undermined my love for my father, but has rather given me understanding and compassion.

A Reflection

It is amazing that in the Gospels Jesus talked such a great deal about His Father, and the way His relationship was with Him. He wanted to introduce His Father to both the disciples and the people. This gave awareness and insight into the depth of Jesus' relationship and the affection He and His Father had for one another. The usual word for father in the New Testament is pater, however Jesus added another special word, abba, which relates to closeness and intimacy in the relationship. '*I lead them with cords of human kindness, with ties of love. To them, I was like one who lifts a little child to the cheek, and I bent down to feed them,*' (Hosea 11:4). This is the Father's Heart to a nation, and nations are made up of individuals, but whoever we are and whatever is the issue, we are all included in that love. Jesus said, '*No one can come to me unless the Father who sent me draws them,*' (John 6:44). This is the Father working with the Son and the Spirit, drawing us by the strength of the Father's love, and by the attractiveness of His grace to meet Jesus. Here we see the Trinity working in glorious harmony for our sake, and expressing a divine love to us that is beyond anything this world could offer. Love draws love; love is the magnet of love, and as we are drawn to Jesus in this way, we have a revelation of the Father to us. This is the role of the Father to us personally, for nothing has changed, and the challenge to us is to be open-hearted and not orphan hearted. We will see in a later chapter that, as we come into an understanding of abba, and also appreciate rather than neglect the term pater, that healing and freedom from past issues, which have persisted in our lives undergirded by the orphan heart, will begin to be exposed for healing to take place.

Consider the following:

Encounter – We all need encounters with God, and sometimes they may be quite unexpected, sudden and spontaneous, but it is also taking time to be still in His presence and soak in His love. Do not mistake stillness for immobility.

Engage – This will lead to involvement, for it is crucial to connect and commune with our Heavenly Father. As sons and daughters, this is our rightful place, by being as close as we can to Him.

Embrace – Some of us have never been close to our earthly fathers, yet God's desire is to be close to us. This may be difficult and certainly challenging, for it is most probable that the pain of the orphan heart will be exposed, yet as love exposes pain, that same love will bring healing.

My response to this encourages me to pray to my Heavenly Father and say, 'draw me close to you.'

THE FATHER'S BLESSING

Toronto

One of the key encounters that impacted me in my Christian walk, was what happened in a small church in Toronto, Canada in 1994. It was known as the 'Toronto Blessing,' a term that found its origin in the British press. John Arnott and his wife Carol, who led the church, called it the 'Father's Blessing,' which is more appropriate. It was not Toronto's blessing, it was from our Heavenly Father! It was a sovereign move of God, and it was certainly up to Him where He decided to pour out His love in that particular way, and amazing it was. The underlying principle was an increased awareness of the Father's love. The word increase is an understatement, however, as the rich presence of God was amazingly encountered, and impacted the multitudes of people that were present from all over the world. It seems there were over a million people from the UK alone, that attended the meetings and conferences during the first ten years.

People, including many pastors and church leaders, streamed in from all over the world. They were challenged, and touched deeply within, in a substantial way, with many emotional hurts from childhood healed through the Father's love. It was a revolution to many lives including my own.

The events that occurred are not unique when considering the history of revival, and this outpouring of the Holy Spirit continues in some measure to make a worldwide impact on the church. Often revivals were known as awakenings, where people came alive by having powerful encounters with the love of the Father, and it was the same thing that occurred in Toronto.

What surprised John Arnott was the number of people, including many leaders, that came there from British churches. Maybe it was because those who had been feeling a deep hunger for many years suddenly began to hear about God dramatically moving in many lives in an unknown church in Ontario, Canada and so decided to visit there. What was amazing was the number of people that very quickly decided to go and see what was happening for themselves. They were not disappointed, and, interestingly, many of the meetings were overwhelmed by those from the UK. It was God's provision that a much larger building became available just down the road, and it was not long before that building was filled with seeking people.

Often the meetings were not that quiet. It was not just the buzz of excitement, but the fact that so many were released from the deep pain of the past, and when that sort of release happens, emotions are exposed and often powerfully. All sorts of manifestations occurred, and for some, it was not an easy time as they found a few of those things difficult. What was seen affected many from the UK, and part of that was that the 'stiff British upper lip' disappeared from their lives! It was wonderful to see those who had been set free from so much bondage whilst coming into a new depth in their relationship with their Father God. You will read about my response, as God exposed my deep hurts to His healing love. I will never forget it. There is no doubt there were some challenging issues, but what Chris and I saw was a godly stewardship of the unusual responses, ably led with integrity, by John and Carol Arnott and their excellent team. It meant that the people there were in a safe place. The scripture is clear when it says, *'Without oxen, a stable stays clean, but you need a strong ox for a large harvest,'*

(Proverbs 14:4 NLT). We all want a wonderful harvest, however, sometimes there is a mess to deal with, yet from Toronto, people went home, to every part of the world, strengthened and ready for the harvest.

It was sometime in May 1994, that my wife, Chris, and I were having lunch with some very good friends at a restaurant just north of Toronto. For many years I had visited churches in Ontario, which included working at an International Teaching and Ministry base, and periodically Chris came with me. This occasion quickly became a Holy Spirit time, a 'kairos' moment, right in the middle of the meal. Ken began to describe a major family issue, tied into a bitter root judgement, which had affected him. As he talked about it, I realised that He was telling me this because God had revealed to him that I had the same problem in my family. I knew straight away that it was to do with my father, and that evening I turned the whole thing over to God, for something had begun to be sown in my heart. The next day there was a leader's lunchtime meeting at the old Toronto Church just up the road from where they are now, and John Arnott had invited me to join them. There were many leaders there, and the theme was the Father Heart of God. It was a soothing, challenging, and powerful time, and as I opened myself up to the Holy Spirit in the worship, something happened. It was a though I went into a sort of trance; my legs buckled and I fell across the chairs. It was not an out of control experience, but as the presence of God was so strong, I chose to go with it.

I had taken Ken's words and his loving concern to heart, and I already had repented of my attitude of bitterness and judgement. It was no wonder that my hidden pain came to the surface because I was in this fantastic atmosphere of the Father's love. Between two and three hours of deep ministry and release took place on those chairs, and I remember some of the leaders and other friends constantly coming up to me, looking after me, and ministering to me. It was a very personal time, as memories of issues with my father surfaced, and all I wanted to do was to open up to the Holy Spirit and allow Him to have His way to heal past hurts. At one point, I looked up through my tears and thought I was the only one left in the meeting, only to realise that everyone was on the floor being touched by God. Somehow, the amazing worship touched my wounded spirit, and it was as though the hurt child of the past came to the surface full of fear and loneliness, which allowed the Holy Spirit to bring deep healing. Although the release of pain was intense, I felt safe with friends around me, and I was in a place where my Heavenly Father could pour out His healing love in such a wonderful way. I know that this was one of the most significant times in my life, as I gave the right to Father God to touch my orphan heart with His love. I know too, that I was one of tens of thousands of people who found deep healing within their lives at Toronto Airport Christian Fellowship.

Thousands of words have been written about what happened in Toronto. Controversial? Of course! There is no doubt though that evangelical and charismatic Christian culture was dramatically impacted. I wonder what the press and the religious groups of the day would have made of the strange manifestations in a fairly small upper room where 120 women and men were worshipping on that day of Pentecost. Remember, it was a tornado of wind that suddenly manifest in the room; the heads of the people caught on fire, and they all spoke in languages the had never even heard of. No wonder they ran out into the street! One would have expected a torrent of criticism, particularly from people that were not there. Is it not intriguing how the Church was born!

What happened to me in Toronto came out of my own experience of my Heavenly Father's love all those years ago when HIs love touched my orphan heart. The whole concept of the Father Heart of God in Toronto so resonated with me that it helped me to grow from that powerful encounter, and in doing so I came into deeper healing than I had ever known before. There were some 'fleshly' and demonic manifestations, but to me, they were distractions, as I wanted to get closer to my Father in worship with an expression of joy. The Toronto church leadership became well aware of these issues, and they were dealt with clearly and righteously. I am thankful for what happened, as it opened my eyes to much more of the Father Heart of God with His expression of love; what an amazing help it has been in seeing my own orphan heart being healed.

Why Toronto?

I have often wondered why, how, and where previous moves of God and revivals began. It is not difficult to speculate and come up with several reasons why they happened, but amidst the different answers, one stands out, and that is the sovereignty of God. What took place in a small unknown church was that God spontaneously broke into people's lives with a revelation of His love, and they, together with thousands of people worldwide, have never been the same since. This happening was the genius of God. These were not famous, or even infamous North American Christians, but more like an army of ordinary people who were being deeply touched by the heart of God. There was nothing contrived, or any agenda, except that of God Himself, yet the meetings went on night after night for a considerable period. A core group of people, from which many ultimately became leaders, led by a man with an entrepreneurial spirit, John Arnott, learned to skilfully handle the meetings in whatever way the Spirit moved. Probably the British were a little more confident in visiting Canada, as it is a Commonwealth Nation, rather than travelling south to the pizzazz of the USA, however, they were in for a shock when they got there, because it probably did not happen, for most people, in the way that they expected. Any reader of the history of revivals will concur, because in Toronto the spontaneous seemed to be continually present - things happened that were unexpected as people's lives were turned upside down, often with deep emotional release. The revelation of the Father's unconditional love together with His outrageous grace became keys to influence the dynamic worship. The orphan hearted and the prodigals were coming home to get healed, reconciled, and restored to their loving Heavenly Father.

Looking back, it seems that everything was set up well, including some clear prophetic words about the move of God. However, nobody got close to realising the enormity of what was happening or even the length of time the renewal would last. God had planned it and certainly moved in an unusual and sometimes mysterious way in order to release His plan and purpose to the nations. You may be amazed to know that there are conferences still going on there, particularly as 2019 was the 25th anniversary of the Father's Blessing.

Unconditional Love and Outrageous Grace

There were many attributes of the heart of God that the people were made aware of in Toronto, through relationships, teaching, and revelation. Two of them, which still affect us, are foundational, and crucial in our walk with God. They are the Father's 'unconditional' love and His 'outrageous' grace. They present a challenge to everyone, but to those that have an orphan heart, they are fundamental and can be life-changing. These areas are some of the characteristics from the heart of God that are of central importance to our mindset and belief systems. Therefore, it is imperative to not only grasp hold of them, but also to gain understanding through revelation, so that they become meaningful in our daily relationship both with Father God and in the way we relate to others. Maybe we need a revolution in our lives that will bring us to a point where the unconditional love and the outrageous grace of God become dramatically deep and meaningful in everyday life.

Love

One of the fundamental principles of Christianity is that God is love. However, with some Christians, particularly those affected with orphan hearts, it is a common thing to have a distorted view of the God of love, because of the way most people understand it. So often it is connected with, 'what can I do to please God to receive His love?' There is nothing we can do to make God love us, and there is nothing we can do to stop God loving us. There are no conditions. God loving the world means exactly what it says, and the way to respond to this is to take it at face value. He loves the world completely, no matter what condition humanity is in. This love is constant in its intensity to the point whereby He sacrificed His Son on our behalf. There is no discrimination or exception, everyone is included. It has opened a door to eternity and has brought Heaven to Earth so that we can in Jesus be rooted and grounded in this love, (Ephesians 3:17). There is no greater love than to lay down your life, which Jesus did so that we might receive His life and know transformation in ours. In the language of the Bible, God's love can be summed up in two words, 'agape,' Greek New Testament, and 'hesed,' Hebrew Old Testament.

Agape is the highest form of love there is. It is not merely an attribute of God, it is His intrinsic nature, His lifeblood, and it determines His character. God is love and He loves in the completeness and the perfection of that love, making it its deepest, truest, and total expression, and one that is only found in Him. Agape love is selfless, sacrificial, but voluntary, as well as spontaneous, lavish, and given without expecting anything in return. This love is beyond emotion, feeling, and sentiment because it is the heartbeat of God. This is well illustrated by John lying on the bosom of Jesus, (John 13:23 NASB). You cannotget any closer than hearing the heartbeat of God. It expresses such intimacy. Our words for love and out human love get nowhere near agape, they are just mere tokens, and could never be compared with the unfathomable, immeasurable and inexpressible love of God.

The word 'hesed' is found throughout the Old Testament, and it expresses the essential part of God's character. The word is built around God's covenant relationship with His people through which He portrays a steadfast faithfulness, *'though the mountains be shaken and the hills be removed, yet my unfailing love for you will not be shaken nor my covenant of peace be removed, says the Lord, who has compassion on you,'* (Isaiah 54:10). As well as this, it indicates God's generosity and kindness to His people. There is no one kinder than God in time or eternity. At a critical time in the history of the people of Israel, God came down to where Moses was and revealed Himself. He described himself as *'abounding in love and faithfulness, maintaining love to thousands,'* (Exodus 34:6-7) and again a God *'who shows love to a thousand generations,'* (Exodus 20:6). As with agape, this love is much more than emotion and sentiment, but action with compassion, mercy, and faithfulness to the individual, as well as nations. It is unrelenting, extravagant, unrestrained and lavish. Hesed is a great pointer to the New Covenant where agape comes into its own, such as when Jesus tells Nicodemus that, actually, *'God so loved the world,'* (John 3:16) not just the Jewish nation.

Through all of this, my revelation was that agape and hesed, the Father's love, are unconditional. This is not easy for the orphan hearted to grasp, for it reveals the heart of God in a way that no one would expect.

1. Unconditional Love

Bear in mind that most people, if not all, have issues with this. To think that God manifests love with no conditions is radical. Religion does not cope with this. We have all been to the place, me even recently, where we think we have to do something to influence God to accept us. I remember coming to my senses realising that I was saying to God, 'I can help you sort this through.' Naivety, pride, or deception? I would say a touch of all three. Even though the mind prompts us, we cannot do this. We need to realise, probably again, that we take these sort of thoughts captive to the obedience of Christ (2 Corinthians 10:4-5) and get on living with God accepting the fact that He cannot need our help to make something happen, especially as it already has been established before the foundation of the world!

The purest of the pure is unconditional love. This is love that eclipses any other love, and thankfully it persists regardless of any circumstance. This love is relentless, it is tireless, unstoppable, unceasing, constant, and incessant. God's love is open-hearted and generous to all with no exceptions. Unconditional love is known as affection without any limitation or reservations; it is to love completely, no matter what happens, no matter what changes, and with no power and control involved in making it conditional. It is God saying, 'you do not owe anything in return.' When Jesus was on the cross there came a point where He cried out, *'it is finished,'* (John 19:30) then He died. What right have we, therefore, to attempt to continue that which is finished? This is God freely and willingly giving His love, and saying it is ours to keep, yet many live in conflict because of the father of lies, who goads them into seeking approval when God has not placed any conditions on anyone. It is important to note that this love is a love that God initiates; it is not any kind of response, which is precisely what makes it unconditional. If His love were conditional, then we would have to do something to earn or merit it or to somehow satisfy His wrath. Love is not something God chooses to do, because love is God, and God is love; it is the core of His being. Unconditional love opens the door for intimacy to the point at which God says, *'but the people of Jerusalem said, the Lord has abandoned us! He has forgotten us. So the Lord answers, can a woman forget her own baby and not love the child she bore? Even if a mother should forget her child, I will never forget you,'* (Isaiah 49:14-15 GNT). Our relationship with God is not a formal, impersonal one, but a relationship in which God knows us affectionately and intimately. This intense love consistently and continually gives, for it does not regulate or restrain in any way to make us earn it. We are loved just as we are.

Boundaries and Conditions

We live in a world that does not love; it tells us that to receive love, it must be earned, achieved, or performed for. We also live in a legalistic world, and we learn this legalism by seeing it modelled and demonstrated in every aspect of life, including the church. If you have to do something or live in a certain way to receive love, that love is conditional. If love is given to you freely and without reservation, it is unconditional. The literal meaning of the word unconditional is without conditions, and this becomes real to us when we realise what conditional love is. It is a wrong attachment to another, which depends on behaving in a certain way to gain approval and acceptance. God cannot do that; His love does not depend on us acting in any particular way trying to please Him. God's love does not give benefits if we conform, because it transcends all behaviour, and is completely and utterly selfless. Nothing can stand in the way of unconditional love, 'can anything separate us from the love of Christ?' No, neither life nor death, angels nor demons, or any power anywhere, including the present or the future can separate us from the love of God (Romans 8:35-39). For the orphan hearted, this is not an easy thing to accept, especially if you have not totally believed that the Father loves you. At times we try so hard to please God, to impress others, and to be determined to be as good as we can. It becomes stressful, laborious, and it cannot work, so we feel more orphaned. However bruised we are, He will never crush us. '*I make the dry tree flourish,*' (Ezekiel 17:24). '*At least there is hope for a tree: If it is cut down, it will sprout again, and its new shoots will not fail. Its roots may grow old in the ground and its stump die in the soil, yet at the scent of water it will bud and put forth shoots like a plant,*' (Job 14:7-9). No matter what our past is like and how it still affects us, no matter what we are like today, and no matter what we think we will be like in the future, He longs to draw us into His embrace. There is no need to hide away because we think we are unloveable. We think hiding keeps us safe, but being hidden is not a safe place, as our first parents found out. God knows who we really are, and whether we know it, like it or cannot accept it, it cannot matter to Him, because '*love keeps no record of wrongs,*' (1 Corinthians 13:4). If unconditional love means to love completely, no matter what happens under all circumstances, why is it, that orphan hearted people have an expectation that there should be some form of repayment? It is because they believe there have to be conditions attached. If that is true, they find themselves surrendering the right to choose to someone else, which gives that person the right to control them. To give the right to another to control a person is ungodly. This is shown with comments such as, 'fulfil my expectations, and you will be loved,' or 'fail and I will not love you,' The point here is that God sees the person as they are, including the scars, and the pressure to perform that pushes them towards perfectionism. However, despite all of that, every individual is still the Father's delight.

Are there conditions around the acceptance of unconditional love? The only condition that God gives us is that we unconditionally accept unconditional love. It is possible for the orphan hearted person, consciously or unconsciously, to add their conditions, such as the 'just in case' syndrome. It is the feeling that we may need to help God out 'just in case' He cannot manage. There is a continual danger that needs to be recognised because if there are no conditions, people can do what they like. Bad behaviour cannot stop God loving us, but if we undermine the healthy understanding of our worth and value, we will begin to undermine and devalue our identity. Boundaries in this context are important, as they are not conditions that impose and restrict, but are necessary as a line that would be wrong to cross, and that we know in our hearts would not be good for us. Does God bring discipline? In many ways, yes, but often it is our irresponsibility that opens a door for the enemy to affect us. Wrong choices can lead to difficult personal consequences. Unconditional love is more than a kind of love, but rather a way of loving. God's love is stubborn! It is a dogged determination not to change, but to stick to a course of action, being inflexible and defiant, for God will not be moved in His love toward us, and whatever we do or say we cannot persuade Him otherwise. His unconditional love leads to unconditional acceptance - it is absolute, and no performance could ever achieve unconditional acceptance.

Consideration

Many scriptures express the love of God, and amongst them, there are three words that dramatically show the expanse of this unconditional love.

Lavish

*'See what great love the Father has **lavished** on us, that we should be called children of God! And that is what we are,'* (1 John 3:1 NIV).

Lavish is a wonderful word full of a variety of meanings such as profuse, abundance, excess, without limit, extravagant, generous, bountiful and exuberant. It is as though God overdoes things for our benefit, and it is this that will not only touch but fill the orphan heart. The imperative, 'see,' gives direction to stay focused on the quality of the Father's love, and the words, 'what great' implies astonishment. We know the Father loves us, but to say He has lavished His love on us is something else, as it portrays an action whereby we see the immeasurable extent of God's love, and that in itself makes it breathtaking.

Perfect

*'We need have no fear of someone who loves us perfectly; his **perfect** love for us eliminates all dread of what he might do to us. If we are afraid, it is for fear of what he might do to us and shows that we are not fully convinced that he really loves us. So you see, our love for him comes as a result of his loving us first,'* (1 John 4:18-19 TLB).

There is no room for fear with God's love, particularly as it is His perfect love. It is complete, full, consummate, mature, pure, yet genuine, and sincere. Perfect in the character of God means perfectly perfected and completely complete. Yet fear is a stronghold, or maybe it should be called an empire, as it is so vast across the world, and is utterly dangerous, as it can restrict a person developing in every area of their lives to the point where nothing is done. After the death of Jesus, the disciples met behind locked doors because they were afraid of the Jewish leaders, when suddenly Jesus was standing among them, and He said, 'peace be with you,' (John 20:19). Fear dissolved as peace was spoken. It has its roots in the garden where Adam said, 'I was afraid, so I hid,' (Genesis 3:10). Both the man and the woman made excuses and withdrew from God, which is what the father of lies wanted to begin his empire. To the orphan hearted, fear, and being hidden, are related, and it is no different today. Of course, God knew where Adam was, He already knew the answer to His question, 'where are you,' but He just wanted a response, and He is asking the same question to the orphan hearted today. So many are hidden, some wear masks, some are still filled with shame, and they do not know why. Consider Paul's advice to Timothy about fear, *'for God has not given us a spirit of fear and timidity, but of power, love, and self-discipline,'* (2 Timothy 1:7 NLT). He also brought a powerful revelation to those in Rome, *'for you did not receive the spirit of slavery to fall back into fear, but you have received the Spirit of adoption as sons, by whom we cry, Abba! Father,'* (Romans 8:15 ESV). This oppressive spirit leads us to serve fear, which is sourced in Satan, however, we are not going to be hijacked into that again, because, as sons, we have received the Spirit of adoption, and have been brought into the family of God, whereby we can speak to God as with intimacy and affection calling Him Abba. There is only one Father who can release this powerful and perfect love, and it is this love, that casts out, drives out and banishes fear.

Poured

*'Now hope does not disappoint, because the love of God has been **poured** out in our hearts by the Holy Spirit who was given to you,'* (Romans 5:5 NJKV).

The word 'poured' is linked to water, and means abundantly imparted, or an endless filling, quickening and invigorating of all of our faculties and powers. It can even mean to gush - think of an oil well in that context. We are drenched in His wondrous love, which is filling us with an extravagant consciousness of His presence. This is nothing to do with a drip, a drop, a trickle, or a stream, but it is a river continuously overwhelming us with His love. There need not be any disappointment, or hope deferred, because it is the reliable Holy Spirit pouring out this love, and He cannot stop! He is our hope and our assurance for the release of divine love. The outpouring of the Spirit and the experience of the Father's love are inextricably linked. If the love of God has been poured out in our hearts by the Holy Spirit, then the responsibility of the orphan hearted must be to surrender to Him, and give Him the right to reveal this love, so that His overwhelming presence becomes a reality.

2. Outrageous Grace

If love is the being and the essence of God, then grace is like a river, which flows out from that source into every area of our lives. Love is the heart of God, and very much intertwined in that is grace. Grace is often defined as God's unmerited favour, which means God giving us something good that we do not deserve. Grace is different from mercy, which could be defined as God not giving us something bad, which we do deserve. Grace is the idea of something completely undeserved, unmerited, unwarranted, unearned and very much unlooked for. We can never achieve it ourselves, although many have tried, and then have found out they could never get there. Grace emphasises the difference between the limitless kindness of God and the forlorn poverty of humanity. God is kind, which means He is considerate, attentive, thoughtful, good-hearted, helpful, caring, compassionate and sympathetic, and that is more than enough to draw anyone into His heart. The reason why is that God is personal, however, the orphan hearted can easily make Him impersonal just by choosing to be distant. Grace has to be more than a concept for us to understand and enjoy it, it has to be personal, as it relates to the mercy, compassion and favour that Jesus continually gives. To the religious and ruling parties of Jesus' time, His grace was interpreted as shocking, outrageous, scandalous, indiscriminate, senseless, irrational, unfair, irreligious, ridiculous, absurd and offensive. But, to the ordinary person, it was revolutionary, personal, a revelation, a challenge - it was life with compassion and mercy leading to freedom and liberty in His

Kingdom. The people were astonished at seeing a new side to God - His goodness.

There are two areas that demonstrate that grace is so prominent and different in its definition in comparison to God's other characteristics and qualities.

i. Grace is Unfair

Jesus told a parable that was revolutionary to the relationship of a landowner and his workers, (Matthew 20:1-16). The agreement for a day's work was made, and the promise of payment was kept. However, as the day went on, the owner needed more workers, and whilst he was hiring them he said, 'I will pay you what is right.' This happened several times until the last ones hired had very little time left to work in. At the end of the day, the men were ready for payment, but the owner called the last ones first, and paid them the same amount as those who were first taken on; it did not matter how long they had been working. In the eyes of the men, the owner had violated the natural order of justice by paying an equal wage for unequal work. This, according to the standards of the world then, as well as today, would be considered outrageous, but what was seen was the generosity of God, which is His grace. When God acts, He does not act according to the tendency of human justice of being fair, He acts with grace, which is unfair. In the eyes of the men who started work earlier in the day, paying the same wage to everyone, no matter how long they had worked, was unfair, but had they not agreed to the wage in the beginning? It was not up to them how much money the others should get; it was the owner's responsibility, and he was exceedingly generous. The issue is not that of receiving more, it is receiving enough, and grace is enough, and it turns out to be more than anything we have, or will ever have. Did not God say to Paul, 'my grace is sufficient for you,'? (2 Corinthians 12:9). Sufficient is always enough, no matter what the problem is. God's enough is a far greater provision than we could ever conceive. Is fairness based on what we deserve? God is unfair because if God dealt with us fairly, none of us would survive. The fact is we deserve nothing, and that is why grace is unfair; we are not entitled to anything, but we have everything. God's economy is like that, it is not fair, for everybody gets more than they deserve. The mercy of God is that nobody gets justice, because everybody gets grace. There is nothing to compare grace with. Grace is not a contract, it is a miracle, and our joy is to receive what we do not deserve. Even at Calvary, the grace of God was incredibly exposed, when one of the criminals responded to Jesus, (Luke 23:39-43). This is the epitome of grace. There was no time for anything except a response from the heart, and whatever life this man had, whatever crime he had committed, grace for him was still the same as it was for everyone else, even though it was in the last minutes of his life. He deserved nothing but got everything. The last was first; this is outrageous grace.

ii. Grace Confronts Belief Systems

Grace is a challenge to the deeply embedded mindset and belief system of every person, including the orphan hearted, because they are always motivated to do something to deserve God's love. What sort of mindset do we have regarding our God? Is He like a benign headmaster, a ruling tyrant, a controller, or a manipulator? This type of mindset is an open door to fearfully hide in, and self-protect, when the pressure is on. Yet, there is a better way, because however risky we think grace is, it is far much safer than hiding away. When you trust grace, you trust the heart of the Father, and to the orphan hearted that is a major step forward, as it undermines the wrong assumption - that they are unacceptable and unloveable. To feel safe is to take thoughts captive, and begin to live from the motivation of the heart when dwelling in the shelter of the most High, (Psalms 91:1).

Some believe that God has a chart with their name on it, and at the end of every day He grades them on their performance and then decides by examining it, how much should He love them - is it more, or less, or perhaps they do not deserve any love at all on that day. Imagine carrying a copy of that day by day, and being under massive pressure to perform to an unreachable standard. This would also include being motivated by fear, that controls every step, just in case it is not in line with God's demands and standards. The pressure would be to do more to make sure of being accepted and valued, and the focus would always be to come first, which exposes a selfish disregard of others, and God.

Does the orphan hearted understand this? Of course. As much as they can, the orphan hearted person tries to determine their worth. What's the point of trying to earn love, when it comes by grace and favour? Earning love brings with it the danger of losing it; if we do not have to earn it, the danger is not there, because we receive grace through faith in our loving Father God. If you say you do not deserve it, that is true because you cannot do anything to deserve it, except for being grateful. 'God did it for us. Out of sheer generosity, He put us in right standing with himself - a pure gift. He got us out of the mess we're in and restored us to where he always wanted us to be. And he did it by means of Jesus Christ,' (Romans 3:24 Message).

Outrageous

To the human way of thinking, the grace of God is so far beyond the boundary of respectability that it appears to be excessive, shocking and scandalous. Outrageous grace is not some sort of favour that can be achieved by being good; it is the gift a person receives by just being God's child. As God pursues humanity, He comes in His goodness and grace on the basis that no one has anything to offer Him in return, and to those who mess up, He continually shows His grace even though it is undeserved. Grace looks beyond my faults and sees my needs, and even though I deserve judgement God still accepts me. The religious and civil leaders in Jesus' time could not understand the way He lived and how He accepted 'the sinner.' They were scandalised, because Jesus accepted the 'wrong' sort of people. This is 'amazing' grace, that accepts the orphan hearted, just as much as the rest of humanity.

It is clear with a term such as outrageous grace that there is the danger of moving to either one of two extremes. First, there is legalism, which has an emphasis on rules and regulations, and which opposes the expression of grace, particularly when it is interpreted as frivolous. This sort of thing would annoy, or even be considered offensive, making it unacceptable to many in the church. It is not difficult to try to limit, restrict, or modify grace so that it is not as shocking or scandalous as it first appears, but something is lost when this happens. Where God has given liberty with a release of passion, we should never enslave people to man-made rules. Our relationship with God is primarily a matter where everything flows from the heart without a religious filter saying, 'we do not do it that way.' If grace is put in a box you bring restrictions, which can become unnecessary laws. Jesus deliberately moved outside the box, and that provoked the religious and civil leaders to anger because He undermined their religious culture. It was so unnecessary, as it opened the door for control, but maybe that is why Jesus deliberately healed on the Sabbath when He could have waited another day.

David dancing before the Lord with all his might, and wearing a priestly garment as the Ark returned to Jerusalem, may well have got him thrown out of the church even these days, (2 Samuel 6:14). His wife, Michal, not only despised him but berated him with his so-called vulgarity. However, David's reply summed up his fiery love for God, 'I will become even more undignified than this, and I will be humiliated in my own eyes. But by these slave girls you spoke of, I will be held in honour.' Her reaction to David brought her barrenness, and Michal never had children, (2 Samuel 6:22-23). Religion will not change the orphan heart, only feed it with rules and regulations. The orphan hearted will often tend towards a 'spiritual' obsessive-compulsive disorder. One of its meanings is a predisposition towards perfectionism, and that is the antithesis of grace. Grace will be suffocated and its life squeezed out. It is saying, 'I am right,' 'my way is right and what you do is wrong.' There's not much left except judgement, (Romans 14:10).

The second extreme is hyper-grace, which describes teaching that emphasises the grace of God to the exclusion of other vital teachings such as repentance and confession of sin. Teachers of hyper-grace fail to note God's other attributes of holiness and His call for followers to live righteous lives. They teach that there is no need to deal with sin any more since God has forgiven all sin, past, present, and future. It is a mixture of truth with error. Grace is not an excuse for doing wrong, it does not give us permission or a licence to sin; we are not free to please ourselves, we are free to please Jesus.

'Shall we go on sinning so that grace may increase? By no means! We have died to sin; how can we live in it any longer?' (Romans 6:1-2).

'For you have been called to live in freedom, my brothers and sisters. But do not use your freedom to satisfy your sinful nature. Instead, use your freedom to serve one another in love,' (Galatians 5:13).

A Reflection for the Orphan Hearted

It is important to consider these points with an open heart, and then to respond honestly to God as He speaks to you:

- Outrageous grace and unconditional love will lead to reckless confidence in living with God and sharing His love.
- Christianity is a love affair, for His love empowers us with grace so that we would know a depth of affection and intimacy.

- God loves you as you are, not as you should be.
- God offers us something which is unlike anything else that we have ever found or experienced.
- The death of Jesus on the cross was because of God's grace, not the grounds for it.
- We are not to be made as people who will become more acceptable and nicer, but brand new creations ignited with the Spirit of God.
- Allow yourself to be loved in your brokenness by stretching your mind and your heart to accommodate God's all-embracing love in Jesus Christ.
- I think am bad enough to receive God's grace, but I am not good enough to do anything about it, except to receive it with thanksgiving.

ABBA FATHER

Abba - An Astonishing Word

As well as being defined as following Jesus, a Christian is one who has God as Father. This means family, and a Christian's foremost privilege and deepest desire is to experience God as a loving Father, and to have an assurance that He can be approached with love and affection and without fear. We know that all the names of God are important, but one of the most significant is 'Abba,' as with it comes a very clear awareness of what sort of relationship God wants with humanity. The New Testament was written in Koine (common) Greek, which was the familiar language of the Roman Empire, and was something that made its writings accessible across that vast area. Jesus would have known Koine Greek, as it seems that the district that He lived in was influenced by Greeks, for there was a large Greek colony only a few miles from where He lived, at Sepphoris. He also had more than a working knowledge of Hebrew, as His knowledge of the scriptures pointed to His ability to read and understand Hebrew, such as reading from a Torah scroll written in Hebrew in a synagogue, (Luke 4:16-17). However, it is more than probable that Jesus' native language was Aramaic, which was the common Jewish language spoken during this time. This would mean that whenever He addressed God or talked about Him as 'Father,' He would have used the word, 'abba,' which is an Aramaic term meaning endearment. Most, if not all, Jewish people would have thought it was impossible to use this term when talking to God, because it was overly familiar. Judaism taught that anyone could talk to God, but only in a particular or set way, and they would have been adamant that the term abba was too intimate to use when speaking to God, and therefore was highly unacceptable. Aramaic and Hebrew are closely related, both were Semitic languages that existed in close proximity in the time of Jesus at the eastern end of the Mediterranean. Where it is used in the New Testament, abba is transcribed into letters but left as an Aramaic word. Aramaic was as similar to Hebrew as Swedish is to Norwegian, or Portuguese is to Spanish, and Aramaic speakers freely borrowed vocabulary from the Hebrew language, and Hebrew speakers did the same with the Aramaic language. Abba was borrowed by Hebrew speakers and used in the sense of 'Daddy,' and even today, the word abba can be heard on the streets and in the homes of Israel. In fact, no child, even after they have reached adulthood, addresses their father by the Hebrew word for 'father,' but rather uses the Aramaic word, 'abba.'

This remarkable word, as well as being revolutionary in Jesus' time, is revolutionary for many today. Sadly, some would consider the use of abba disrespectful, and others would be negatively affected by the wounds of their orphan heart, regarding how they see and communicate with God in using the word. All sorts of warning lights might go on, indicating to them the need to distance themselves, because of the potentially disturbing thought that God could get that close to them, because in their experience there has been a lack of a father's love, affection and intimacy. The father might not be around for a number of reasons, but even if he were still around, they might see that he behaved as though he were absent. Probably the cry of their hearts would be, 'how can I love God as a Father, when I do not feel loved by my earthly father?' It might be a lack of understanding or even fear, but it would be very real to them and could become a restriction that would hinder them in their walk and growth in their relationship with God. They might find it easier to relate to the other word for father in the New

Testament, which is the Greek word 'pater.' We will see though, that both words, whether used together or individually, are pivotal in the Christian life. As the core definitions for abba and pater are opened out, considered, and understood, it will become clear to see how fundamental these two words are in our relationship with God: abba identifies with cherish and pater with nourish.

The Revelation of Abba

This Aramaic word was a commonly used term that expressed affection which would lead to trust and confidence in a person. It signifies the close, intimate and trusting relationship between a father and his child. Abba is both deeply intimate and familiar, as well as formal and profoundly respectful. It seems that it can mean either one or the other depending on the circumstances of the conversation, such as from a child to their father, or as when Jesus used abba in the garden of Gethsemane (Mark 14:35-36). This would have not been a formal conversation, as it was a deeply emotional and personal time. In the scriptures, abba is only used when referring to God, and it is used in a way that implies a close and caring relationship. What stunned the disciples, surprised the common people and shocked and offended the ruling parties, was the way in which Jesus spoke to and about His Father. He did this knowing that no one in His culture ever addressed God directly as 'my Father,' and to say it made an impression is an understatement, for how can you talk to God Himself and call Him an everyday family word. The Jews thought that the gap between themselves and God was too great for them to use such a familiar expression. They did not even address God by His name in either it is spoken or written form - Yahweh, but Jesus had a different and distinctive way in speaking to God. It must have been spiritually traumatic for so many, because suddenly this man turned up introducing a new way of life, talking about the Kingdom of God, His Kingdom, and then talking about God, as well as talking to God, as though He intimately knew Him! It was so revolutionary, that it turned Jewish religious culture upside-down. Jesus addressed God as a child would address their father, and it needs to be understood that this is an amazing thing to say, because it is intimacy with deep affection, such as that reserved normally for parents and children. Abba is a distinctive and unique word, which is sacred to the child. Abba was also a family word, and it was not permitted for a bondservant or slave to use it to address the head of the house.

Cherish

This word is important in defining abba, as it gives clarity to its meaning. Cherish describes abba as giving protective loving care, and treating someone with great tenderness, affection and expressing a love that can be interpreted as a special love. Abba Father is devoted to us, as He esteems, admires and appreciates us. Another distinction of abba, which develops out of cherishing, is that He treasures us. To treasure emphasises a careful guarding of something or someone precious, and of great worth and value, and this is how Abba Father sees us. There is a parable that Jesus told concerning a field that had treasure hidden in it. '*The kingdom of heaven is like treasure hidden in a field. When a man found it, he hid it again, and then in his joy went and sold all he had and bought that field*' (Matthew 13:44). Could it be that one perspective of looking at this parable is that the man who found the treasure in the field, and then went sold all to be able to buy the field, was God himself? Grace being free to us is certainly exceedingly costly to God. God so loved us that He sacrificed the treasure of His heart, His only Son, so that we could be with and intimately know God. This would mean a love so extravagant, a love greater than we could imagine, that moved God to do everything He could to get us to a place where He could cherish and treasure us. The promise to His people in the Old Testament was the same, '*Now if you obey me fully and keep my covenant, then out of all nations you will be my treasured possession*' (Exodus 19:5). This promise has been extended to us, therefore we are esteemed precious, highly valued in His sight, and cared for beyond measure. We are always in His mind, and that shows the extent of His devotion to us.

Beloved

Beloved is not a word used that much in the English language these days, however it is used in the scriptures, and is very much connected to abba. Anyone can be loved, but the word beloved is used to define someone who is dearly loved, with a greater, or even a more extreme love. The word is scattered throughout the Old Testament, although more than half of those used are found in the Song of Solomon, where the King and his bride express their deep affection to each other. Interestingly, God called Solomon beloved (Nehemiah 13:26 ESV). In the New Testament, the use of the word extends to include the Father's love for His Son, as well as His love for us. Jesus is not only the centre of God's love but, He, the beloved of God, invites us to share in the relationship that He has with His Father. When Jesus was baptised in the Jordan at the beginning of His ministry, the heavens opened, the Holy Spirit descended on Him like a dove and the Father's voice cried out, *'you are my beloved Son; with you I am well pleased'* (Luke 3:22 ESV). This showed the strength and depth of the relationship that the Father had with Jesus. God underlined this by saying, 'I am well pleased,' or continually delighted, which expresses the utter passion of infinite delight and pleasure that He has with His Son. *'Here is my servant, whom I uphold, my chosen one in whom I delight; I will put my Spirit on him, and he will bring justice to the nations'* (Isaiah 42:1). Delight can mean 'takes my breath away,' which is an amazing response for the Father to have. Becoming a Christian brings us into the close relationship that Father God desires. *'To the praise of the glory of His grace, by which He made us accepted in the Beloved'* (Ephesians 1:6 NKJV). The word 'accepted' has its roots in the word grace and means that He has made us objects of His grace. In following Jesus, we are adopted into the family of God, and the Holy Spirit gives testimony to us that not only are we God's children, but we are also recipients of His lavish love because He delights in us (Romans 8:15; 1 John 3:1). We need to know that God's acceptance is different from our human form of acceptance, and what this does to the orphan hearted distorts the fact that whatever happens, God's love never fails us. God's acceptance of us is eternally established - it cannot be changed, for God has no intention of doing so! This incredible act of His love gives us a confident trust in Him and His promises, because of His unending grace and favour. Therefore, we are not only accepted, but we are accepted in the beloved, that is, in all that Jesus is. Our relationship with Father God is summed up in this glorious revelation, 'I am my beloved's and my beloved is mine' (Song of Songs 6:3).

Challenge

The treasure that the man in the parable suddenly found, was something that transformed his whole outlook on life, as it restructured his values and priorities. The concept of God as abba, that Jesus showed, brought into focus the magnitude of the possibility of intimacy with our Heavenly Father. Intimacy with God means the deepest part of a person having a relationship with God; it needs to include vulnerability as well as trust. God's plan from the beginning was to make humanity in His image (Genesis 1:27) and knowing that we are made in the same image as God establishes an enduring bond that cannot be replicated. Jesus is the object of the Father's love, and because we are in Christ, we too are the objects of the Father's unconditional love. It cannot matter how we feel, for God's acceptance of us is nothing to do with how we feel; it is more how He feels, and what He has established eternally, because His feelings for us are unchanging.

When faced with this, many of us, including the orphan hearted, find that there is a conflict concerning how to get there and how to recognise any issues that might hinder us. Certain truths which will prepare us to make an honest response and to come out of hiding and come closer to the Father, need to be acknowledged. Remember Adam and Eve remained hidden, and we know what happened there:

- We know God loves us, but do we know God likes us?
- Grace is God's acceptance of us; we are received with approval and are pleasing to Him.
- Faith is my acceptance of God's acceptance of me.

- God loves us despite our failures.
- It is not who we are first and foremost, it is where we are - in Christ!
- As this truth is accepted, we will be free to enjoy our relationship with Him in a brand-new way.
- God does know everything about us anyway, so talking to Him honestly will be a step towards personal freedom.
- 'You shall know the truth [Jesus] and the truth will set you free' (John 8:32).
- 'Trust in the Lord with all your heart, and do not lean on your own understanding. In all your ways acknowledge him, and he will make straight your path' (Proverbs 3:5-6).

There is enough here to encourage the orphan hearted to make honest choices, recognising that God has already released His grace to enable them to make the right decision.

The Lord's Prayer

The number of times that Jesus spoke about God being His father shocked the ordinary people as well as the religious and civil leaders; He continually talked about His Father. However, when they heard Jesus pray to His Father, they were overwhelmed because it was so different from the way people prayed normally. It was the name He used that became a sensation, because nobody would ever have ever used that name in talking to God. It was not unusual that Jesus prayed, because everyone prayed, for the nation of Israel was known as a people who prayed. Children were taught from a very young age, that you should say your daily prayers three times a day, and these included 'The Shema,' as the centrepiece, (Deuteronomy 6). Jesus lived in a society where the public reading of the scriptures was in Hebrew, therefore prayers had to be spoken in the same language. The disciples would have heard Jesus pray often, and the way He prayed not only attracted their attention but would also have touched them deeply to the point where they could not let the issue go because it was so different.

At one time, Jesus was talking to them about giving advice on how not to pray. He talked about insincerity, hypocrisy and posturing in prayer, as well as those heaping up empty phrases with too many words, (Matthew 6:5-8 TPT). It seems that He was trying to lead them to a type of prayer that was more intimate and relational, and relatively short! Another time when Jesus was praying, the disciples who were with Him came up to Him and asked, 'Lord, teach us to pray.' He said, 'when you pray, say, Father' (Luke 11:1-2). As He spoke, there would probably have been an immediate tremor of shock in the disciples, because Jesus used the Aramaic word for father, which is abba. There are many places in the Old Testament where God says that He is the Father of Israel, but He is never addressed as such. Jesus was saying, 'this is what your God is like,' and He can be approached in a very close and intimate way, which is completely different from any other prayer that would have been made to Him. Jesus was teaching His disciples and the people to pray in the common language, which was very simplistic, yet heartfelt. He was not giving them '**a**' way to approach God, He was giving them '**the**' way, and in doing so He endorsed Aramaic as the acceptable language of prayer. Jesus was talking about prayer being a language of the heart not a sacred language, as part of a sacred culture, and in that, He was portraying God primarily as a tender and compassionate Father full of grace. It was a term of endearment, yet respect, and of a close relationship, because it is family. Jesus was showing the heart of His Father because He knew that helps to shape the people in prayer.

Jesus opened a door for us to come close to the Father in prayer. This may constitute a challenge, but to the orphan hearted it is more than that, because praying to Abba Father gives an expectation of closeness and vulnerability. Past relational issues will cause some people to back off but be aware that speaking to Abba enables us to open our hearts to the intimacy and affection of our Heavenly Father. Thankfully, God never abandons His commitment of love to us; it is wonderfully constant, and we can be assured that He will never forsake us. In spite of the tug of fear of rejection, fear of failure, condemnation and other pressures that attempt to undermine our response to God by bringing back to our minds the pain of past relationships, we need to remind ourselves that there is a way forward. Why should our thoughts rule us when we are women and men first and foremost led by the Spirit of God, and not by the way we think? We can harmonise our thoughts with His Spirit, and then can undermine the strongholds of the mind by taking captive every thought and making them obedient to Christ, (2 Corinthians 10:5). We know that we please God by our commitment to His unconditional love, which is motivated by His outrageous grace, and therefore we can *'be transformed by the renewing of our minds in order to know His good, pleasing and perfect will,'* (Romans 12:1-2). The way forward is to bring Abba right into the forefront of our lives, including our minds, as this will give God the right to begin to expose the orphan issues that have brought so many restrictions and hindrances in our walk with Him.

The Holy Spirit is the key to revealing Abba to us, as we will see later, so we can, therefore, choose to ask Him to help restore our minds. *'Instead, let the Spirit renew your thoughts and attitudes,'* (Ephesians 4:23, NLT). The Greek word for 'renew' is used only here in the New Testament, and means to make new, but involves a supernatural event. However, we have a responsibility as 'we put off' (v22) meaning to renounce the old way of life, and then, 'we put on the new self' (v24) by opening ourselves up to the life of God. We are new creatures in God's new creation, and it should not only be our positive response, but also our legal right to resist the ploys of the enemy, who has access to undermine, torment, afflict and deceive the mind. We can learn to say no, which is part of the reforming of our new mindsets and belief systems. We have the authority to overcome in Jesus' name. The orphan hearted can and will get to the place where yesterday's problems become quite secondary to communing with Abba, for there is a precious place of security in the Father's love, as I and many others have experienced.

Little Children

There is a mandate from the scripture, which calls us to be as little children in our response to Father God and His Kingdom. If Jesus taught that it is fundamental in our relationship to God to use the endearing term abba when talking to Him, surely we need to understand the significance of why a child uses the same term when talking to their father. In the first century, children were more peripheral to society, and were somewhat undervalued, and shown little respect. While families accepted and loved their children, society merely tolerated them; the innocence of childhood lasts a lot longer these days. What Jesus did was to use a child to teach us how our response should be to God. How can we say abba if we are not childlike? The disciples were not concerned about children, so they scolded the parents who brought their children to Jesus. They were more concerned about their own status and who was going to be the greatest in the Kingdom.

'At that time the disciples came to ask Jesus, who is considered to be the greatest in heaven's kingdom realm? Jesus called a little one to his side and said to them, learn this well: Unless you dramatically change your way of thinking and become teachable, and learn about heaven's kingdom realm with the wide-eyed wonder of a child, you will never be able to enter in. Whoever continually humbles himself to become like this gentle child is the greatest one in heaven's kingdom realm,' (Matthew 18:1-4, TPT).

'Listen to the truth I speak: Whoever does not open their arms to receive God's kingdom like a teachable child will never enter it,' (Mark 10:15 TPT).

One way of understanding what Jesus was saying is to understand the theory of 'attachment' (this will be looked at in more detail in a later chapter). Attachment is a deep and enduring emotional bond that forms between the child and its parents, and it is how the powerless baby gets its primary needs met. This bond is usually well established before the end of its first year and will become the foundation and source for future stable relationships. We know that we cannot see the Kingdom of God unless we are born again (John 3:3), and to help Nicodemus in his confusion Jesus explained that He was not talking about physical new birth, but a spiritual rebirth. *'If anyone is in Christ, he is a new creation; the old has gone, the new has come!'* (2 Corinthians 5:17). This sovereign act of God fosters an attachment, which becomes a spiritual bond through the Holy Spirit, who introduces us to Abba (Galatians 4:6-7). We become Christians by God's grace through our faith, for it is the gift of God to us, however, if we come as a child would, we would remain childlike in the Christian life. This is to do with heart attitude, and not growing into maturity. We attach and we stay attached, but in a childlike way, and get our primary needs met through getting our cherishing and nourishment from the one to whom we are connected, namely Abba Father.

A child is teachable, willing to learn, and to receive care, free from prejudices. To become as little children means not being self-reliant, but reliant on God. Children utterly trust their parents to love, care and provide for them in their daily needs. They are humble and teachable and have an innocence and purity, for there is nothing hidden. Jesus wants each of us to possess that childlike faith, which is pure, unassuming, and humble. This allows us to receive from God without an appearance of pride or of being pretentious. The attitude of the disciples highlighted their arrogance due to their self-importance about their status more than anything else in their response to the children. Are we childish or childlike, meaning not acting like a child, but being like one? It allows us to resolutely believe that God is who He says He is. A child trusts parents without a second thought, for trust to them is total dependence, which is an essential and necessary reality. As children who rely on their parents' provision for daily needs, we should humbly depend on our Heavenly Father for provision in every area of our lives. To encounter God is to have our childlike heart spontaneously open to receive as much love as is possible, with an audacity that simply asks. Probably to many, which includes the orphan hearted, this way of responding to God would be difficult, but no-one is saying forget your intellect. It is more to do with the pride of being childish in attitude, so humility will need to be in the ascendency. Fundamentally, the message of the gospel offends the proud, as it insists that we have open hearts to Father God who then will touch us in our need. The challenge is not to live with only one foot in sonship, and therefore to still be able to slide back into an orphan attitude. A child has no fear when approaching their abba, for love cannot give room for fear. It is the same for us, for we can make the right choice, and deal once and for all with these heart issues that hold us back in our childlike faith.

Pater

The word father when translated in the version of the Old Testament is 'pater.' It is a word that compliments 'abba,' with its root signifying 'nourisher,' and it relates to provider, protector and parent, which all connect to the word creator, being the one who imparts life. To nourish can also mean provision, which not only builds up and strengthens, but also sustains, gives support and encouragement, all of which underline the expression of pater in a practical, personal and spiritual way. God declares Himself to 'be father to the fatherless, a defender of widows' (Psalms 68:5). Pater, in this context, shows the tender character of a loving God in the Old Testament, where it is rare for God to be referred to as Father, and, even then, it was relatively impersonal and far from the New Testament term abba. There is no reference in the Old Testament of an individual speaking of God as Father. As we have seen, when Jesus came onto the scene, He only addressed God as Father, and never referred to Him by any other name. It was as though a sudden change took place, for Jesus began to use the name Father in a personal and tender way, which had not happened before because it was not the way the Jews had a relationship with God. In the beginning, God said 'let us make man in our image,' (Genesis 1:26) and as Father, pater, He passed on the potential for likeness. It is probable that image and likeness describe one concept, as in the two sides of a coin. It would seem that both terms point to reflecting His nature. We were made to be like God, as He has given us certain characteristics, such as to think for ourselves, and our relationship with Him, which give us the ability to communicate with Him, but parts of that image have been distorted and lost. When Jesus came with the message of the Kingdom of God, He introduced us to His Father in order to see image and likeness restored, and it can be, for as we reflect Jesus in our daily living, we reflect the Father. Through Jesus, we bear His image and reflect His nature, for God purposed that we should be conformed to, or match, the likeness of His son (Romans 8:29). All of this comes out of our Heavenly Father who is the life-giver, pater, and it was the term used throughout the Old Testament. When Jesus came, He began to use another word, abba, and, when used together with pater, this brings an amazing harmony of cherishing and nourishing. In my walk with God, I have unwittingly taken the term Father [pater] for granted and not realised or lived in the fulness of its meaning, and it is only relatively recently, that I have begun to perceive the truth of abba. We need a restoration of pater and a revelation of abba!

My father was not an abba, but more a pater. He was conscientious in his provision to my mother and me, but I would say his nourishing was out of duty because it was the only way he knew how to express his love. If I was told I was like my father, I would understand that as not being something very complimentary, because, as mentioned previously, he was an angry man. Occasionally we display the image of our fathers. God's likeness, however, is something different, and whether orphan hearted or not, it has been established we are sons and daughters of our Heavenly Father and can reflect His image. Imagine being told, 'when I see you I see something of God.' I long to be seen in His likeness. I have observed through the years, that some people have unfounded fears of God leading to a grave apprehension of a dependence upon Him, because they bear deep wounds from their earthly fathers who had disappointed them time and time again. The image of a father brings pain to them rather than delight, as they could never measure up to their own father's expectations or demands. They understood control with intimidation, domination and manipulation. In my case there was never the intimacy of being cherished by my father because of his self-centred ways, and his inability to show emotion other than that of the negative sort. Maybe he did not know how to, because he was never shown how by his own father. It is wonderful to know that there is a way through this though, for Jesus is not only the way, but the truth and the life (John 14:6).

The Union of Abba and Pater

The joining in the New Testament of the words 'abba' (Aramaic), and 'father,' (pater Gk), is fundamental to our life in God. Interestingly, it is rarely used in this way, yet it highlights the substance and necessity of their union. Pater can literally mean **the** Father and is connected to abba, but not in place of it, so it is valid to say, 'Abba the Father.' There is a big difference in saying God is 'a' father when He is known as **the** Father. This gives God His rightful place, as there are many fathers, but there is only one Father who is God. The name 'Abba Father' is only found in the New Testament three times, being Mark 14:36, Romans 8:15 and Galatians 4:6. Only two people used these words - Jesus and the Apostle Paul, and in doing so, each expressed a rich intimacy, which characterised their personal relationship with God. Although both are valid in their own right, the synergy of these two words has a powerful influence, which releases revelation with a depth that strengthens our foundations in God. It is necessary to realise that the use of both words spoken together is much more powerful than just the use of one or the other. The key to the release of pater is its link to abba, for nourish (pater) needs to be impacted by cherish (abba), which releases the capacity to see its full meaning, as it becomes a fundamental union undergirded by the power of the Holy Spirit. Nourish without the mix of the intimacy of cherishing loses its dynamic. The problem that many have, is an unspoken assumption that pater, being formal respect, and abba, being familiar intimacy, are mutually exclusive, which implies that our response to God must be either familiar or formal. That may seem good, but the best is to be both familiar and formal, discerning which and when as we respond to God. The Old Testament excludes familiarity, although there are a few exceptions, such as King David publicly dancing as the Ark returned to Jerusalem (2 Samuel 6).

However, things completely changed when Jesus came and spoke to His Father with words of affection and intimacy. In Middle Eastern society, the father would rule as head of the household, demanding the most respect and exercising absolute authority over his household often with a lack of affection and intimacy. What Jesus did was to turn everything upside down in the way He not only communicated with the Father, but also communed with Him! It was quite shocking to them, but it was the way forward. We are designed to live in a family, and it is our privilege, as well as our deepest need, to experience God as our Father, and to be able to approach Him without fear, but with an assurance of His loving care. It is important, therefore, to learn to use these two distinctive words concerning fatherhood together. We need to have care not to put too much weight or emphasis on one of the words to the detriment of the other. For as much as abba describes the privileged, intimate relationship we have with our Heavenly Father, we also know that He is worthy of our full respect.

Abba Father

The following three scriptures that encompass 'Abba Father' in the New Testament are unique and distinctive in the way in which they impact the reader, but, amazingly they are not mentioned elsewhere in the Bible. The response Jesus has towards the Father in His deepest hour of need shows us much that is important in our relationship with Him. Also, there is the role of the Holy Spirit as a tutor, teacher and helper, (John 14:16 & 26) in leading us into the close relationship, that we can have with Him. The task of the Holy Spirit, who is the promise of the Father, is to introduce us to the most affectionate word there is in our relationship with our Heavenly Father, which is abba.

Mark 14:35-36

'Going a little farther, he fell to the ground and prayed that if possible the hour might pass from him. Abba Father he said, everything is possible for you. Take this cup from me. Yet not what I will, but what you will.'

Just before the most heartbreaking and anguished time in Jesus' life, He went to the garden of Gethsemane with some of His disciples, and He began to pray in a deeply distressed and troubled way; this was an incredible challenge, as He had an almost impossible decision to make. Gethsemane aptly means 'oil press,' and Jesus was overwhelmed with sorrow, and due to such extreme emotional stress, He sweat drops of blood. He did the only thing He could do, He spoke to His Father most intimately, addressing Him as 'Abba Father.' There was nothing formal about that, it was utterly passionate, totally trusting and so childlike, as He struggled with what He saw ahead. Jesus surrendered His will to His Father, and this prepared the way for all believers to speak to the Father in the same close way. What an amazing outworking of the relationship He had with His Father! The Holy Spirit led Jesus in and through that deepest need, and moved Him to cry out, 'Abba Father.' It is the same Spirit that leads us in our unique relationship as adopted sons, encouraging us to say the identical words to our God in whatever situation, difficult or not, we are in.

Galatians 4:3-7

'But when the set time had fully come, God sent his Son, born of a woman, born under the law, to redeem those under the law, that we might receive adoption to sonship. Because you are his sons, God sent the Spirit of his Son into our hearts, the Spirit who calls out, Abba Father. So you are no longer a slave, but God's child; and since you are his child, God has made you also an heir.'

Here the Apostle Paul is declaring something fundamental regarding the transforming steps to becoming a Christian, and as well as being a revelation, it becomes revolutionary to a person's life. The orphan hearted person often gets stuck in the process of becoming a son after a previous life of slavery to sin, and the oppressive bondage of the basic and dark principles of the world. Slavery was a common practice at that time, and a person who was a slave was the property of someone else, as they were legally owned and wholly subject to them. Paul is saying we have come out of the law that would control us, but now, through the grace of God, we are redeemed and can come into the full rights of sons.

This is a key insight into the role and work of the Spirit in our lives. Consider the strategy of the Holy Spirit, as He inspires and encourages us because He is committed to tutoring us in showing us the way forward in our relationship with the Father. As we open our lives to God, we position ourselves to be adopted into sonship, for God has already established that we are sons, and it is now up to us to possess that which in God's eyes is already ours. What God did was to send the Spirit of His Son into our hearts, and He gives testimony to the truth of the indisputable fact that we are sons, and as He continually speaks into the core of our lives, the revelation spoken will become a passion, which will quickly develop into a desire for Abba Father. Our responsibility is to not only listen as the Holy Spirit calls, but also to allow the words Abba Father to permeate into the depth of our beings so that they become part of us. He speaks into our hearts constantly, reminding us of the passion of the Father, whose desire is to get close. The challenge is to give the Holy Spirit the right to have His way with us, as He tutors us to come into the most intimate relationship, which is gloriously possible with our Heavenly Father. *'He will teach you everything and will remind you of everything I have told you'* (John 14:26 ESV).

I believe that over the years of being affected by my orphan heart, I did not grasp hold of the remarkable work that the Holy Spirit did in my life regarding Abba Father. It undoubtedly happened, and His voice was continually speaking those wonderful words to me, but my spiritual awareness in that area was dulled, and I was in a backwater. So many other areas in my Christian life were growing and expanding, and things were happening, but it took several years for me to be fully aware of the Holy Spirit is work in revealing Abba Father to me. The orphan heart will attempt to undermine our response to the Holy Spirit, and to draw us away into independence when what is necessary is for us to rely on Him to bring us into this essential truth.

Romans 8:14-16

'For those who are led by the Spirit of God are the children of God. The Spirit you received does not make you slaves so that you live in fear again; rather, the Spirit you received brought about your adoption to sonship. And by Him we cry, Abba, Father. The Spirit himself testifies with our spirit that we are God's children.'

This takes it further, with the Apostle Paul declaring that the Spirit we received has not only brought us into the revelation of adoption, but has also extended that to sonship. We have been liberated from slavery, which locked us into fear, and have been brought into the family of God as children of God, 'for where the Spirit of the Lord is, there is freedom' (2 Corinthians 3:17). Suddenly, we have before us an amazing change of direction, as we move from the dominating condition of slavery with fear, to the overriding characteristic of adoption, and first and foremost, all we can do is to declare that. In the previous scripture, it is the Spirit within us that calls out Abba Father, but now we can progress to the point at which we ourselves cry Abba Father. It is not the Spirit calling, but us, motivated by Him. The word is a loud cry, full of desire and passion, to the extent that no-one would miss it, and this cry declares that we have been liberated from all the orphan issues that have afflicted us for many years, and that by adoption we are sons and not orphans.

The Holy Spirit testifies to us that as believers we are God's children and are accordingly invited to cry Abba Father. For by the Spirit, we now have the confidence to address God in this way, because of the relationship we have with Him in through His grace. It is amazing to know that we can pray to the Father with the same sense of warmth and intimacy in our relationship with God that Jesus Himself enjoyed. The newborn believer is powerfully moved from within to cry out Abba Father with an assurance that they now are sons and daughters who possess an intimate, unbreakable relationship, and oneness with the Father now made real and personal through Jesus, with the New Covenant in His blood. Over the years, so many, including me, have missed out on this vital part of our inheritance, but now I can rejoice, that not only have I experienced the joy of crying Abba Father, but also the closeness of being cherished in the fulness of my Father's love.

Barabbas - The Counterfeit Son

During the Second World War, the English Prime Minister Winston Churchill had a dirty tricks department, and its operatives were not sent undercover to Europe, but to the USA! They went to persuade America to come into the war, and this was known as a 'high-level seduction mission,' which used any charming way possible, as well as blackmail, bribery, spreading lies and even plotting to kill. This conspiracy highlights the devious ploy of Satan at the very end of Jesus' life, where he used any scheme possible to deceive the people to choose to crucify Jesus. This was the ultimate use of identity theft, because it took away everything that Jesus had and was, and gave it to another, a 'counterfeit son.' We read that, 'the thief comes to steal, kill and destroy (John 10:10), and at this point, Satan created his own 'Final Solution' to try to get rid of Jesus once and for all.

A custom had developed during the Passover festival which gave the Jews the choice to release a prisoner. Pontius Pilate used this method to appease the people in an effort to keep the peace. The two men Pilate offered to the people were Barabbas and Jesus. Barabbas was a 'freedom fighter,' an insurrectionist, part of a revolutionary movement, and he, together with others, was in prison because they had been involved in a murder during a recent uprising (Mark 15:6-15). Amazingly, Jesus was accused of participating in similar activities when He was before the Roman authorities. However, as far as Pilate was concerned, Jesus had done nothing wrong. Pilate knew that Jesus was not a criminal, but he did not know who He actually was. Was the choice of Jesus in contrast to Barabbas an accident, or was it premeditated, and malevolent? Here are two messianic figures with their own beliefs, standing, as it were, in opposition to each other, both with clearly different perspectives. The people could see and choose between one who led an armed struggle, who took life to gain a better life with a promise of freedom and a new kingdom, and the mysterious Jesus who also promised freedom and a new Kingdom, but who talked about laying down your life as the way to gain life. Pilate had no option but to put it to the people, as he was under such great pressure. It was a no-win situation, as the people began to chant 'give us Barabbas,' which soon became a frenzied shout due to the crowd psychology of the few stirring up the many. It reached a peak when the mob assumed the guilt of Jesus' death and proclaimed, 'Let his blood be on us and our children' (Matthew 27:25).

If we consider the meaning of the name of Barabbas, the underhand tactics of the enemy become clear. His last name, Barabbas, means son (bar) of the father (abba). Jesus had always referred to himself as the Son of the Father. Barabbas' first name was significant too. Pilate asked them, 'which one do you want me to release to you: Jesus Barabbas, or Jesus who is called the Messiah?' (Matthew 27:17 NIV). Amazingly, Barabbas' first name was Jesus. So what you see is Jesus son of the father opposing Jesus Son of the Father! A man with the same name as Jesus, who Satan used in an apparent triumphal way to deceive the people. Right up to the cross, Jesus was challenged about who He was and why He came to Earth. It is also important to realise that Satan is also a kind of father, the father of lies (John 8:44) and that this event involves satanic malevolence deceiving and confusing the people with a counterfeit messiah. Satan's purpose was to rob Jesus of His identity by stealing His name, as well as His status as Son. Jesus knew that He could have asked His Father to put at His disposal the legions of angels, who would have been watching since Gethsemane (Matthew 26:53) but He did not, He laid down His life, and let Satan have his way. We know why.

We have a responsibility in all of this too. The powers of darkness will do everything they can to afflict us in the core belief of our being, which is the source of our relationship with the Father, Jesus the Son and the Holy Spirit. The enemy will come and attempt to take ground in our lives when things get hard and we are under pressure. He is no respecter of persons; he will kick us when we are down. Are we going to let Satan undermine our relationship with Abba Father, steal our inheritance as Abba's children and plunder our identity, and our right to call God abba? It is understandable that if this were to happen, we would lose our capacity to commune and communicate with our Father God with affection and intimacy. However, it is vital that we know we have a glorious opportunity to take that which God has given us and to press into the inheritance that we have as sons.

IDENTITY AND DESTINY

Some of you will feel relieved and blessed when you consider the definition of these words, but others, including those of you with an orphan heart, will be deeply challenged because the type of relationship you have with God might undermine the concept of identity and destiny. Knowing who you are, where you have come from and where you are going, is fundamental in our walk with God. Knowing who you are and who you want to be is an identity issue. Knowing what you do now and want to do in the future, relates to your destiny. Both are two sides of the same coin; they are as one and cannot be separated.

There are some remarkable verses of scripture about the beginning of our lives. 'Oh yes, you shaped me first inside, then out; you formed me in my mother's womb. I thank you, High God – you are breath-taking! Body and soul, I am marvellously made! I worship in adoration - what a creation! You know me inside and out, you know every bone in my body; You know exactly how I was made, bit by bit, how I was sculpted from nothing into something. Like an open book, you watched me grow from conception to birth; all the stages of my life were spread out before you. The days of my life all prepared before I had even lived one day' (Psalms 139:13-16, MSG).

'Before I shaped you in the womb, I knew all about you. Before you saw the light of day, I had holy plans for you: A prophet to the nations - that is what I had in mind for you,' (Jeremiah 1:5, MSG).

God was there before your beginning, planning for you to be. He then began to form and fashion you in your mother's womb, and watched you grow from conception to birth - He prepared the days of your life. There was not a time when God was not there, and He certainly was not an onlooker! He was involved with us, I believe, with joy and excitement, from that first spark of life in the womb, and has remained with us ever since. This is our Heavenly Father, and in His eyes, we were never orphans and never will be! All of this is summed up as identity and destiny, and amazingly God got the first look by being involved with us even before our parents were! Remember God cannot change His mind about us, regardless of what we think or what we do, for since our beginning He was there with His unconditional love and outrageous grace!

Identity

Putting aside the Christian perspective, the components of identity can be summed up as, how we look at ourselves, how others look at us, and then how we react as we consider the perceptions which others have of us. The formation of our identity includes discovering and developing our potential, which dictates the life choices we make, such as relationships or career. We need to understand that identity is individuality, meaning there is no one else like me; I am unique, with distinctive characteristics in my personality, which were seen as I grew and developed from a child. Connected to this is the fact that our identity is very much influenced by both our parents and by other family members. As a result, few people actually choose their identity, because they internalise the values of their parents. Children very easily define themselves in terms of how they think their parents see them, and if parents see them as useless, worthless, or of no value, they will absorb those things and it will be difficult for them to change those views as they grow older. We are all born with certain areas of need, such as a desire to feel loved, to have a safe place to live, or to be significant, which means our lives have purpose and value. However, if these needs are not satisfied it can lead to a lack of a sound sense of identity, bringing with it an uncertainty regarding who you are.

In light of this, there are two further components that connect to identity which need to be given careful thought. These are self-image, which is how you think other people see you, and self-esteem, which is how you think of yourself. This will be troublesome to the orphan hearted because generally their frame of reference regarding who they are is derived from a negative perspective. It is quite understandable that they might believe a lie about themselves on account of their vulnerability, because children easily accept negative judgements from the authority figures in their lives. What develops as a result is a low or poor self-image and self-esteem, which, when established, becomes more of an undermining factor than an enhancing and guiding voice. This also gives rise to a belief system motivated by negativity, as everything is affected by the continued difficulty of accepting positive comments. In the end, the accumulated criticisms collected over the years create dysfunction in the personality. Therefore, answering questions such as, 'what kind of person do you think you are?' or, 'what do you believe people think of you?' will almost always lead to a negative response. So many of us have learnt to hide, just as Adam and Eve did when they disobeyed God and became overwhelmed with fear and shame, which included separation from Him. We hide by creating sculptured faces, which do not reveal the real you, or we hide our feelings by denying the pain; we can even get to the place where we construct our image to impress other people. Yet conversely, we become apt at deflecting the good things said to us because we know that if we dislike ourselves it becomes very hard for us to accept anything nice, because after all, there is nothing nice to be said. There is a way through, which centres upon our relationship with God, giving us hope as we choose to get close to Him.

'Now may God, the inspiration and fountain of hope, fill you to overflowing with uncontainable joy and perfect peace as you trust in him. And may the power of the Holy Spirit continually surround your life with his super-abundance until you radiate with hope' (Romans 15:13 TPT).

Identity and Relationship

As we consider this aspect of identity and our response to it, we need to be aware of what is missing, because it is a key to us being secure in who we are. First and foremost, our identity lies in **whose** we are not just in **who** we are! It is not that something missing, but someone is missing, as our identity is intertwined in the relationship we have with God. Our value is derived from who we are in God and not from what we do or do not do. When we know we are loved because of who we are, we become healthier in mind and more intimate in expression. Therefore, our significance lies in the truth that we are both recognised and accepted by God, and there is no need to prove ourselves or our value to God. Identity happened because in the beginning, God pursued His creation as He 'came down' to the garden to commune with them (Genesis 3:8). As we are aware, things severely changed as Adam and Eve hid from God and orphaned themselves. They chose to leave their Father. At the beginning of the New Covenant, God became flesh in Jesus and came down to Earth to be with His people. As the Message succinctly puts it, 'the Word [Jesus] became flesh and blood and moved into the neighbourhood' (John 1:14). The forming of identity is a process of the development **of** a distinct personality, and individual characteristics by which a person is known. With Christians, the forming of identity is a process of development **by** a distinct personality (our Heavenly Father) and includes Him giving us the characteristics by which we will be known. As we get to know who He is, the more we begin to know who we are.

One day, Jesus was with His disciples in Caesarea Philippi and He asked them, 'who do people say that the Son of Man is?' They came out with a few ideas, but then Jesus got personal with them and asked, 'but what about you, who do you say I am?' Suddenly Peter had the answer, 'you are the Christ, the Son of the living God.' Jesus knew no one could have told Peter that, but it must have been revealed to him by Jesus' Father in Heaven. Then, amazingly, Jesus revealed to Peter his identity and destiny. They were stood in an area where there was a mass of exposed rocks and Jesus knew Peter's name meant rock, so He began to reveal what Peter would become, and what he would do. Peter's own revelation of who Jesus was prompted Jesus to bring revelation to who Peter was and Peter then began to see himself as Jesus saw him. Once we know who Jesus is, it releases us to know who we are.

'It is in Christ that we find out who we are and what we are living for. Long before we first heard of Christ and got our hopes up, he had his eye on us, had designs on us for glorious living, part of the overall purpose he is working out in everything and everyone' (Ephesians 1:11-12, MSG).

What the orphan heart does within us will undermine our true identity and destiny, because we will get a distorted picture when we look at everything through orphan eyes. It means that our relationship with our Father will be affected, and if our identity is in who we are, that is someone with an orphan heart, we will not come into the best that God has for us. If our identity is wrong, then our destiny will be wrong.

Identity Crisis

When my family secrets, which deeply affected me, were revealed, I was in leadership in a large church in Bristol, and I have often wondered why it happened at that time. It needed to, because leading a church with an unhealed orphan heart is certainly not the best way. Chris had held much of the information for probably two years, and she knew it was time to tell me. I believe she was prompted by God, for in that moment of personal revelation, I had a supernatural encounter with Him. It was as though He had prepared everything and was ready to move and come closer to me than ever before. What happened to me as I became broken was a revealing of His unconditional love and His tenderness and mercy. It touched me deeply and began a process which healed the deep hurts and wounds of my orphan heart. It became clear, as I began to understand the context of my background, that it was time to deal with the past issues that were affecting and hindering me in who I was and what I wanted to be - my identity and destiny. As understanding came to me regarding these areas, I knew it was time to face and embrace them. The key issue with me was an identity crisis! I thought that I knew who I was and where I was going, and in some measure I did, but there was a gaping hole regarding my relationship with God as Father. Most of the events of my early years had been hidden from me. It was more than a loss but rather more a theft - an identity theft. The biblical context relates to a destructive act or a theft.

'*Jesus said, the thief comes only to steal and kill and destroy. I came that they may have life and have it abundantly*' (John 10:10 ESV).

It was as though there had been a theft related to my identity. Looking back, it felt as though so much had been lost with the enemy being given a clear opportunity to harass, afflict and torment my orphan heart. Genesis 3:1-4 reveals it was Satan, the first liar, who seduced and undermined Adam and Eve in their identity and relationship with God as a Father, by deceiving, twisting, contorting and contradicting His words. The way we see ourselves is vital to the way we live, and suddenly, through their disobedience, they saw themselves in a different light. Shame and fear oppressed them, and they chose to hide from God when He came to be with them. They had orphaned themselves from their Father, and the world would never be the same. When Jesus came to Earth, He said to His disciples, 'I will not leave you as orphans, I will come to you,' and that came to pass as the Holy Spirit was given to teach us, that God is Abba Father to every individual. What I had to contend with was this harsh, critical voice within, with the condemning, negative messages, that orphan hearted people seem to internalise more readily. In those early years of our lives, we would have learned a script, formed a negative belief system, and have ended up believing a lie about ourselves. This would have had a detrimental effect on our sense of worth, our value and the way we saw ourselves. We derive our identity from living in a clear revelation of God as our Father and then taking responsibility in learning how to maintain that daily. It is not impossible to get to that safe and secure place, because in Christ we are there already. For through His life, death and resurrection, He has made a way that we can enter into. We have the authority and power in Jesus to live in the victory that He has achieved for us.

Adopted as Sons

The progression from identity, knowing who we are, to sonship, knowing who we are in God, is a vital step in our Christian walk, and there is a need is for this process to grow from understanding to revelation. Nobody adopts a child by accident, and God chose us even though He knows what we are like. Adopted as sons is a powerful and foundational term, and it touches every Christian whether they realise it or not. Those with any sense of an orphan heart will be challenged, because the realisation of the revelation of sonship requires an openness that will lead to, in many cases, deep inner healing. For me, it was the obvious step to take, as the revelation of the Father's love became so significant, and even though it led me into a painful place, it was worth it, because I met God as Father in a way that I had thought was not possible. In the New Testament, 'adoption' and 'sonship,' constitute one Greek word. They converge as one and form a new whole, such as two rivers joining together, as a confluence, creating something with greater width and depth. They are distinct but become fused together, because having one without the other undermines the full definition. The word adoption means 'to make a son,' and is only used five times, and only by the Apostle Paul, in the New Testament (Romans 8:15,23, 9:4; Galatians 4:5). The fifth verse is, 'God predestined [decided in advance] us for adoption to sonship through Jesus Christ, in accordance with his pleasure and will,' (Ephesians 1:5). The Passion Translation is powerful, 'For it was always in his perfect plan to adopt us as his delightful children, through our union with Jesus, the Anointed One, so that his tremendous love that cascades over us would glorify his grace - for the same love he has for his Beloved One, Jesus, he has for us. And this unfolding plan brings him great pleasure!'

Amazingly, adoption to sonship brought God as our Father tremendous pleasure. Our God is not like any other! Who would plan a pathway to salvation, centred around the sacrifice of His Son, before the world even began, and then bring those who believed into His family to father them? It is inconceivable, but it has happened, and we, as frail, fragile and flawed humanity, can have an intimate and affectionate relationship with the God of Heaven and Earth in this way. Did not Jesus say, '*I will not leave you as orphans, I will come to you*' (John 14:18). There is a way to be free forever from the orphan tendencies and predispositions that have pursued and afflicted us to the point of undermining our relationship with our Father God.

When the Apostle Paul wrote to the church in Rome, he compared the Roman adoption laws to the plan and purpose of God in drawing us into His family with status and privilege. Adoption was not part of Jewish law, but as Paul applied Roman law into the scriptures, it became clear that adoption had such a significant influence on those he was writing to. This is not just to the church in Rome, but to those everywhere who follow Jesus. Be aware that Paul is using the following principles as a figure of speech to create a profound truth that to us becomes so meaningful, particularly as we begin to understand God's purposes of desiring a close relationship with us.

The Roman principles of adoption include:

- The child was freely chosen by the new parents, and they entered into a permanent agreement, which formally and legally declared that he was to be treated and cared for as one's own child, knowing that the child could not be disowned, or was in no way inferior to a birth son. The adopted son was regarded by the law as a new person.

- Adoption is a legal action, whereby the person who was adopted into a family gained all the legal rights and privileges, including that of the father's estate, of a legitimate son in the new family.
- He lost all the rights, privileges and responsibilities in his old family because the old life was completely wiped out. This included the cancellation of all debts, and any past issues had no effect - nothing was remembered.
- The concept of inheritance in Rome was not taken on at death, but it was a part of life, and the child became an heir of the father, and a co-heir, together with any siblings, of all the father's possessions, something which was not subject to change.

The Apostle Paul brought out certain principles from the Roman law regarding adoption, which underline the heart of God for all of us. *'God sent him [Jesus] to buy freedom for us who were slaves to the law so that he could adopt us as his very own children,'* (Galatians 4:5 NLT). Through redemption, we are now able to enter into God's plan for family and fathering, which He established before the foundation of the world. God determined not to leave us without help, but to draw us into His family to be a Father to us, so He ordained it and graciously adopted us into His family as sons. Adoption by God has nothing to do with Him thinking we would be worthy heirs; we are not, and the grounds for adoption is based on His grace, and certainly not who we are or what we can do. Adoption is a legal process, and although His justice and law demanded punishment, with exclusion from His presence because of our sins, it did not finish there, for God went beyond that. Jesus voluntarily laid down His life to satisfy the Father's justice, and all the legal demands, by shedding His blood, which paved the way to accept us into His family and to give us status as sons in a relationship undergirded by promise and not law. This is not focussed on the principle of reward or punishment related to behaviour, but on the acceptance of His unconditional love! The promise very much involves the Holy Spirit who is the Spirit of Adoption and Sonship, and as He comes into our lives, the Spirit of Slavery and Bondage are displaced. There is no room for them and they were made null and void; they were superseded, displaced, and evicted, never to return. The Holy Spirit within us gave testimony to the truth of the indisputable fact that we are sons, and in addition, He continually speaks into the core of our lives with the words Abba Father. We now have the right and authority to possess which is rightfully ours as sons, and in doing so, we can challenge our old belief systems and mindsets, and see them change! Through the power of His Word, we can demolish every deception, every ungodly attitude, capture every thought and insist that they bow to Jesus the anointed one (2 Corinthians 10:5 TPT). As we surrender to God as living sacrifices, we can be inwardly transformed by the renewal and reformation of the way we think (Romans 12:1-2). This way will help us to be free forever from the orphan tendencies and predispositions that have pursued and afflicted us to the point of undermining our relationship with our Father God.

Our responsibility is to not only listen as the Holy Spirit calls, but also allow the words Abba Father to permeate the depth of our beings so that they become part of us. He speaks into our hearts, constantly reminding us of the passion of the Father, whose desire is to get into a close and affectionate relationship with us. The challenge is to give the Holy Spirit the right to have His way with us, as He tutors us to come into a relationship with our Heavenly Father. '*He will teach you everything and will remind you of everything I have told you*' (John 14:26, ESV). Our status has changed from an existence marked by slavery and fatherlessness to a new family, characterised by freedom and sonship. This has to go further than logic and reason, for an unveiling and revelation of truth is necessary. This is not just an intellectual truth, but it has to get into the depth of our inward parts. Jesus said, 'then you will know the truth, and the truth will set you free' (John 8:32).

I believe that over the years of being affected by my orphan heart, I did not grasp hold of the remarkable work that the Holy Spirit did in my life regarding Abba Father. It undoubtedly happened, and His voice was continually speaking those wonderful words to me, but my spiritual awareness in that area was dulled, and I was in a backwater. So many other areas in my Christian life were growing and expanding, and things were happening, but it took several years for me to be fully aware of the Holy Spirit is work in revealing Abba Father to me. The orphan heart will attempt to undermine our response to the Holy Spirit, and draw us away into independence, when what is necessary, is to rely on Him to bring us into this essential truth. '*For in Christ Jesus you are all sons of God, through faith. For as many of you as were baptised into Christ have put on Christ. There is neither Jew nor Greek, there is neither slave nor free, there is no male and female, for you are all one in Christ Jesus. And if you are Christ's, then you are Abraham's offspring, heirs according to promise*' (Galatians 3:26-29, ESV).

Destiny

Everyone indeed ends up somewhere, but only a minority end up somewhere on purpose. We need to know where we are going, particularly with our Heavenly Father planning everything, 'For I know the plans I have for you, declares the Lord, plans to prosper you and not to harm you, plans to give you hope and a future' (Jeremiah 29:11). 'My life, my every moment, my destiny—it is all in your hands' (Psalms 31:15) the Passion Translation. Remember destiny is knowing what you do now, today, and want to do tomorrow. Identity to destiny and adoption to sonship are progressive, and very much inextricably linked. Destiny is realised sonship, which means we do not just look to the very end of everything when Jesus returns to the Earth, but we are aware that our destiny starts right now, because we are sons now. Of course, we wait with anticipation for its fulness, but we wait in the tension that we hold, which is the now and the not yet. Today, our destiny is in and through Jesus; He is our destiny! 'Through our union with Christ we to have been claimed by God as His inheritance. Before we were even born, he gave us our destiny; that we would fulfil the plan of God who always accomplishes every purpose and plan in his heart,' (Ephesians 1:11 TPT). Our destiny hinges on a clear sense of identity built on the revelation of our union with Christ, and of God as our loving Heavenly Father. Destiny is dormant in many, and it needs to be re-awakened, understood and pursued. This is not a time for passivity, for destiny includes finding the way God is going, and going that way. The orphan hearted can have a tendency to settle, but it is necessary to make the right choices and move forward. *'This is what the Lord says: Stand at the crossroads and look; ask for the ancient paths, ask where the good way is, and walk in it, and you will find rest for your souls'* (Jeremiah 6:16).

An heir is someone who has a legal right of inheritance, who becomes a beneficiary following someone's death. We are not only heirs of God, but co-heirs with Christ. *'Now if we are children, then we are heirs - heirs of God and co-heirs with Christ, if indeed we share in his sufferings in order that we may also share in his glory'* (Romans 8:17). Not only was Jesus the testator, but, because of His resurrection, He became the executor too! As heirs we inherit the Kingdom prepared for us (Matthew 25:34) but it is not only the future, for the Kingdom is now! As Jesus is the heir of all things, (Hebrews 1:1-2) so we as co-heirs share all things, including destiny, with Him. Our interests are fused, for what belongs to Jesus belongs to us, which means we benefit in our God-ordained inheritance. This is grace, amazing grace. If that is not all, we have the presence of the Holy Spirit, 'and because of him [Jesus], when you who are not Jews heard the revelation of truth, you believed in the wonderful news of salvation. Now we have been stamped with the seal of the promised Holy Spirit. He is given to us like an engagement ring is given to a bride, as the first instalment of what's coming! He is our hope-promise of a future inheritance which seals us until we have all of redemption's promises and experience complete freedom - all for the supreme glory and honour of God,' (TPT). What a guarantee! When you have Jesus you have everything, the way, the truth and the life. There is nothing we can do to attain this other than possess it, because it is already ours, and has been so from the beginning of time.

Inheritance is fundamentally possession, and this brings us to another amazing aspect of the character and heart of God. Not only do we possess an inheritance given to us by Him, but conversely, we are His inheritance, His possession! 'Remember that the Lord rescued you from the iron-smelting furnace of Egypt in order to make you his very own people and his special possession, which is what you are today,' (Deuteronomy 4:20 NLT). This is also taken up in the New Testament, 'for you are a chosen people. You are royal priests, a holy nation, God's very own possession. As a result, you can show others the goodness of God, for he called you out of the darkness into his wonderful light' (1 Peter 2:9, NLT). We can understand how God is our inheritance, because when we receive Christ, we become the beneficiaries of his unconditional love. That, in itself, is stunning, but for the scriptures to say that we are God's inheritance, is remarkable! God, who owns everything in the universe, is thrilled that we are his possession! When the father in the parable of the wayward son said to the angry elder brother, 'my son, the father said, you are always with me, and everything I have is yours' (Luke 15:31). Today this is our portion, whether you are troubled by an orphan heart or not, because we cannot make God love us more or less, and we certainly cannot do anything to make Him accept us. It is all about learning to live in what He already has achieved for us.

Jesus - Identity and Destiny

Jesus lived in glorious security within His Father's love, and this was underlined by the fact that He knew where He had come from and knew where He was going, '*Jesus, knowing that the Father had given all things into His hands, and that He had come from God and was going to God*' (John 13:3, NKJV). His identity and destiny were settled, and He knew it. A strong sense of stability and confidence emanated from Him, as He brought the message of the Kingdom of God to the people, and He often did so in difficult circumstances. Jesus knew His identity was not based on success, popularity, or power, but in His Father's love. At one time, I had no idea what had happened to me regarding my birth and in my early years, as my life was enmeshed in secrecy and deception, which continually affected me in who I was, as well as how I saw my future. It was as though I had some disability mentally, emotionally and spiritually, however when I found Jesus, and ultimately came into the Father's love, things began to change. Now, I know where I have come from, and where I am going, and it is so liberating. I now understand being adopted by God as a son, and have confidence in my identity and destiny, because my orphan heart is more healed than ever. I have a purpose, which is undergirded by my relationship and life in Abba Father.

Both Abram and Sarai were barren, and Sarai persuaded him to take a maidservant (Genesis 16). The plan that Sarai hatched backfired, and Hagar was blamed unjustly and suffered abuse, so she fled. She ended up in a desert, however, the angel of the Lord found her. He said to her, 'Hagar, Sarai's servant, where have you come from, and where are you going?' She replied, 'I am running away from my mistress, Sarai' (Genesis 16:8, NLT). This is such a typical orphan heart example. We're unclear where we have come from, or where we are going, we are just running away. The angel said, 'go back,' and gave her a wonderful promise. We find out who we are and where we are going, when we know who Jesus is. Jesus was secure in who He was, He knew that He had come from God and would return to God. That security and peace undergirded His identity and destiny. Running away is not an option but finding our security and peace in Jesus is imperative, as it undergirds our identity and destiny.

Jesus and Adoption

It could be that one of the most significant examples of adoption in the Bible is Joseph's adoption of Jesus. He assumed the role of Jesus' father, which made a statement of family and fatherhood that God wanted to be highlighted, for He desired Jesus to have an earthly father, which was consistent with His plan for family and parenting. It is amazing to realise that God chose His incarnate Son to be adopted. Many have plenty of reasons why they do not want to adopt, and one is that they do not want to raise another man's child. God did not have to arrange for Joseph to adopt Jesus, for Joseph was prepared, because God spoke to him through a dream (Matthew 1:18-25). His heart was touched, and he chose to adopt Jesus because he wanted to; it was his honour to do so. There is something mysterious and supernatural about this, yet it was in the plan and purpose of God to bless Joseph in this relationship and to show us how much God cares about adoption. God does not leave us isolated when He adopts us. He cannot leave us without feelings of acceptance and love. He pours his Spirit into our hearts and reveals Himself as Abba Father, giving us the experience of being utterly accepted into His family.

Jesus the Father's Son

One of the key areas in the life of Jesus revolved around the way that He saw himself. It is summed up in a very positive self-acceptance, with self-esteem and value, which manifested in strength of security as He faced the powerful issues of life. It became the foundational basis of Jesus leaving His home to go out and proclaim the good news of the Kingdom of God. Jesus was able to fulfil His Father's call because of the relationship He had with Him, and this was so clearly emphasised at His baptism (Luke 3:21-22). It was a crucial time because it was this response from His Father, who interrupted His baptism with an incredible response of lavish affection, that gave Him the impetus to move on in the will of the Father in proclaiming the Kingdom of God. It is also important to us because we have been given that same love. As Jesus came out of the Jordan, and for a few seconds stood praying, heaven opened and two things happened simultaneously: The Holy Spirit descended on Him and clothed Him with power and authority, and the voice of His Father spoke out from the rent heaven. The Father expressed a deep emotional cry, which was a very personal response to His Son. It was as though the whole world needed to hear what the Father was saying, which was a declaration of sealing the family relationship:

- 'You are my son,' this is belonging.
- 'Whom I love,' this is worth, for Jesus was highly valued and esteemed by the Father.
- 'With you I am well pleased,' this gives an ability to cope, for Jesus could rest daily in the trust and pleasure of His Father.

Here there is no pressure to perform, or to feel the need to achieve to be accepted. Jesus had to do nothing to please the Father but just rest in His love. He had nothing to prove. The Father was saying, 'you are my son, chosen and marked by my love, you are the focus of my delight and the pride of my life.' Jesus needed nothing else.

He had received confirmation of who He was, and He received unconditional love and acceptance, something which was not based on a pressure to be, to conform, perform or to please. The Father was pleased because of who Jesus was, not what he was going to do. No wonder Jesus felt safe as He went out into the towns and villages of Israel. He knew who He was, and was secure in Himself and His Father's love, so that He could go and fulfil His calling.

We are Sons!

Everyone needs to know that they are loved and approved of. Where was our first recognised source? Surely it was the family, and it was the same with the Father who affirmed His Son, who was then able to go out following His Father's commission with a great sense of confidence. His worth was in no way determined by what others thought of him, as it was already resolved in His Father's love. As Jesus went about His task with His disciples, it became clear that He was someone who was different. It was not so much the miracles, although they were important, but more of a confident lifestyle, and a secure attitude of who He was, even to the point of saying so! This becomes so important for us because of the pressure of how we see and value ourselves. We do not serve God at a distance; we do not serve God as hired men and women, or as slaves, but as sons - we lovingly serve God, as part of His family. God sees us in the same way as He saw Jesus, and He expresses His love in the same way as He did to His Son:

- 'We are His sons,' adopted into His family, affirmed and accepted totally by Him.
- 'We are loved,' approved with unconditional love, and nothing can take that away. Nothing could make God love you more than He does right now, not greater achievement, greater recognition, greater wisdom, or even greater spirituality. Nothing could make God love you less, not our character flaws, or our past failures or regrets.
- 'He is pleased with us.' We could struggle with this, as most, if not all of us will want to do something in order to gain the pleasure of the Father. That is not the way, for there is nothing we can do to achieve God's approval. We need to stop trying to earn His love which is a love that actually can only be received by faith. God does not withhold His love as an expression of His disapproval. Others might, but He cannot. He has given us the ability and confidence to cope day by day, and therefore we can rest in the trust, pleasure and delight of our Father.

This shows the heart of God for all of us, including the orphan hearted, and it gives us an impetus to deal with these issues that have afflicted some of us for years. God is on our side, He is with us, to help us, and wants to draw us closer to Him in order for us to know fulfilment in who we are and satisfaction in what we do in partnership with Him.

Note: Paul is not being sexist or exclusive in his language when he writes about sons. In Roman law, daughters did not have the same privileges as sons, and if Paul used the language of 'sons and daughters' it would have weakened what he wanted to say about the status and security of Christians. Paul makes a radical statement in that he calls both men and women 'sons' of God, saying that in Christ, women have the same status as men despite the Middle Eastern culture's failure to recognise this. 'There is neither Jew nor Gentile, neither slave nor free, nor is there male and female, for you are all one in Christ Jesus' (Galatians 3:28). Regardless of race, social standing, and gender, we are heirs of God's promise and co-heirs with Christ.

THE ORPHAN HEARTED CHILD

It is important to consider the early years of children concerning the effect that the orphan heart can have upon them. A child's vulnerability within the womb and into its first few years is such that the unforeseen circumstances of life, which may include trauma in relationships, can affect him or her to the extent that hurts and wounds received would very likely be carried through to adulthood. The possibility of dysfunction in their personality is not lost. The way the parent-child relationship is worked out, regarding whether it is good or positive or the opposite of that in nature, will have a significant effect on the development of the child. Regarding my own childhood, there is no doubt that the consequences of what happened to my parents had deeply affected them. As you have already seen in previous chapters, it impacted me, and I carried the effects of those days on into adolescence and adulthood.

Parent-Child Relationships

Other than the fact of our fundamental relationship with God, there is nothing else comparable to the parent-child relationship. It is more distinctive than all of our other relationships, making it one of the most significant in any person's life. This role is crucial in terms of the development of the child. It is the earliest connection a child has - something which places a clear responsibility on both parents to cherish and nourish their child. Children have a clear tendency to seek closeness and a secure attachment to their parents for food, shelter and protection. This relationship will affect them for all of their lives and will become their guide in making future relationships. The parent-child relationship nurtures the physical, emotional and social development of the child. It is a unique bond, or in words that Christians may understand, a soul-tie, which implies a deep connection to mother and father. There is a spiritual content to this, whether known or unknown. Loving parents create loving children, with positive parenting increasing parent-child closeness. This means that children who grow with a secure and healthy attachment to their parents stand a better chance of developing content and fulfilling relationships with others.

Abba Father

We have a God whom we love and worship. We know that He is called God the Father, but do we understand the implications of that? We were in the mind of God before the beginning. 'Even before he made the world, God loved us and chose us in Christ' (Ephesians 1:4). What manner of love did God show? It was the lavish love of Abba Father, which came straight from His heart to cherish and treasure, as well as to nurture, nourish and bring provision. In that context, God inaugurated family at the beginning of creation so that they might fill the earth. He wanted a relationship, and because He desired to be with His creation, He came down to walk and talk with His children in the garden, (Genesis 3:8). God wanted to be with Adam and Eve loving them; He was and is, Abba Father. This same love was there when we were being formed in the womb. God planned to include us in His family, so that we could come into the very heart of His love.

'You formed my innermost being, shaping my delicate inside and my intricate outside, and wove them all together in my mother's womb. I thank you, God, for making me so mysteriously complex. Everything you do is marvellously breathtaking. It simply amazes me to think about it! How thoroughly you know me, Lord! You even formed every bone in my body when you created me in the secret place, carefully, skilfully shaping me from nothing to something. You saw who you created me to be before I became me! Before I had ever seen the light of day, the number of days you planned for me were already recorded in your book,' (Psalm 139:13-16 TPT).

When Jesus began His ministry, He was constantly introducing God as His Father to the people, as is particularly evident in the Gospel of John. Later, the Apostle Paul wrote about the Holy Spirit unceasingly speaking the revelation of Abba Father into our lives (Galatians 4:6). These words not only sum up God's response to His children, but it is also the way He wants His children to respond to Him through the power of the Holy Spirit.

The essence of parenting is the relationship with the child, and the most vital component in that is the giving and receiving of love. This is more than the parents simply being asked if they love their child, because the answer would immediately be, 'yes, of course, I love my child.' My parents loved me, but there was very little expression of that love, and I cannot remember them telling me that they loved me. When a child is born, there are basic human requirements that are vital in its development. Children need to be shown affection through unconditional love, and this creates a sense of belonging and security. Children need to know that they are cherished and cared for with nurturing, nourishing and appropriate communication. Some of this begins in the womb where the baby has the emotional and intuitive capacity to sense their parents love. This awareness means the baby can see, hear, feel, remember, taste, and think before birth, and the beginnings of bonding or attachment happen then. The mother and father need to make a good connection with the unborn child, as it strengthens the bond in their relationship.

It is in these formative months and years that foundations are laid which stay with the child in the rest of its life. When there is a healthy attachment between baby and parent, the baby comes to believe that the world is a safe place. The child is deeply influenced by its parents in what it sees and feels and will open its heart to bond and connect as trust develops. Remember in a previous Chapter, when Mary who was pregnant with Jesus visited Elizabeth, her cousin. She was pregnant too, and when Elizabeth saw Mary, the baby leapt in her womb, and not only was Elizabeth filled with the Spirit, the baby was too (Luke 1:15,41). John was dramatically affected by his mother's feelings and he too was wonderfully touched by the Holy Spirit before he was born. However, when circumstances are negative and traumatic, the baby is still affected, but adversely, leaving a lasting wound. The parents' responsibility for the child starts in the womb, as this is where the unconditional love starts.

If God loved us before He made the world, and if He was there showing us that same love, as we were being formed in the womb, surely He would not stop loving us just before we were born. He did not, and His love as Abba Father became foundational in the parent-child role. God being the perfect Father wants to support every parent and has put within them a latent ability to cherish and provide for their children. Parents can then cherish (Abba), and provide (Father) in their relationships with their children because they know that a safe, loving, genuine and faithful relationship is what children need more than anything else. Following and loving God is such a benefit, but it seems that God transcended this, and in His wisdom seeded into each parent's heart the ability to love their children in the way that He does. God is not insisting that everyone should, first and foremost, follow Him for this to happen, He gives to all parents, with no preconditions. This is amazing, but it is who He is; it is what He wants to do, that is, to give His unconditional love with grace and favour to all parents. The dilemma is that some parents have excellent parenting skills, but some do not. The ideal is that we would all be perfect parents, but unfortunately, we all carry issues, hurts and wounds, which not only affect the way we relate to our children, but can also damage them. God's purposes are not haphazard plans cobbled together, but pure, purposeful and loving. Do we think that our loving Heavenly Father would give up newborn babies without doing everything He could to release His love to them? It must mean giving the ability to every parent to show the same kind of love to their children that He gives to the world.

Orphan Heart

What children need in the womb, and what they look for at birth, can be summed up as unconditional love. Everything develops from the expression of love from the parents. We are created with a longing within for something deep, solid, unchanging and lasting. This desire will be influenced by the people who are closest to the child, that is their parents, particularly in the way that they show their love. The child totally relies on them; they are the child's first and key role model, and the experiences they have in the home environment, whether good or bad, will play an important part in how their identity, and ultimate destiny, is worked out. Needs can be met consistently with loving care, but if they are consistently not met, the child will begin to react in a dysfunctional way, by suppressing the hurt and/or behaving badly. These issues do not go away; they are buried into the child's belief-system, which inevitability continues to affect them into adulthood. Undoubtedly, we would all wish for perfect parents, but we know that that is not realistic. Children cope better with real, honest and authentic parents, not perfect ones. Parents carry their own hurts and wounds, which in certain circumstances come to the surface, and this damage will affect their child. This sort of behaviour leads to an undermining of the heart of parenting, as well as contributing to the development of the orphan heart in the child. I know, because I remember more of my father's angry temperament than anything else.

Adam and Eve, the Orphans

The Garden of Eden was a glorious place of fruitfulness, love and friendship with God, as He came down to be with His family. However, something went very wrong, and the world has been left with the consequences of the sin and disobedience of our first parents. Adam and Eve made a choice to decide their future themselves, something which was motivated by the deception and manipulation of Satan. Their decision pushed them away from the Abba Father relationship they had with God, which not only led to severance from Him, but opened a door for fatherlessness, things which deeply affected them. They became orphaned from their Heavenly Father by their actions, and God had no alternative but to banish them from the place of fellowship and communing that they had had with Him. Satan was given the opportunity to take so much from them, which cursed future humanity, and separated them from the closeness to God that Adam and Eve had. They felt abandoned and rejected, and it was their irresponsibility which led to that, but most of all they realised that they were orphans, isolated from their Father. What started there continues now, and many women, men and children feel the same, motivated by their orphan hearts, and often oppressed by orphan spirits. Thankfully, God sees the bigger picture and a way to redemption was made, taking Jesus, God's Son, to the cross where a divine exchange took place that allowed humanity to come out of the effect of the orphan heart into sonship.

There are several things that we can take into consideration in the parent-child relationship which will bring further clarity to the way the orphan heart manifests and roots into the child.

Roots and Wings

'There are two lasting bequests we can give our children. One is 'roots' and the other is 'wings.' A child who knows he's loved unconditionally is a child with roots; he'll stand the storms of life. Give a child self-worth, teach him to dream, to have vision and you'll give him wings.' (Hodding Carter, Rheinhart & Company, New York, 1953)

This very apt and pertinent quotation has helped many to bring definition and purpose to their communication with their children. This is not limited to childhood, for we as adults can apply this life-giving principle into our lives, which will undoubtedly challenge everything about the orphan heart that would want to control us. Children are born to have roots within a safe and nurturing atmosphere in which they can grow and prepare for the time when they leave home and begin to fly. Roots define where we have come from, establishing where we are, and wings define where we are going and how to get there. They give stability, nourishment and a sense of belonging. Roots are an analogy for the foundation of life as wings are for the future. Roots are the first part of the plant to appear after the seed germinates, making them vital for the plant's growth and fruitfulness. The parable of the sower highlights that healthy roots require healthy soil (Matthew 13:3-9). The seed sown is the word, and the soil represents the heart and mind of those in whom the word is sown. The seed takes root, grows and produces fruit depending on the state and suitability of the soil. A child who is continually seeded with unconditional love will have strong roots to withstand whatever comes their way. The good soil will support and nourish the root, and ultimately the entire plant. Parents have a responsibility as to what kind of soil they create, and what seeds are released into that soil in their desire to create a stable and nurturing home. The soil will support whatever seeds are sown and be fruitful, however, if negative words that relate to love that is conditional, or consistent rejection and abusive behaviour from a parent are sown, the child will be affected accordingly. If there is no unconditional father's love, the process of seeds, roots and fruit will be detrimentally affected, which will lead to dysfunction with the establishment of the orphan heart. Children are prone to easily believe anything, particularly if it comes from their parents. If a lie is seeded consistently into the heart of the child, the child will accept it as truth, and begin to live the lie.

Strong, stable and secure roots produce powerful and invigorated wings that bring glorious freedom to fly. Out of the unconditional love will develop self-worth, which is value, acceptance and esteem. This leads to self-awareness, which is being secure in identity and relationships, and teaching the child to dream and have vision (purpose in life), will produce the wings to fly. It will also bring freedom and liberty, which the child desires in future life. Orphan hearted children do not fly well - their wings will have damage and they won't get far. Such children will have difficulty in fulfilling their destiny.

Tumbleweed

A helpful illustration of the plight of orphan hearted children, who do not receive the love they need, is that of the tumbleweed. It is a plant, especially found in a desert, that breaks away from its roots, and is driven or tumbled about by the wind as a light rolling mass, scattering seeds as it goes. As they mature, they dry into a rounded tangle of branches, and tumble being blown about by the wind, often covering long distances spreading seeds as they roll along. Tumbleweeds are easily uprooted when the wind blows because they only put down maybe one or two roots, which are small, frail and shallow, therefore there is no depth. A tree, such as an oak, puts down many roots that go very deep. Even during strong winds, the oak stands firm, because its root structure is strong and stable. The tumbleweed is not like that; it is totally at the mercy of the wind. There is no specific direction other than whichever direction the wind is blowing, which could be any direction, so there will be no sense of purpose or stability. A tumbleweed is always vulnerable, and therefore easily picked up, out of control, and tossed about helplessly by the wind.

The orphan hearted child and adult without unconditional love in their life will only have one or two roots in their life, and these roots are not very deep, bringing with them the risk of constantly being uprooted when the pressures of life, difficult issues in the family, or other circumstances, such as trauma, suffering and tragedy take hold.

However, if a person has deep spiritual roots through unconditional love, they will stand firm no matter what comes to them. Even though life cannot hurt any less, and even though the struggles of life continue to affect them, they will keep strong in their Heavenly Father's love. *'Then Christ will make his home in your hearts as you trust in him. Your roots will grow down into God's love and keep you strong'* (Ephesians 3:17). The orphan hearted are very much like the tumbleweed and cannot decide for themselves where to go; there is a loss of direction. The prophet Jeremiah picks it up powerfully, *'he's like a tumbleweed on the prairie, out of touch with the good earth. He lives rootless and aimless in a land where nothing grows. But blessed is the man who trusts me, God, the woman who sticks with God. They're like trees replanted in Eden, putting down roots near the rivers - Never a worry through the hottest of summers, never dropping a leaf, serene and calm through droughts, bearing fresh fruit every season'* (Jeremiah 17:6-8, MSG).

Attachment

God was intimately involved with us before we were born, He was present at our birth and it was He who pre-programmed us to form bonds or attachments to others. He also imparted to our parents the ability and capacity to love and care through His 'Abba Father' nature.

When considering the parent-child relationship, it is important to be aware of the theory of attachment propounded by John Bowlby, a British psychologist and psychiatrist. This accomplished work posits that very young children have an intuitive need to develop a close emotional bond with parents or a caregiver, who are available and responsive to the child's needs. This will develop a strong sense of security with good social, mental and emotional development. The bond formed will impact behaviour for a lifetime, as it shapes the child's relationships into adulthood. It has been suggested that children come into the world biologically pre-programmed to form attachments with others because this will help them to survive, as well as to form a secure base from which to go out into the world. It was found that attachment was characterised by clear behavioural and motivational patterns. For example, when children are frightened, they will seek comfort from their parents or primary caregiver. Attachment is an emotional bond with another person, and it is considered that the effect of the earliest bonds formed by children with their parents, particularly sourced in physical and emotional care, continues throughout life.

- It is clear that attachment is a basic and powerful human need, and that the child's experiences of relationships in its early years will shape the way they coexist socially in their development to adulthood.

- The first experiences of a child are its most significant ones. Early parental relationships are therefore crucial, for they will either give the impression of the world being a safe place - one in which the child knows they belong, or give them a completely different message, which will say to them the world is unsafe, making their attachment insecure and more dysfunctional. If adverse attachment experiences in childhood, such as neglect, rejection, or a traumatic circumstance occur, this may well lead to mental or emotional problems later in life. Sometimes an adult may not have any idea why they would react relationally or socially in an illogical or extreme manner, not realising that the problem was established in their infancy, and now lodges in their unconscious memory beyond their recall. God as our Father longs for good parenting, however, it is obvious that this has not happened with some parents. There are many children left with a legacy of neglect and hurt, because their emotional, and physical needs have not been met. Some children can be left with trauma, which could be the result of abuse; verbal, mental, emotional, sexual or physical, and this will undermine any sense of security they have. Children are not made with the ability to cope with these issues in their early years.

- Just as an attachment formed with parents will impact behaviour in the child which may last for a lifetime, a broken attachment will also impact the child's behaviour for a lifetime. The negative and undermining effect on the child will begin a process of distancing, isolation and eventually abandonment, which eventually presents as an orphan heart. A baby has no understanding, thought process or language, and so only responds to feelings. In its vulnerability, the child will have to adapt its behaviour to survive.

Toxic Parents

There are no perfect parents, and all parents are different. It almost seems a travesty, as well as accusatory, to use the word toxic concerning parents, but if we consider the full breadth of the word's meaning, it can become a helpful definition. Various traits can be considered toxic, for example, one or both parents may be narcissistic, have other personality disorders, be mentally ill, abusive, emotionally immature, and alcoholic or addicted. These destructive things happen when parents impede their child's development by causing them harm, such as hurt and wounding, which may or may not be physical, but do affect their emotional and mental state. Toxic behaviour is anything that poisons or contaminates a relationship leading, in this case, to a limitation of the child's growth. It becomes an abusive relationship with the vulnerable child being affected often from their early years, and as it continues the child may well believe it is part of their normal way of living. Many people do not realise until adulthood that their formative years were subject to harmful family circumstances. Some children believe that it is they not the parent who is responsible for the toxic relationship, and therefore take on the guilt themselves whilst also suffering from deception. It is probable that the problem stems from the fact that many of these parents have experienced neglect or dysfunction themselves while growing up, the problem continues to grow, as they go on to reproduce these same hostile behaviours when raising their own children.

Certain toxic parental situations can be obvious, but others are less so.

Most parents genuinely do their best to provide their children with a secure and wholesome life, but even good parents can accidentally make mistakes. It is, however, necessary to distinguish an honest mistake from an enduring pattern of behaviour, because some parents go far beyond the occasional mistake, and move into the toxic category, because constant repetition of the same behaviour can no longer be regarded as just a mistake, but rather becomes a toxic action. Toxic parents can be intentional in their behaviour, but often, they're just utterly self-centred, making sure that everything revolves around them, and they do not understand that their children have their own emotional needs and desires that need to be met. There is a difference between intentional and unintentional behaviour, yet sometimes the unintentional reaction can be just as abusive. Although it may not mean much to the parent, it can still cause emotional and mental damage that ends up affecting the child years later.

Most of us probably rarely exhibit toxic behaviour, however, it is the degree of consistency or the intensity of that behaviour that is key here. Many will recognise that, but some will not, and they will carry on regardless, demonstrating that they themselves rather than their behaviours are personally toxic. This type of person would be motivated by deep wounding, and would not be able, or might even refuse, to take responsibility for their actions, feelings and needs.

Poor parenting is a series of actions that can seriously harm a child's behaviour and perspective. It is not restricted to a single act but is more of a collection of these actions that contribute to a harmful effect on the child. Most poor parenting may not be intentional, but this does not reduce its negative impact on the child. Some parents are not aware of the consequences of these actions, and some might not even care. A child with toxic parents would just assume that their parents are typical, and without any basis for comparison; the child would consider that other families operate by the same dysfunctional rules as theirs, and that everyone's parents are harmful, distant or controlling.

Toxic parents cause harm and pain to their children, leaving them to cope with psychological problems, which continue to influence them throughout their lives. In some cases, it almost seems that some parents are virtually immune to any help that could lead to positive change. Some have no awareness of their problems, others refuse help, and put up barriers, blaming their children, their parents or other circumstances; in other words, they refuse to take responsibility for their behaviour. This would leave the child with a sense of loss, which would lead to anger, because of what has been stolen from their lives. They would feel rejected, and would want to protect themselves, or take on the blame, which would only lead to them rejecting themselves. All of this feeds the orphan heart and enhances the power of abandonment, isolation and loneliness.

In this feeling of hopelessness and despair, there is an answer, for it is possible to overcome the effects of toxic parents. It is necessary to be aware of what it means to have toxic parents, and to recognise the ways in which they are dysfunctional, however, it is important to start with a personal response to God our Father who has an amazing ability to heal the orphan heart.

Signs of Toxic Parenting

There are certain areas of toxic parenting that are important to recognise and understand, as they are foundational to the restricting and undermining of growth and development in the child, as well as in contributing to the development of the orphan heart. It has been recognised that some children grow up thinking their parents' toxic behaviour is normal, because it is all they have seen and are so used to it. This harmful behaviour can cause such emotional and mental damage to children that it would continue to affect them as an adult. One important area to recognise is the ability for parents to make children in their own image. It is not difficult to do the same things to our children that our parents have done to us. This is repetition of a dysfunctional experience from childhood, but instead of being the victim, the victim becomes the perpetrator, which is a complete change of role. If the parents' own traumatic wounds from the past haven't healed, it is likely that they will inflict those same wounds on their children.

There are many indicators of toxic behaviour, which can be classified in two ways. The first is related to the parents regarding what they say and do, and the second to the child in how they receive and cope.

Narcissistic Parents

Toxic parents cause pain and trauma, and this will mean significant and lasting psychological problems for their children. They are narcissistic in behaviour, which is a major key in how they relate to their children. Life is all about them, and everything they do or want their children to do for them is done to satisfy their own deep needs and desires. This self-centred relationship is characterised by control, dominance, manipulation and intimidation. Their abusive behaviour is projected onto the child in many ways including, unmanaged emotions, anger, disrespect, silent treatment, unrealistic expectations, blame, and having no regard for the child's boundaries, privacy and personal space. Basically, they are always right and nothing else matters. It seems that the impartation of 'Abba Father' by God to the parents is disregarded, or in some cases used as a manipulative tool.

The Hurt Child

A child reflects its environment, whether good or bad. There are so many things in life that are beyond a child's control, so children depend on their parents to keep them safe and secure physically, emotionally and mentally. If their life is full of abusive and dysfunctional parenting, the child will not feel safe and secure and so will carry lasting wounds which will continue into adulthood. This would include disappointment because their expectations in childhood had not been fulfilled. If the child doesn't get the love it wants, the abuse and rejection will lead to pain, which the child will try to relieve by a process of numbing those parts of them that desire love. The longing for love and approval in a child is so strong that they will do whatever is necessary to try to gain that approval. If a child perceives that they are not loved, they will think that they are not worthy of love and will perform to win parental love out of a fear of being rejected. When everything is about the parents and never about the child, it becomes almost impossible for there to be any sort of a positive relationship. This means there would be an insecure or anxious attachment, which would develop into an inability to trust parents to take care of them. An insecure attachment leads the child to live out of a wrong belief. Each child carries decisions into adulthood that are scripted. These life scripts are very much influenced by parents, and they relate to behaviours, thoughts, emotions, feelings and survival patterns which become part of their belief system. The problem is that messages received and believed by the child may not be true, but they become accepted and then incorporated into the way they see the world from a toxic family situation, for example, a core belief maybe, 'I am unlovable,' which is an orphan hearted response.

How a child handles trauma in toxic and abusive situations is critical for their survival. Children learn to withdraw and close down, but in an extreme situation, they will freeze the memory or even dissociate to survive. The memory of the experience will be relegated beyond the conscious to the unconscious memory. For a child, dissociation is a survival strategy. Its purpose is to take a memory or emotion directly associated with trauma and encapsulate, or separate it, from the conscious self. Any type of trauma, physical or emotional, can arise from stressful experiences from the child's earliest prenatal development. A child learns that they cannot run physically from trauma, so they separate or dissociate themselves from the situation by escaping to a safe place deep inside them. Once the child has learned that escape mechanism, it becomes a survival technique which can be used repeatedly during childhood. In a toxic family relationship, dissociation has been described as one of the symptoms experienced by some victims of multiple forms of childhood trauma, including physical, psychological, and sexual abuse. The child may not be able to describe the trauma as an adult can, so they dissociate in order to deny and suppress the feelings of hurt and pain. Fight and flight are not an option to a child, but just like a rabbit in headlights, they freeze to survive. Nothing is ever buried dead; memories are frozen, and will remain so, but sometimes they percolate back into the conscious area, thus causing more dysfunction.

A further area which can be defined as a stronghold is shame. A child may feel guilty for doing something wrong, however, the toxic parent will shame the child by constantly telling them that they are wrong. It then becomes an extremely painful experience for the child of believing that they are flawed, therefore unworthy of love. If a child grows up in a neglectful, abusive and dysfunctional family, shame becomes an inevitable consequence. Children are particularly vulnerable, because the development of their identity is based on their parents' reactions to them, and if it is consistently negative, shame will become toxic. As these negative feelings become established, the child will withdraw, creating negative and critical patterns which would have a lasting effect on their self-image and their ability to function day by day. This is where the orphan heart can begin to develop, and ultimately become the controlling factor in the child, affecting every relationship, including that with God as Abba Father. We can take heart though, for, 'my past does not have to define my future!' God has provided a way out.

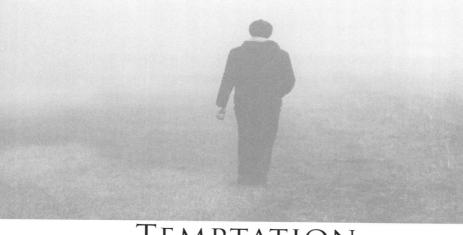

TEMPTATION

This chapter is as important as any other in the book because it opens up a subject that is crucial for the orphan hearted person to have clarity on, as well as giving us an awareness of how to respond to temptation. In the midst of it, there is a need to be understanding, which not only brings revelation, but also the necessity of taking responsibility to make right choices and decisions. The danger is that of being indecisive, which in itself creates an opening for the enemy to take advantage of. Doing nothing, as many have found out, is not an option. This would become a dilemma because it would undermine our relationship with Abba Father.

In defining temptation, it is important to be aware that it is an external event happening on the outside of a person rather than an inherent disposition of mind and character. The inducement to sin, which is seductive, comes from outside, and the pressure to give in for an easy and often immediate pleasure or gain becomes the deception. It is always self-gratifying but seeing it as a snare or a trap would encourage you to be more intentional in making the right decision. No-one can escape the influences of temptation; there is no bias or prejudice for it is not confined to any age group, race, gender, intellect, or social standing.

Temptation, in itself, is neither good nor bad, it is what you do with whatever or whoever is tempting you. One thing is clear though, if you have given in to temptation, then your thoughts and desires are contrary to the thoughts and desires of God. Satan uses the temptation to bring us down, but God takes the opportunity to use these temptations to strengthen us. Temptation is a part of the Christian life, but remember it is not a sin to be tempted; it is giving into it that results in sin. *'The temptations in your life are no different from what others experience. And God is faithful. He will not allow the temptation to be more than you can stand. When you are tempted, he will show you a way out so that you can endure'* (Corinthians 10:13, NLT).

Temptation can be meaningful because it can be a way by which faith is tested. As long as we are in this world, we are exposed to temptations, so being alert is important. There is a mandate that we can keep, *'keep watch and pray, so that you will not give in to temptation. For the spirit is willing, but the body is weak'* (Matthew 26:41, NLT). There is an incentive here as well as a blessing, because if there is temptation there is also a place to overcome, and in Christ, we can demonstrate that we have the victory, and live in it day by day.

Temptation, Desire and the Orphan Heart

The orphan hearted person presents an opportunity for the enemy who will tempt people in the weak areas of their lives. It is not difficult for Satan to take advantage of those who are vulnerable. Considering the things which give emotional, mental and sometimes physical pain that orphan hearted people can have, it is not surprising that they are targets to be tempted. Many are 'sitting ducks,' especially if they are inconsistent in their response to God as a Father. The enemy, who is no respecter of persons, will take advantage of this, and undermine their relationship with God by tempting them in areas that he knows they struggle in.

Therefore, it is important to come to a place where troublesome roots are recognised and then dealt with. Discerning the fruit can expose the root issue, so asking God to give more awareness of what is going on in the heart is necessary. If we know we can do something about this, we can be confident in taking responsibility because we know that God will help us. I did not know much about my early years but, at the right time, God brought revelation, primarily about His unconditional love for me, and that became the key to my inner healing and deliverance, which released me to know God as my Father. This key is knowing Him with affection and intimacy, not just knowing about Him.

The word 'desire,' covers a whole range of basic human yearnings and longings, including each individual having the spiritual potential that can lead to a deep response to God, which will bring fulfilment in their lives. Satan takes the God-given desire in a person, and perverts it through the deceptive subtlety of temptation into something negative and unnatural. *'But each person is tempted when he is lured and enticed by his own desire'* (James 1:14 ESV). It is this powerful desire in the wounded orphan heart which conceives and gives birth to sin. Orphan hearted people want to protect themselves from further hurt, and the enemy will try to trigger emotional reactions in order to persuade the person to sin. Desire is a paradox; it can be good or bad, but when God Himself becomes a person's greatest desire, everything else will be in its rightful place. We need to be alert to Satan's devices because he would have no hesitation in stealing anything he can, including our identity.

Being Vulnerable

The general definition of being vulnerable is that of being in a situation where there is a fear of being at risk to harm either physically, mentally or emotionally. This could be with anyone known or unknown, including those close in relationship. The orphan hearted person is more vulnerable to temptation because the enemy knows they are more susceptible to being emotionally, mentally or spiritually wounded, and therefore he makes them a target. Why is it that emotional vulnerability in a person is more often than not considered as being weak, frightened, easily hurt, or inadequate and flawed? Being vulnerable is unavoidable in our day-to-day existence, but it is mostly perceived as having a sense of feeling uneasy, uncertain, or unsettled - things which provoke anxiety and rejection. Could it be that a fear of emotional exposure makes it easier to self-protect, hide, or keep yourself locked up within so that nothing shows?

Vulnerability needs to be looked at in a different light because it can be a tremendous source of strength, and it can sometimes be necessary for honest connections in personal relationships. Life is risky living and if uncertainty is evident, it can bring fear that will attach itself to every aspect of daily life. However, vulnerability can give birth to a feeling of empathy, and an understanding of each other fashioned out of love, both of which lead to personal worth and a knowledge of belonging. The challenge is to embrace and accept our vulnerability rather than to create the internal emotional conflict which tends to overflow in difficult situations. Being open-hearted means positive emotional exposure; being orphan hearted is to close down and hide. Openheartedness leads to a release of personal freedom and security in the way you see yourself, with an acceptance of how God as your Father sees you. Having the emotional courage to share feelings with those who are important to you, strengthens relationships. Would the orphan hearted person risk getting hurt and rejected or would they be happier to avoid the word vulnerability altogether? Would we risk further disappointment in order to have the chance of accomplishing strong relationships with one another and the closeness with our Father God that we have always longed for? This is an opportunity to change how we have seen vulnerability as a negative tendency, and to begin to see it as something positive that will change us for the good.

Temptation in The Garden

The outcome of the temptation of Adam and Eve in the Garden of Eden was pivotal in their relationship with God and each other, as well as something that affected the rest of mankind. The purpose of Satan was to destroy something that had hardly begun, and that was the Father relationship, which God had desired with His creation. The enemy knew that capitalising on the weaknesses and selfish desires of Adam and Eve by seducing and deceiving them with lies and half-lies, would fulfil His primary goal of drawing them away from God, and of destroying the depth of relationship they had with Him and each other. The essence of temptation is the ability to manipulate and misdirect the God-given desires towards sin, and in so doing undermine any response to God. All our basic desires ultimately come from God, who has given us longings and needs that emphasise our dependence on Him and strengthen our relationships with each other. Any distortion of these will bring negativity in our lives, and further manipulation will turn love into lust and honour, respect and personal accomplishment into pride. In this context, Satan is clever enough to offer a counterfeit for God's best, as he knows that what he has is not genuine and will not bring fulfilment. Satan as the serpent was crafty, cunning and subtle, and was able to seduce firstly the woman, and then, soon after, the man who was standing next to her witnessing everything. It seemed that Eve was beguiled, but Adam abdicated his God-given responsibility.

The best-case scenario for the devil and the worst for Adam and Eve was to tempt Eve. It would not only affect Eve in her relationship with God but would also undermine her relationship with Adam. He failed to take his responsibility and submitted to his wife's desire by eating some of the fruit, which implicated him. Satan not only severed their relationship with God, but also damaged their relationship with each other to the point that their mutuality was changed by God, making the relationship that more difficult. 'And you will desire to control your husband, but he will rule over you' (Genesis 3:16 NLT), which means dysfunction and division. This was never in the plan of God, but it has remained so ever since. The purity of the almost innocent relationship they had with God and each other in the Garden of Eden was stolen. However, God has made a way out through redemption in Jesus at the cross, enabling humanity to come into a restored relationship with God as Father and friend.

Reconciliation has become of key importance, as not only have we been reunited with God, and in our relationships with one another, but mutuality has been restored regarding how we relate together as man and woman. Satan did not deny that God had spoken - that was too easy to discern, but he simply questioned whether God had really said what Eve thought He had said. He was making Eve, in her insecurity, question God's credibility with words like, 'if God really loved you, would He keep something wonderful from you?' It is a short step to denying God's word, 'you will not surely die' (Genesis 3:4-5) and the trap was sprung! Satan substituted his own lie telling her she would 'be like God, knowing good and evil.' Is this the same sin that Satan had in wanting to take the place of God?

It got to the point where her desires turned in the wrong direction and Eve had to gratify them immediately. '*When the woman saw that the fruit of the tree was good for food and pleasing to the eye, and also desirable for gaining wisdom, she took some and ate it; she also gave some to her husband, who was with her, and he ate it*' (Genesis 3:6). This is lust of the eyes, with the fantasy turning into reality. She also saw the tree was good for food, which is lust of the flesh, and then she saw it 'was desirable to make one wise,' which opens a doorway to power. The flesh began to pull her away from her obedience to God, and she yielded to the overwhelming desire to gain pleasure. Satan was telling Eve that she could be a god, and feel valued and have significance, but she was being deluded into becoming proud. He didn't tempt Eve in isolation, because Adam was with her. Adam knew the truth because God told him, but Satan introduced doubt and entangled Eve in deception, leaving Adam to surrender his responsibility and position to choose to do what he knew was wrong.

God's purpose was a mutual dependency in the relationship between Adam and Eve, but that was undermined, and it crumbled away to the point where society still living in the consequences of it today. What Adam and Eve were duped into seeing and desiring is comparable to the outline in the Epistle of John, 'do not set the affections of your heart on this world or in loving the things of the world. The love of the Father and the love of the world are incompatible. For all that the world can offer us - the gratification of our flesh, the allurement of the things of the world, and the obsession with status and importance - none of these things come from the Father but from the world' (1 John 2:16, TPT). Seemingly, Eve was not as certain about God's command as Adam was, so Satan saw Eve as the one more susceptible to deception. This is not choosing to tempt the weaker vessel, because Adam willingly chose to follow her; he seemed to know what he was doing, but Eve might not have understood what she was doing. The silence of Adam was deafening until God asked the question, and he immediately transfered the blame to the woman (Genesis 3:12). If anything, Adam acted as the weaker vessel in this context by relinquishing his God-given rights. They fell for the lie, which flattered them, and were led into the trap of loss and death.

How does this affect the Orphan Hearted?

What the temptation of Adam and Eve shows us, is that there are two areas which it is imperative to grasp hold of. This is not only for the orphan hearted but for all, for everyone gets tempted, however, not everyone is as vulnerable as the orphan hearted person.

First of all, the word 'desire' needs to be understood, because the enemy will use this to attempt to turn us towards making a wrong choice resulting in sin. Even though desire is God-given, Satan can deceive us, so that we begin to use something from God to fulfil our own needs.

Secondly, having a greater awareness of the areas that Adam and Eve went through is essential, particularly regarding the pride of life, which could be described as a wrong desire for power over others. Being prepared is necessary, for the more we become mindful, the more we can take action to defend ourselves from the wiles of Satan. We will see later how Jesus went through a similar temptation in the wilderness, and how He handled it. The enemy knows our strengths and weaknesses and he will attempt to undermine our relationships, as well as our confidence in God and our identity. Carrying unhealed wounds and hurts day by day is certainly a disadvantage for the orphan hearted, but Satan, being no respecter of persons, will continually tempt and harass in similar ways to those which Adam and Eve faced. He enticed them to find their own identity and destiny independently of God by feeding upon the lies he deceived them with. It did not take long for fear and shame to arrive, but it was too late, and hiding seemed the only option. Nothing changes, as is still the same today.

Temptation in The Wilderness

It was for our sakes, as well as God's purpose, that Jesus went into the wilderness and was tempted. It was just before beginning His ministry, that Jesus, full of the Spirit, was led into the wilderness for forty days of fasting where Satan came to Him to tempt Him (Luke 4:1-13). Jesus had just been through a remarkable manifestation of the Father's favour and approval at His baptism, and the words spoken to Him at that time became rooted deep within. He was immediately was sent out by the Spirit into the wilderness, and was with the wild animals, and later angels attended Him (Mark 1:12-13). It was an opportune time for Satan to attack Jesus in that barren place, with all kinds of subtlety and trickery, as he realised that he might be able to entrap Him before He began His ministry.

Jesus is known as the second man or the second Adam (1 Corinthians 15:45-49) who came to earth very much like a new Genesis or a second creation, as one bringing life with the hope of resurrection. Through the first Adam we experience death, but through our redeemer Jesus, the second Adam, we experience eternal life. The first chapter of John's Gospel explains that Jesus came to Earth as the Word made flesh, and He dwelt or tabernacled amongst us, just as God did in the beginning. In the light of that, Jesus, as the second Adam, needed to be subject to temptation in similar ways to Adam and Eve. We need to know that these temptations are common to everyone today, and because of that, it can be understood why Adam fell, but Jesus overcame. It is important, therefore, to consider these temptations with their possible consequences, including how they can affect the orphan hearted person.

Satan undermined God's word to Adam and Eve concerning the tree of knowledge of good and evil by deception with three subtle allegations, each of which tempted them to seek to establish their independence and identity separate from God. They are connected to the 'pride of life,' and can be described as arrogance and worldly wisdom, which the Apostle Paul refers to as the conflict of the sinful nature (Galatians 5:19-21). Adam and Eve became delusional in their attitude and superior in their actions as they declared that their way was the right way - the only way, and one which made God redundant. Satan tried these same three temptations on Jesus during His forty days in the wilderness. He attempted to motivate Jesus to fulfil His desire in a lustful way leading to pride, prestige and power, which is idolatry. This means that if He gave in to any of the temptations, He could not have carried on to serve His Father's purposes and His calling. The temptations in the garden and the wilderness are interrelated, with each having an intention to exploit or even abuse by undermining a relationship with God.

Satan's first temptation was an attempt to get Jesus to be uncertain about His Father's care, which would lead to mistrust. He wanted Jesus to use His power in an independent way in order to satisfy His own needs, so he attempted to provoke Jesus' desire with words like, 'if you are God's Son why are you hungry?' 'Why starve yourself, just turn a few of these stones into bread.' Satan was challenging Jesus to prove that He was the Son of God by doing a miracle. Perhaps the same whisper that was given to Eve in the garden was an attempt to deceive Jesus, 'if God really loved you, He would not keep something you needed from you, would He?' 'If God really cared for you would He did would he leave you in a wilderness without food for forty days and forty nights? Of course not, He would want you to make provision for yourself.' Satan began to twist and misrepresent God's words to make the lie more presentable because it was mixed with a little truth. However, Jesus already knew that He had His Father's approval, so there was nothing to prove. The fact of the matter was that Jesus had the power to do exactly what Satan was suggesting. Did not He multiply food during His ministry to feed some 4,000 and 5,000 people (Matthew 15:29-39;14:13-21). Jesus used His divine power when it was necessary to feed and serve the people but did not use it to simply fulfil His own needs.

Was there a touch of irony here when Jesus miraculously created bread to feed the people? Jesus used the word of God to reply to Satan's taunts, '*it is written Man does not live by bread alone, but on every word that comes out of the mouth of God*' (Deuteronomy 8:3; Matthew 4:4). This is connected with our relationship with Father God, and how we live 'on every word' He gives us, 'for the Lord gives wisdom; from his mouth come knowledge and understanding' (Proverbs 2:6). The challenge is to focus in the right place, because our deepest needs are beyond the physical.

For his second temptation, Satan took Jesus to Jerusalem and had Him stand on the pinnacle of the temple, which was its highest point, rising to at least five hundred feet above the Kidron Valley. A leap from there and the appearance of the promised protection of the angels would have been a spectacular event, which would have been in full view of all the assembled people. This would have been headline stuff, and what if they had had cameras at that time? The temple was the epicentre of Jewish worship and national identity. It was, in its time, a magnificent structure dominating the whole of Jerusalem, as it sat on the top of Mount Moriah from where it could be seen for miles around. Everything seemed to lead to the temple, and everything emanated from it; it was the perfect place for Satan to choose.

Satan said to Jesus, 'I see you really do trust in God, so why not show how much you trust Him by doing something spectacular, which will show everyone that you really do have confidence in Him.' 'Why do not you leap off and show the people that God is with you and that you are their Messiah.' It was an attempt to test God's promise of angelic protection; to get Jesus to create a crisis and then manipulate God to save Him. The assumption was that, as He was God's Son, God would have had no choice but to help. Satan was attempting to stimulate selfishly the desire in Jesus, which is within everyone, to gain approval from God, and to have that approval paraded very publicly. He even artfully used scripture to prove his point, when he quoted the words of Psalms 91:11-12. They referred to Jesus being protected by angels, and it seems that Satan wanted Jesus to doubt the promised angelic protection. Satan clearly understood that Jesus knew this Psalm, and as much as it was talking about David, it was also a prophetic word about the coming Messiah, the Son of David, which Jesus knew was Himself. However, Satan left out, 'to keep you in all your ways,' which was an attempt to distort the text to say what it had never promised, by deceiving Jesus to test God. Jesus again replied with scripture to the contrary 'it is also written, do not put the Lord your God to the test,' stating that it is wrong for Him to abuse His power (Deuteronomy 6:16; Matthew 4:7).

What is shown here is that Jesus had a very clear grasp and understanding of the Scriptures, and no perversion of them would have confused Him causing a lack of trust. Interestingly, the angels were there to care for Jesus after Satan had left Him (Mark 1:13). Imagine too, if Jesus had asked for help from the twelve legions of angels, who were straining to break through and save him, but He was, rather, committed absolutely to His Father's will (Matthew 26:53). It is a mistaken idea that the greatest display of faith is in some spectacular demonstration. The mark of a man or woman of faith is not showing faith in God by performing to the people a miracle or by doing something supernatural. The crowd would have hailed Him Messiah if He had jumped, but He did not and they did not, however, they did hail Him as Messiah when He came into Jerusalem sat on a donkey. There was no supernatural demonstration then, just humility.

The third temptation from Satan was to offer Jesus 'all the kingdoms of the world and their glory,' if He bowed down and worshipped Him. What an inducement to avoid the cross! Jesus was offered a shortcut to His Kingdom with the cheap attraction of power, authority and of being exalted, yet Jesus knew that He would suffer and die before He entered into His glory (Luke 24:26). If He had submitted to Satan, perhaps He could have enjoyed the glory without enduring the suffering. The enticement of power was great because Satan had declared he already had the nations to give to Jesus. Satan was not wanting Jesus to prove his Sonship, he knew He was, it was more of a coming between the Father and the Son and an undermining of the strength of their relationship. Even though Jesus did not dispute Satan's claims, He knew that this way would lead to Him losing everything. Jesus knew that if He had taken His inheritance then, it would have been outside of God's plan and purpose, and it would have meant conceding that Satan had the right to own the nations and their glory, and that worshipping him would give him absolute lordship. There was a promise that was finally reinforced in scripture, which Satan wanted to pre-empt, 'the seventh angel sounded his trumpet, and there were loud voices in heaven, which said: The kingdom of the world has become the kingdom of our Lord and of his Messiah, and he will reign for ever and ever' (Revelation 11:15). It was something that would definitely happen, but not in the way Satan wanted.

The response of Jesus was authoritative and concise, 'Jesus said to him, away from me, Satan! For it is written: Worship the Lord your God, and serve him only' (Deuteronomy 6:13; Matthew 4:10). Satan finally came up with a specific and direct proposal to Jesus, but it fell on deaf ears because Jesus' response was one of no compromise. The consequences of compromise were vast, but that was not to be, for Jesus would not be seduced, as there was no way that Jesus was going to deny God's sovereignty and enter into idolatrous worship of the devil, so He told Satan to leave.

The Spirit and the Word

In the struggle that Jesus had with Satan in the wilderness, two key areas sustained Him: 'The Word and the Spirit.' When Jesus entered into the wilderness He was already filled with the Spirit (Luke 4:1) and even as He contended with the pressures upon His human nature, it was clear that in His weakness He was strong in the power of the Spirit, which released Him to speak the word of God with confidence and authority. The Word in itself is authority and power, and this was able to penetrate the deception and trickery of the enemy, meaning that Satan had no answer to the words of Jesus as He quoted scripture to him. Jesus trusted God's Word totally, which gave Him the impetus to stand His ground. Although there is a distinctiveness between the Word and the Spirit, there is a glorious harmony as they go hand in hand together. It is like two mighty rivers coming together in a confluence where something greater, deeper, and wider will happen, because as the Spirit expresses and the Word manifests, divine energy is released. Notice that Jesus left the wilderness in the power of the Spirit (Luke 4:14) which was different to when He entered. Something powerful had happened!

As followers of Jesus, we have that same divine link to the Word and the Spirit, for as they were part of Jesus, they are part of us. We are commanded to, '*take the sword of the Spirit, which is the word of God*' (Ephesians 6:17) and begin to live by every word from the mouth of God (Matthew 4:4). What Solomon's bride set her heart on was a closeness and intimacy in her passion and desire and so from her heart she said, '*Let him kiss me with the kisses of his mouth, for your love is more delightful than wine*' (Song of Songs 1:2). This can be interpreted as God kissing us with His Word, which underlines the fundamental meaning of 'Abba,' that is to cherish. Therefore, day by day, we can know the kiss of God as He communes and shares His word with us, which will nourish, nurture, and strengthen us. As Jesus said to Satan, 'worship God and only serve Him,' and what Jesus did, we can do the same. As we dwell in the stronghold of the Word of God, we can rely totally on the certainty that God has spoken to us. It is then that the battle diminishes because as Satan is confronted with the Word and the Spirit, he knows there is no way to victory. Therefore, the way to resist temptation is that in our vulnerability (remember not weakness) we submit to the Word of God knowing that we have the Spirit working with us and in us. '*They triumphed over him by the blood of the Lamb and by the word of their testimony; they did not love their lives so much as to shrink from death*' (Revelation 12:11). However, there is an inditement here for us to seriously consider. Jesus rebuked a group of Jewish leaders about the way they used the Scriptures, 'you are in error because you do not know the Scriptures or the power of God' (Matthew 22:29). The challenge is to focus, open up to the power of the Spirit, and know the Scriptures with diligence. Jesus is the living Word and our relationship with Him is paramount in our quest to know greater liberty in sonship.

There is a further challenge that the enemy will use to trap us regarding how we respond to God in our application of the Word and Spirit. The danger is that we get caught in the trap of striving to please God and seeking His approval with performance and perfectionism (this will be developed further in the next chapter). Jesus went into the wilderness having the approval of His Father firmly established in His heart. There was no need for Jesus to seek it because it was already His. His Father had taken the initiative and declared so, which created security in His identity and His relationship with His Father. Once we realise that God has given His approval we can rest in His favour and not strive to gain it anymore. If God has given His Word to us, there is no need to keep on going back for a little more, because this will give an impetus to Satan to question and undermine our trust in God. Striving gives no peace, but resting (abiding) in what God has said and done will give peace. '*Then you will experience God's peace, which exceeds anything we can understand. His peace will guard your hearts and minds as you live in Christ Jesus*' (Philippians 4:7 NLT). It is the peace of God that protects us not ours.

Consideration

Although the temptation of Adam and Eve in the Garden parallels that of Jesus' temptation in the wilderness, certain specifics need to be highlighted as they show us which way we should go as temptation affects us. Adam and Eve lived in a perfect place, which overflowed with abundance, and it must have been exhilarating, especially when God walked with them. Although it seemed that they had everything going for them, they were duped into making wrong choices, which have affected us all. They were cast out of Paradise and driven into the wilderness, but Jesus freely and willingly entered the wilderness to regain Paradise for those who lost it. Jesus the last Adam (1 Corinthians 15:45) took back the ground that Adam and Eve lost. Similarly, Jesus underwent temptation; He met Satan in an environment that was barren and dangerous, inhabited by wild animals (Mark 1:13). Jesus was alone and had been fasting for forty days, but He overcame the wiles of the enemy. However, Adam and Eve who had had the best of everything stumbled and fell, and although they were deceived they were responsible. The temptation was made to look as though it would meet a legitimate need, but the woman, followed by the man, allowed their own desires to take them in the wrong direction, which was disobedience.

Being tempted is not a sin, it is when we yield to it that it becomes sin. Adam and Eve's downfall began when they engaged with Satan, which was a fatal mistake. You do not try to hold the attention of Satan, you just do as Jesus did, and send him away. Jesus did not argue, philosophise or debate with Satan, He came into the wilderness with the Spirit and the Word and delivered the Scripture as the living Word to Satan. Jesus was able to do that, because preceding the temptation, at His baptism, His Father had declared from a literal open heaven that Jesus was His Son whom He loved and approved of (Matthew 3:16-17). What Jesus did, was to ignore the trickery of the enemy by underlining His trust in His Father, proving to Satan He was God's faithful and obedient Son. Jesus went into the wilderness with no external pressure, but then, in His humanity, experienced the force of temptation as Satan attempted to beguile Him. He showed us that the issue is the heart, where He had deep security in His Father's love, rather than in a certain location.

What Satan attempted to do was use the word, 'if,' and in the three temptations he said to Jesus, if you are the Son of God, why not do this, (Luke 4:3,7,9). This small word was being used to undermine Jesus' sense of identity, dependence and relationship with His Father. However, the words of His Father were still ringing in His heart, giving Him great assurance that He knew who He was, where He had come from, and where He was going. To Jesus, God's Word has never changed, and His Word has never changed for us! 'If' can be a powerful word that will begin to turn us to act on our own and thus independent of God. It is crucial that we, as orphan hearted people, look seriously at these temptations, as a clear understanding of them could bring further understanding regarding the ways the enemy would want to affect us today, and such consideration would give us keys to enter further into freedom.

THE PURSUING FATHER

Probably the most well-known parable that Jesus taught is known as 'The Prodigal Son.' However, a better title for it might perhaps be 'The Pursuing Father,' as that does the parable more justice by putting its emphasis in the right place. I am sure that I am not the only one who thought I knew the story well, however, I have come to realise that there is much more that needs to be considered regarding all three of the characters in the story - not just the younger son, but his older brother and, even more, so the father.

There are cultural presuppositions that our western mindsets need adjusting to, as well as hidden truths giving a sense of mystery that is there to be revealed. Jesus used a method of teaching, the Parable, that is foreign to our culture, but being somewhat aware of the necessity of having some understanding of His society before attempting to understand the parable from our western point of view, would be a helpful thing. There is no doubt that there is much for the orphan hearted person to consider regarding the two sons, and particularly the father, whose character shows us the heart of our loving Heavenly Father, who is very much part of the mystery of the Kingdom that Jesus spoke about to His disciples.

'The disciples came to him and asked, why do you speak to the people in parables? He replied, because the knowledge of the secrets (or mysteries) of the kingdom of heaven has been given to you' (Matthew 13:10-11). A mystery, here, is not something unknowable, but it is something to be revealed, and in this parable, as in most of them, the things concerning the Kingdom of Heaven, can be seen and known by revelation. Jewish people at that time looked to the future coming of the Kingdom, but what Jesus was saying was that the Kingdom of God is also a present reality, which made the parables relevant. The family members in this parable could, perhaps, be regarded as dysfunctional, divided and distant from each other. Yet, there was one who, amidst the very difficult situation the family was in, exuded a love that was far beyond that which would have been expected by anyone who understood the situation. Of course, it is the father, whose actions are astonishing, thus making him to be the main character in the parable, but it also shows us how 'Abba Father' can be to us today.

Parable

The purpose of parables in Jesus' teaching was to focus the listener on God and the nature of His Kingdom, for these are an essential part of the Gospels. Jesus did much of his teaching in parables and was radical in the way He applied the Scriptures to the people. The use of parables was well established among Israel's first-century rabbis. The fact that Jesus used parables, in His unique way, is evidence that He was amongst the rabbis functioning in a rabbinic world. They used parables to illustrate the various applications of the old covenant law to encourage the people to live according to the will of God, but Jesus used them as a means of giving new revelation of His Kingdom and His Father's love. He brought the future hope of the Kingdom into the present reality, something which had quite an effect on the people because His teaching was so different from that of the other rabbis. Jesus spoke in parables not only to apply the Scriptures to His audience, but also to draw spiritual truths from everyday life, which enabled the people to connect with Him, as well as to what He was saying.

The difference was very quickly recognised by the people that heard Him, *'when Jesus had finished saying these things, the crowds were amazed at his teaching, for he taught with real authority—quite unlike their teachers of religious law,'* (Matthew 7:28-29 NLT). He was dynamic, inspiring, yet uncompromising as He spoke words of life, and the people and the other teachers recognised it.

A parable is an effective vehicle, which is simple yet powerful, that can be used to demonstrate to a person how God wants to enable them to find depth and understanding of how to live in this world and to realistically relate to Him. It compares one thing with another by placing them side by side - in juxtaposition. Its root can mean 'to throw alongside,' and Jesus would be teaching and suddenly 'throw' in an illustration by telling a parable to help the people understand what He was saying.

Parables often incorporate elements of surprise and hyperbole, and they are taught in such an interesting and compelling manner that the listeners' attention can be held to the degree that they cannot escape their truth. In general, they draw on an uncomplicated down to earth subject in order to illustrate a deeper and profitable personal lesson. This is certainly so with the Parable of 'The Pursuing Father' and his two lost sons, which, as we will see, Jesus used to not only challenge, but to shock and startle the people, particularly the critical Pharisees and teachers of the law, who took offence (Luke 15:1-2). The use of parables goes back to the Old Testament prophets. Nathan, for instance, told the famous parable of the rich man's theft of the poor man's sheep in order to confront David for the king's sin with Bathsheba (2 Samuel. 12:1-15). *'I [God] spoke to the prophets; it was I who multiplied visions, and through the prophets gave parables'* (Hosea 12:10). This gave an impetus for the parable to become a popular teaching vehicle for Jewish rabbis, including Jesus.

Prodigal

Most people would think that they would understand the meaning of the word prodigal, and in this parable, it seems, at first glance, to imply a rebellious person who runs away. However, this term could be regarded as ambiguous, as it can also be taken to mean something completely different, that is lavishly extravagant, or one who wastes money by spending it with reckless abandon, or even gives it with great generosity. In the context of this particular parable, the latter could, perhaps, be seen as a more appropriate definition than that of a rebellious person who runs away, and this interpretation rightly opens up the parable to the father of the two sons.

The word prodigal was not used in translations of the New Testament until a revised Latin translation of the Bible (Vulgate) was printed in the 16th century, and then later in the King James Version, however, it was still only used as a heading in order to highlight the parable.

What is important for the orphan hearted person to consider is why Jesus told this parable as the final part of a trilogy. Parables have common themes, and it seems that the subject here was so important that Jesus used three to emphasise the message. Jesus highlighted the fact that the Pharisees and teachers of the law were criticising Him for His love of lost people, for they wanted to separate themselves from the 'sinners' and 'outsiders.' However, in these three parables, it was clearly stated that Jesus wanted to pursue such people, love them, and, in tangible ways, show them that the Kingdom of God was breaking into this world.

The first parable is about the goodness and compassion of a shepherd who leaves the flock to find the one who is lost. This seriousness of the lack of care of sheep [people] is exposed in the book of Ezekiel, where he is commissioned to prophesy against the shepherds {leaders] of Israel, and he describes the anger and judgement of God to the shepherd who lacks the responsibility of provision and protection (Ezekiel 34:2). Obviously, the lost sheep should be found, *'for this is what the Sovereign Lord says: I myself will search for my sheep and look after them'* (Ezekiel 34:11). There is a prophetic leap into the New Testament where Jesus described Himself as the Good Shepherd who would lay down His life for His sheep (John 10:11). The Shepherd was so pleased and relieved he had found the sheep, that he invited his friends and neighbours to celebrate and rejoice with him (Luke 15:6).

The second parable looks at a woman who had lost 10% of her savings, which would have been a considerable sum for her. Accordingly, she placed great value on finding that coin. Her emotional response to losing the coin was meaningful, as it highlighted her efforts to search for it carefully and diligently. The woman celebrated in the same way as the shepherd did with her friends and neighbours, after she had found it (Luke 15:9).

The emphasis of the third parable, is the significance of the two sons being lost and the profound nature of the father's love, as he pursued both sons with compassion and tender mercy. This parable will be considered in more detail below, and, as we compare it, we will see how much the orphan hearted person matters to our Father God, because what is lost and hurting is so valuable that it moves Him to pursue, embrace and celebrate His son's return. It is important to realise that the third story told by Jesus here, brings family relationships into focus - not just between the sons and their father, but also between the brothers. There is also much that is not said about why there was family dysfunction, and even some of the issues that Jesus mentions are not answered but left open-ended. One in particular concerns the older brother, which in itself was a challenge to the listeners, because it provoked them to consider how they would respond to their Heavenly Father as Jesus deliberately did not give an answer.

All three parables are the subject of recovering the lost, which is the explanation of why Jesus received the 'rejected' and ate with them: they are lost, and He wanted to restore them. We can all be genuine sons but still lost sons, however, we can return to the Father and be accepted, because the Father has never rejected us and never will. It is important to remind ourselves that whether the people listening realised it or not, the two sons represented everyone in the room. They were a diverse and divided group, with, on the one hand, the tax collectors and sinners, but on the other hand the Pharisees and the teachers of the law on the other.

Jesus wanted each person listening to see themselves in the story. It is a parable which calls for personal examination and response. Both sons were lost; it was not just the younger son who went away to a distant land, but his older brother was lost too, even though he remained at home. The younger son was actually already lost before he left home: it is not a case of where you are located, it is more to do with an attitude of the heart, rather than distance. We will also see the extreme reactions of all three characters, with the two sons not understanding their father's love, nor able to love each other, and, in addition, their prevalent anger. These were the clear symptoms of a deeper crisis, and it is not difficult to see instances where the orphan heart could have been manifest through the sons. There is much to be learned including the father's response, which was one of love, mercy, and compassion, and that in itself was an unexpected response and would have been seen to be extreme by many.

The Younger Son
Inheritance

After Jesus had introduced the main characters in the parable, the listeners were suddenly jolted into a sense of shock, because, out of his anger and pain, the younger son made a demand of his father that was shaming and devastating, and which then led the family into further division. Those listening, which included the Pharisees and the teachers of the law, would have been appalled, because they knew the consequences of such a request. The son had asked for his inheritance before his father, whom we can assume was healthy, had died. What everyone, including the father, would have understood, was that the son wanted his father dead. It is as if he had said, 'why do not you just die and let me get on with my life, and by the way I want my share of the inheritance.' This is a request that would have been unthinkable in a Middle Eastern culture, and it indicates the desperation of the son to get away from his home as soon as possible, and to probably never return. The shame and humiliation would have been overbearing for the father, but he would have been left with the debilitating thought that, 'my son wants me to die.' The son wanted his 'freedom,' but freedom from the father becomes a denial of sonship, and is not freedom at all, for it leads to slavery. It is almost as though he is choosing to orphan himself, rather like Adam and Eve did.

The father knew what he had to do, and it was not the traditional Middle Eastern response, which would have been to angrily strike his son across the face and drive him out of the house in response to his outrageous request. At best, he would have been disowned and disinherited, which would have meant that he would not have been allowed to return home as part of the family, but at worst he could have been stoned. He did what was already established in his heart, that is to abandon his father and move as far away as he could, because he had no intention of being a faithful son. It would have been like a mortal blow to his father who reacted in a very different way to that in which a father in that culture would have done, because he laid down his life for his son. This is a real demonstration of unconditional love, for he gave his son what he really wanted - no words spoken, no questions asked, as the father gave his son the freedom to reject his love and leave. However, in his heart, he also gave his son the freedom to return.

The laws of Inheritance at that time stated that a father could make a will before this death, but there was no custom in the culture of entitling the son to his share whilst the father was still alive. If a man had two sons everything was divided into three parts with the firstborn taking double and the other son a third (Deuteronomy 21:17). The older brother received his share at the same time, and, although he did not ask for it, he did not refuse it either. Interestingly enough, nothing is said about him until the end of the parable, yet custom and tradition would have demanded his involvement from the beginning, but he was nowhere to be seen at that point. It is probable that the father was a man of stature, influence and property, with the farm being the focus of the community. To divide everything up prematurely would have been a monumental task that no father in that culture would have normally ever agreed to, but this father did. It was not just about dividing up his living, it would have been more like dividing his life between his sons. It is not easy to describe the depth of pain that the father would have been in, yet little did he know that things would get even worse.

'Not long after that, the younger son got together all he had, set off for a distant country and there squandered his wealth in wild living,' (Luke 15:13). This means that he took his share of the family property, had 'a quick sale,' and left. Shock and horror would have continued to affect the crowd listening to Jesus, because selling off land that had been in the family for generations would have been tantamount to a betrayal of the father. The son then quickly disappeared to a distant country.

A Distant Country with only Pigs as Friends

Many orphan hearted people can relate to the distant country even though they are physically at home. Here was a lost son full of anger and pain running away as far as possible from his father and brother. He left the Promised Land and went to a Gentile country, which, in the Jewish culture of the time, would have been associated with exile and danger, where he lived extravagantly, squandering his wealth in dissolute company. Through his irresponsibility, the son ran out of money, then friends, and it looked as if he would not have been able to sink any lower, but then a famine arose causing much suffering, and consequently he becomes destitute and began to starve. He was alienated, lost and very much alone, for no-one gave him anything; the question to be asked is what could he have done to survive?

He had no choice but to accept any job that was offered, and he was forced to hire himself out as a servant.

It would have been humiliating enough being a servant to a Gentile, but that was not all, because he was told to feed pigs, and what was worse was that he was given no food, so he ended up eating the pig's food! The shame would have come on him layer by layer, which must have been further affliction on top of the rejection that was setting in. If there had been a synagogue in the town, he could probably have got some help, but he was defiantly independent, choosing to feed unclean animals, which was against Jewish law, particularly when some believed that pigs had demons! No normal Jewish family would have ever acknowledged who he was, let alone accepted him if he had tried to come home! The ultimate indignity for a Jew would have been to work with pigs, because pigs were designated as unclean animals (Leviticus 11:7-8). The younger son had reached rock bottom, and there was no help from anyone, and nowhere else to go. He wanted freedom but had to become a servant as he lost his sonship, and it was as though he was as good as dead.

Return

It was at that moment that a seed thought germinated deep within him, which was, 'If I stay I die, so I need to go back.' 'When he came to his senses, he said, how many of my father's hired servants have food to spare, and here I am starving to death' (Luke 15:17). There was a sudden realisation that brought him up with a start, and he began to think of his father's servants, who would have been so much better off than he was.

Coming to his senses is not the same as repentance, though it may well be the beginning of it, but being sensible is not the same as a change of heart, and he might well have felt sorry just because he was hungry and hurting; it seemed that the only option left was to go home, and he knew that that would be very difficult. On the other hand, being home would be far better, because he knew that he could probably persuade his father to take him back. So, with that in mind, he prepared a speech saying, '*Father, I have sinned against heaven and before you. I am no longer worthy to be called your son. Treat me as one of your hired servants*' (Luke 15:18-19 ESV). He thought being a servant would at least be better than remaining where he was, although it would mean him not being part of the family. Amongst those listening to Jesus, many would have had a good awareness of the Scriptures, because they recognised that the son's words were not from the heart, but similar to the insincere words that Pharaoh spoke to Moses amidst the plagues. '*Then Pharaoh hastily called Moses and Aaron and said, I have sinned against the Lord your God, and against you. Now therefore, forgive my sin, please, only this once, and plead with the Lord your God only to remove this death from me*' (Exodus 10:16 ESV). However, Pharaoh's scheming and manipulative stance did not work, and neither did the son's calculating words. Even though he had prepared a speech, the father ignored it and won his son by love.

Home

'The deepest dream of human longing is to belong, to find a place of unconditional acceptance where we can be at home,' Roland Evans.

Finally, the younger son made a choice and began the journey home. In spite being at rock bottom, being destitute with absolutely nothing and with no alternative, it still seemed that it was a struggle for him to return to his father even though he was prepared to let go of his sonship to become a hired hand. He knew that in his mind he would have to face an enormous barrier to get back to his home, and that was his father. He wondered how his father would react to him, and, on top of that, the tightly knit village might publicly reject him forever. As he was slowly walking back with nothing except a few rags for clothes, and still smelling of pigs, it is possible that the son was wondering whether he would even see his father for a few days because he would probably have to wait in shame somewhere out of the way, and then subordinate himself by kissing his father's feet before being flogged. But something unexpected happened, because, as he looked up, he saw a figure running towards him. Shock and horror, it was his father! He scrambled to get his prepared speech ready, but it was too late, for the father was right in front of him. *'But while he was still a long way off, his father saw him and felt compassion, and ran and embraced him and kissed him'* (Luke 15:20 ESV). This was such a surprise and would have been completely unexpected! In the parable, Jesus told of the father who was watching and waiting for the return of his son, because he had not given up hope. With great feeling and a manifestation of love, the father forgave him with no recriminations. What the father was doing was restoring his son unconditionally and was amazingly doing so in public before the village onlookers.

Jesus made it clear to the listening crowd that this father was different, and his actions touched the son's heart who began to realise that his father had always felt like this about him. The son could say nothing, as there was no opportunity for him to do so because the father gave him no room, and all he could do was accept and then rest in the overwhelming grace that flowed from his father.

Repentance is not just coming home, but it is being welcomed home by the father. And that was not all, for the father wanted to remove any lingering doubt that the son and the rest of the community might have had about his motives. With his father's arms around him, the son attempted to share his speech, but he did not get very far, as the father started giving further instructions to his servants to publicly endorse the acceptance of his son. 'But his father said to the servants, quick! Bring the finest robe in the house and put it on him. Get a ring for his finger and sandals for his feet, and kill the calf we have been fattening. We must celebrate with a feast' (Luke 15:22-23 NLT). What the father did, in a lavish act of generosity, was to fully restore his son to his rightful place in the household.

First, there was a robe, the finest and best robe in the house, possibly a sort of Joseph's coat of many colours, which would have been seen as a restoration of honour to the son. It was a symbol of righteousness, meaning that everything had been made right, and through forgiveness the son was covered by the father's love.

Secondly, a ring was put on his finger, giving him authority and power, including the right to conduct business in his father's name. This seal of sonship guaranteed his position, which gave him immediate access to his father.

Thirdly, sandals were given for his feet, as in those days, servants would have had bare feet, but sons would have worn sandals. These sandals would have been an instant declaration of forgiveness and restoration to sonship and inheritance.

Somewhere in all of this something began to happen in the son. It seems that the continual release of love, grace, compassion, mercy and forgiveness from his father got to him, so that he gave up trying to seek approval. That led to a breaking, which freed him to accept that he has been found and inspired him to receive his sonship. The father's younger son was completely restored with the broken relationship healed, and with great joy, the father called for the fatted calf to be slaughtered and a banquet to celebrate the father's joy that his son had returned home. *'And bring the fattened calf and kill it and let us eat and celebrate. For this my son was dead, and is alive again; he was lost, and is found. And they began to celebrate'* (Luke 15:23-24). The banquet here was a symbol of joy at which the person who least deserved to be at the table was the guest of honour.

It is important for us to understand the way that the father talked about his son returning home, because he used the language of resurrection, which can be used in several ways. To the father, the son was so out of reach, to the point at which it was as though he was dead. When the son made a choice to come home the original text says, 'and having risen up he went to his father' (Luke 15:20). The Greek word is 'anastas,' which is the word used for Jesus' resurrection (Luke 24:7).

This is more than symbolic, because what the son did was worth the judgement of death. Also, when the father was dividing his possessions among his sons, it was as though he was giving his life away to them. There can be no doubt that something would have died within him, which would have become a deep experience that he would have carried until his son was safe and secure back at home. It shows the intensity that the father felt because his loss was so great, yet his joy was even greater when his son returned. For the father, it would have been like a resurrection. Maybe Jesus was indicating what was going to happen to himself in the future, but of course, the listeners had no idea that he would be proclaimed dead and then resurrected. They could, however, have related it to coming out of exile either from Egypt or from Babylon, and for some, living under Roman rule would have been the same, for they were waiting for the Messiah to appear and lead them out in victory. The father had found his lost son, and in his eyes, it was a though his son had come back to life, something which could be interpreted as resurrection.

Christians are resurrection people, but some with an orphan heart still live as though they are lost in a far country. The consequences of the orphan heart can be seen in the lost and hurting son, for they are not far from the surface. However, Jesus is showing that there is hope and confidence to be gained for all orphan hearted people as they make the right choice to come home, and finally know an acceptance and security in their loving Father God. The whole story turned the culture of the day upside down, because the way the father behaved was different to the way in which a father would have normally behaved in those days. Jesus made the father the centre of the story, and although the two sons played a vital part, He concentrated principally on how the father handled the serious family issues that took place principally with his unconditional love, compassion and grace. We also need two consider the way that the father reacted to the younger son's demands and ultimate disappearance, because in the parable, Jesus places this father alongside His Heavenly Father, showing the listeners that our God would pursue his sons and daughters in the same way to bring them home.

The Older Brother

Meanwhile, after the banquet had started, the older son, who had been still working out in the fields, came closer to the house and heard the sounds of celebration. He saw a servant and asked what was going on. 'Your brother has come, he replied, and your father has killed the fattened calf because he has him back safe and sound' (Luke 15:27). Suddenly, Jesus introduces the older brother into the parable; he knew nothing about what was going on, and no-one had noticed he was not at the party.

Perhaps he felt ignored. He was not mentioned in the early part of the parable though he should have been, but he had disappeared to work in the fields partly to isolate himself. He might have kept himself deliberately from the family, showing the contempt he had for his father, as he probably was not close to either his father or brother. Being so out of touch and not realising where his father was, highlights the fact that although he was physically close to his father, he did not know him. There was no doubt that he worked hard and well on the farm, but it was not so much out of loving service, but more like working for a master than for his father. There was no life in it, and it exposed his hardness for heart, which was devoid of any sense of relationship.

The parable begins with the younger son causing bitter conflict in the family, with his insistence that he received his inheritance immediately as he wanted to leave home. With such an issue, the cultural requirement would have normally been to require the older son to mediate between the father and the younger son and to help heal the broken relationship in the family. This did not happen, for the older brother remained silent and did nothing to mitigate this major family problem. The father was left to decide what to do himself, and he ended up dividing the inheritance, not only for the younger son but for the older brother too (Luke 15:12). The older brother's share, according to the law, would have been double because he was the firstborn, and it would seem that amidst all of the relational problems going on, he gladly received his share. His refusal to be involved with his family would have been critically noted by the listeners, however. The younger son left, and the older son was silent.

When, later on, the older brother heard that his brother had returned home, everything within him exploded, and he became angry and refused to go in (Luke 15 28). In most scriptures, the translation for this is 'angry,' however this does not draw out the full meaning of the Greek here - it might be better to say that he was 'furious' or 'enraged,' both of which indicate a deep-seated reaction. There may have been justifiable reasons why he felt like that, but surely he should have been filled with joy that his brother had returned. In fact, he was feeling the opposite because he was sorry that his brother had returned, for he did not want him home. It became clear that he had no respect for either his brother or his father, in fact, it showed that he did not love them.

He did not want to not go to the banquet, and as the years of bitterness overflowed, he humiliated himself in front of everyone. It would have been customary for the older son to act as a host in greeting, serving and caring for the guests, but he refused to get involved and remained outside, so the father had to endure humiliation again, as he went outside to plead with his son to come in. As the father came alongside to comfort and encourage him, the lid came off his son's feelings, and venom of disrespect, anger, blame, false accusation, manipulation and control, against his father and his brother, burst out of him.

'But he answered his father, look! All these years I have been slaving for you and never disobeyed your orders. Yet you never gave me even a young

goat so I could celebrate with my friends. But when this son of yours who has squandered your property with prostitutes comes home, you kill the fattened calf for him' (Luke 15:29-30). What this dramatic reaction brought about was the exposure of the heart of the older brother; it was not good because his talk was intensely negative about himself, his father and his brother, and the points below highlight his negative reactions:

- He showed contempt to his father. Basically, he was utterly rude.
- He thought he was a slave living in complete obedience to his father.
- He was proud enough to boast that he never disobeyed his father's commands yet refused to go into the banquet.
- He worked out of duty in preference in being a loving son.
- He accused his father of never giving him anything to enjoy.
- He tried to control his father through intimidation.
- He rejected his younger brother and would not even mention his name.
- He was quick to accuse (falsely) the younger brother.
- He refused to forgive them.
- He exposed his self-righteousness and unwittingly aligned himself with the Pharisees and teachers of the law.
- There was not one hint of family love, for everything was centred around him, which was motivated by self-pity, and of course, it could not have been his fault, so he blamed his father and brother.

All of this can be summed up by the older brother taking offence, because of what was said or done by his father and his younger brother, which he understood to be very damaging to him. It is not difficult to react in the way he did because he felt deeply hurt, and resentment with a bitter root judgement had taken hold. All of this was unnecessary, because offence is the result of a choice. A person 'takes' offence, and if the will is there it can be stopped. If it is 'taken,' it is owned and becomes much harder to get rid of. Understanding how to let go is crucial.

Amazingly, his father demolished his arguments in one sentence, *'and he said to him, Son, you are always with me, and all that is mine is yours,'* (Luke 15:31 ESV).

This shows where his motivation lay regarding his son, because it came straight from a loving heart, which demonstrated that nothing said or done could ever affect the way his father felt about him. Clearly, the older son had no understanding or awareness of the love his father had for him. What the father's answer implied was that the older son had had the opportunity to ask the father for a party, to have friends over to celebrate, even to ask for anything he wanted, but he had never done so. Amongst everything that had happened and been said, the father remained steadfast in his attitude and behaviour to both sons with words that are fundamental to the commitment our loving Heavenly Father has for us. As we look at the way that this father handled his two wayward sons, we will see and should become more aware of how our Father responds to us.

A Comparison of the Two Sons

No one can be sure that the sons were orphan hearted, but it is clear that their behaviour and emotions highlight many of the consequences of this. Allied with my own and other people's experiences, it is helpful to consider what happened in this parable, because so many of their attitudes and reactions juxtapose with the orphan hearted. What is also necessary to emphasise, is how the father radically responded to both sons with his unconditional love and overwhelming grace, and how this can be compared with how our Heavenly Father communicates with us! The two sons were brothers, and in many ways quite different, but when we compare their lives and the way they chose to live, we can find many similarities which can be summed up in the following comments:

- They were lost, and a person cannot need to go far to be lost - they do not have to actually leave home.

- They were angry, and they made sure that their father knew it.
- They were in a dysfunctional family, which gave them a distorted view of their father.
- They had hardened their hearts, with the younger son deliberately running away and the older brother staying home, but still very far away in his heart.
- They were desperate for acceptance, so would work to seek approval. The younger son wanted to work as a servant after returning home, but the older brother who was at home confessed that he thought he was a slave even though he was still at home. They viewed their father more as a master and employer.
- They both used control and manipulation in an attempt to get their own way.
- They had no concept of sonship.

Sadly, it can be seen that the attitude and behaviour of the two brothers kept them far from it. It would be helpful, therefore, for the orphan hearted person to give this parable serious consideration, and to allow its challenges to become personal in order to make choices to change.

'Love is large and incredibly patient. Love is gentle and consistently kind to all. It refuses to be jealous when blessing comes to someone else. Love does not brag about one's achievements nor inflate its own importance. Love does not traffic in shame and disrespect, nor selfishly seek its own honour. Love is not easily irritated or quick to take offence. Love joyfully celebrates honesty and finds no delight in what is wrong. Love is a safe place of shelter, for it never stops believing the best for others. Love never takes failure as defeat, for it never gives up. Love never stops loving' (1 Corinthians 13:4-8 TPT). This is the goal that we should all be aiming for.

THE PURSUING FATHER AND HIS TWO LOST SONS

Seeking Approval Through Performance

'God can do anything, you know - far more than you could ever imagine or guess or request in your wildest dreams! He does it not by pushing us around but by working within us, his Spirit deeply and gently within us' (Ephesians 3:20 MSG).

Before looking at the main character in the parable, it is necessary to consider an area that so many orphan hearted people grapple with, stumble over and even get locked in to. The two sons were affected by it, particularly the older brother, who seems to have made it his lifestyle, and it seems it became a stronghold which controlled him. I am referring to the performance driven life - something which also includes seeking approval and striving for perfection. Performance to gain approval is an attitude, not simply a set of behaviours, which often develops in childhood and is based on the lie that, 'I am not acceptable just because of who I am, I am only acceptable when I live up to and achieve perceived family, church or societal standards.'

Both sons had a tendency to perform; the younger son would have used performance in being a hired hand to get approval as a son, and the older son very dutifully performed like a slave to gain approval. When put together, performance and approval can lead to something quite different to what they amount to when used individually. If I perform out of an agenda that motivates me to seek approval, it is highly likely that manipulation and control will play a part too. We all want approval because it is good and meaningful to receive it, particularly when it comes from those we respect. However, demanding approval is so disparate, 'I demand to be accepted,' or 'I demand to be loved,' which is considerably different from 'I want to be accepted,' or 'I want to be loved.' One is healthy and the other is flawed, because you cannot make people accept or love you. Saying, 'I must have acceptance or love' will lead to a wrong perception of having to be driven in order to gain approval by being successful. It exposes the underlying issue of the orphan heart around the way a person will perform to gain acceptance from God and others.

Not everything we do in our lives depends on how well we perform. Someone can work hard, work well, and be fulfilled in accomplishing much without being performance orientated, but instead taking responsibility as they rightly focus on what they are doing, and any commendation will not be used for motivation, or manipulation, because they are not reliant on appreciation or approval from others. For such a person, any correction is always used as an opportunity to improve rather than taken as a sign that something is wrong, and thus usually taken personally. They have a security and confidence in their own opinions even when others disagree; they are not people pleasers, and so won't be used in that way, telling people what they want to hear or be impressed by. Jesus is a good model of that.

There are others for whom their belief system is such that performance has become a lifestyle, and if they were honest, they would admit that they felt trapped. The danger is that they might get caught up in a never-ending cycle of trying to prove their worth to themselves, to others, and even to God, and fulfilment never quite arrives. It is as though they never accomplish enough, no matter how hard they try. In such circumstances, performance then becomes a cruel taskmaster, stealing away any sense of satisfaction, peace, and rest in God, but instead something that injects anxiety and insecurity into the person. However much they try, performance-orientated, orphan hearted people appear differently on the outside to what they do on the inside. They might come across as competent and self-assured, however, on the inside, insecurity and loneliness reign. They require constant affirmation as they attempt to find their security in what people think of them, and they will demonstrate an ability to change in their response to people, like a chameleon, to gain acceptance and approval.

Fear of rejection and fear of failure would be high up on their agenda, so they would know how to protect themselves when there is the possibility of confrontation and might even use anger to intimidate others. Any hint of criticism would not be handled well, because this would speak of failure, and might make them feel unloved and rejected. All this would lead to an unhealthy concern for what people think, and this problem is exacerbated when orphan hearted people become Christians, because they carry their striving and desire to please into the church community, feeling the need to perform for God to gain His acceptance and approval. To them, grace and unconditional love would seem complex and distant, and so they become vulnerable and sensitive to either criticism or approval from others.

Most orphan hearted people have a need to succeed. They fear success as much as failure, and they easily become workaholics with a propensity to behave in a difficult manner, such as:

- Striving for compliments, but at the same time struggling to accept them.
- Having difficulty in receiving criticism, because they are compulsively defensive.
- Taking responsibility for everything, if possible, and then becoming

over busy or even overwhelmed, which leads them to lament that they are always tired.

- Tending to blame others, and often using anger to make them fearful.
- Receiving gifts, because they always have to attempt to please the giver by a corresponding gesture.
- Trying to control people with intimidation and manipulation.

A consideration of other people would be high up in such a person's thoughts, because the objective is the need to be special in the eyes of others. Therefore, it would be deemed necessary to place a higher premium on what other people think or say about you, but this might lead to a wrong dependency, or even a co-dependancy, which would affect their relationship with Father God. Comments such as, 'fulfil my expectations, do what I say and I will love you,' or 'because of what you did, I will never love you,' would undermine their esteem, value, and worth, and open a door to deception. However, there is a revelation that is foundational to a secure life in God: 'If we do not have to earn God's love, we are in no danger of losing that love.'

Perfectionism

What the enemy wants us do, is to get us into the unending cycle of striving towards the 'impeccable' standard of perfection, something which includes setting high performance standards and requires an intense self-evaluation, along with the pressure of how we see the judgment of others regarding us. When identity gets entangled with ministry, more emphasis is put on both praise and criticism from others regarding the way we perform, both of which can lead to dysfunction in our relationship with Abba Father. Perfectionism is basically an addictive personality trait characterised by a person's striving for flawlessness, but it leads to unhealthy relationships, because of a fear of disapproval and rejection; this includes self-rejection, which would be in the form of personal criticism such as pronouncements and inner vows. It can become a vicious and toxic cycle because, on the one hand, there is a desire for success, yet, on the other hand, there is a fear of failure, which together can lead to discouragement and depression.

Perfection is an impossibility in real life, but those living in unreality will continue striving and driving themselves in their attempts to succeed but will end up exhausted by the continual attempt to make it. When living by this way of thinking, mistakes are not allowed, yet thinking you have accomplished something only to see the goal posts moved, becomes demoralising, with the consequence of emotional hurt and pain. This underlines the person's perception of their own inadequacy, particularly whilst viewing others who seem to easily achieve their goals with self-confidence and minimal effort or stress.

Regretfully, after becoming Christians, some carry their striving and desire to please into their church environment. This undoubtably feeds the need to seek approval from God to gain His love and acceptance. There is little room for the motivation of His grace and unconditional love in their lives, as they wrongly believe these fundamental characteristics of Abba Father are too far away to help.

Perfect Imperfect

Being a perfectionist is an imperfection! It is generally considered that perfectionism is not possible. There is a difference between the idea and the actuality, and the idea of perfection is unreachable. It gives the impression that it is the ultimate, and that you cannot get any better, meaning you are perfect! Not only is it unreasonable and flawed, but it is reckless and opens the door to deception, which undermines godly success and fulfilment. It is possible to be less than perfect and to be satisfied without having to strive to get to a higher standard, which becomes a torment because the bar keeps getting moved, meaning that you never reach your goal.

Perfection is often a conceived belief established during childhood. It is easy to carry on living by the rules we learnt in childhood, rules which were, and still are, restrictive in the way we live. These were unchangeable and legalistic, and it is probable that many of us, as adults, still come up against traditions and unwritten rules in a church situation where comments such as, 'we do it this way, or 'we do not change' still happen. It then becomes difficult not only to hear God's voice, but also to believe what we think we hear, and in such circumstances, we start to question our worth, value and identity. There is never a demand to say that you must be perfect; it is more like a seed that created a thought pattern in childhood, that begins when parents and teachers and others impress, sometimes unwittingly, on the child the belief that anything less than perfection is failure. It is like a student getting 8 A's and a B, with the parents questioning why a 'B' without reference to the success of the A's. All the child hears is disapproval, because their efforts did not result in perfection. In the light of this, certain attitudes need to be considered:

- 'I have to prove myself and succeed.'
- 'I always have to do more.'
- 'I could do more.'
- 'I ought to do more.'
- 'I should do more.'
- 'I must do more.'
- 'If I am not successful, I am a failure.'

Danger

There is a scripture which could easily derail our perspective on being perfect. *'Be perfect, therefore, as your heavenly Father is perfect'* (Matthew 5:48). If the word 'perfect' is taken at face value, it can bring confusion, as it appears to contradict what has been described. However, the original meaning of the New Testament Greek word, 'teleios,' is better translated as mature or complete, not perfect. We are called to maturity, not to something that is impossible to attain. The truth is, God does not require us to be perfect, but to live in the completeness of Christ, by loving unconditionally and wholeheartedly. Like the Apostle Paul we are on a journey, '*I press on toward the goal for the prize of the upward call of God in Christ Jesus*' (Philippians 3:14 ESV).

Do not strive or struggle with this, but instead follow the words of Jesus, as they are foundational to our faith, '*love the Lord your God with all your heart and with all your soul and with all your mind. This is the first and greatest commandment. And the second is like it: Love your neighbour as yourself. All of the Law and the Prophets hang on these two commandments*' (Matthew 22:36-40). As we move forward following the way of Jesus, we will see the lies of performance and perfectionism begin to disappear.

Beliefs

What we believe can help, heal or hurt us. Our beliefs are important because the way we behave results from them. They shape the way we think and hence affect the quality of our relationships and our work. They are an important part of our identity, as they reflect who we are and determine how we live our lives. We all have our own beliefs, which have developed throughout the course of our lives. Many things contribute to how we see ourselves and our worldview, including family, friends, school, vocation, church and our faith. Some beliefs can become intense and overwhelming, such as that of seeking approval by trying to please people or even God. Our beliefs can sustain, vision and empower us or, conversely, limit us, so the way that we think is crucial, because believing a lie about the way we see ourselves will trap us, and put us under a form of control which is ungodly. In this context, certain beliefs would be exposed, some of which would have been built into us at an early age, yet would still have the power to affect the condition of the orphan heart in later life:

- 'If I do wrong, I will not be loved.'

273

- 'If I am wrong, it means that I am bad.'
- 'If I do not live up to my family standards, I will not belong.'
- 'I am loved more when I work hard and generate a lot.'
- 'I am only as good as what I achieve.'
- 'The amount I do is more important to me than how well I do it.'
- 'My desire is for complete control, so I will try hard enough to get it by whatever means.'

Jesus and Approval

Looking back, it seems ironic that it was the first day of April 1981 when I sensed the calling of God to give up my professional job and go into the ministry. The honouring and respectful thing for me to do at that time was to see my parents and tell them about my decision. I knew it would be a difficult thing to do, because my father had a problem with God, as well as with the fact that I was a Christian. He had also been very proud of my career as a Chartered Surveyor. As Chris and I spoke to them, I knew that his anger was coming to the surface, and suddenly he got up and rushed out of the house. He did not return, so we then left for home, and all seemed to be ok until, in the middle of the night, the phone rang. It was my father, who in a drunken rage threatened me. My father utterly disapproved of me regarding who I was, and the way I had chosen to go.

However, I was not going to let my father control and intimidate me, because I knew that I had the approval of my Heavenly Father, which gave me the assurance and security that I had done the right thing. If I had submitted to my father's demands, I would not be writing this today. Who knows what would have happened? Things did get better, but I do not think he ever really forgave me. However, I am free to make my own decisions, particularly with Abba Father in the centre of my life.

We all desire to feel loved, accepted, and affirmed, but many know all too clearly that they are not fulfilled in this vital area. However, when Jesus was baptised at the beginning of His ministry, something very dramatic happened, that filled him with a sense of purpose and became foundational to how His Father saw Him (Luke 3:21-.23). It was a public affirmation, demonstrated with joy and delight, as Jesus came into the wonderful expression of His Father's love. It was a supernatural event, with the heavens being dramatically torn open and the voice of God proclaiming, 'you are my Son, whom I love, with you I am well pleased.' Amazingly, Jesus was acknowledged before the people, which gave Him the strength and confidence necessary to fulfil what the Father had ordained.

It is important to note here that He had not yet even started His ministry, He had not done anything, and nobody knew who He was! What was He to do? Perhaps a good dramatic performance would give Him credit, elevate Him up the social scale giving Him value, esteem, and a position of prominence, acceptance and approval? All of this was not necessary, for Jesus did not need to prove anything, because His Father had given Him everything that was needed. What the Father did, was to publicly approve Jesus before He went out to proclaim the Kingdom of God, making His task completely detached from any sense of performance that could be used to seek approval. It meant that He had already been accepted and approved before anything else had happened, therefore He was able to minister totally out of a pure relationship with His Father, not needing to prove or even win His Father's love by performing well. The Father did not say, 'as long as you perform well, or if you do this, or you must do that, then I will love you and pleased with you.' Jesus had not begun His ministry, therefore it was nothing to do with performance; it was purely relational.

For the orphan hearted person, the desire is to do well to gain approval, but this can become a permanent trap, which will always be about us and not about our Heavenly Father. We need to know that in the same way the Father personally affirmed Jesus at His baptism, He has also personally affirmed us, and there is nothing we can do about it, and we do not need to make any attempt to try to perform well in order to gain God's approval.

We cannot earn the grace of God. God's approval does not depend on our performance, so we can just soak and experience God's love, because our worth is not dependent on how well we perform. Sons do not strive for or chase after significance - it is not wrapped up, driven, or dominated by our productivity. We are not employees, we are sons!

We start by knowing that we are simply beloved sons - with no conditions, no terms, no contract, no nothing, except to receive and immerse ourselves in our Father's love. It is most important to realise and understand that we are not given favour because of who we are or what we do, but because of who Jesus is and what he did. His favour became our favour when the Father declared us to be new in Christ, *'Therefore, if anyone is in Christ, he is a new creation. The old has passed away; behold, the new has come'* (2 Corinthians 5:17, NLT).

Activity is not synonymous with identity. If my identity gets wrapped up in performance, I will overreact when praise or criticism comes from others, because I will end up being driven towards perfectionism, which will feed my performance mentality to try to achieve more.

The most important thing for us to understand is that we are not given favour because of who we are, or for our performance, but because of who Jesus is, and what He did for us. If we are in Christ, why is there any need to live for approval when we know that God the Father thinks the same of us as He does His Son? Many carry the pressure of disapproval, which is often imbibed deeply within, especially if it was related to childhood issues. It is important to make some godly choices to deal with the issues of performance, perfectionism and approval, because the more you continue you will find the cycle becomes toxic, and the danger is, that you become obsessive and begin to live by the 'enough' syndrome, which would involve the following:

- 'Enough is never enough.'

- 'You are not enough.'
- 'You must continually perform to be enough.'
- 'You need something from somewhere else to make you enough, therefore you strive to achieve to be enough.'
- 'God is not enough to make you enough.'

Grace

If the gospel, which is God's love to us, is just a challenge to do better, we will hit a wall, and we won't get to where God wants us to be, that is to fully enter into his purposes. So often, we have tried to do better and failed, whether by trying to keep more rules, doing more activities, or doing more works, but it has only resulted in discouragement and disillusionment. The Apostle Paul strongly confronted the Galatians by exposing their foolishness for attempting to keep the law, and in doing so, turning away from living in the Spirit by going back to living by their own works (Galatians 3:1-5). This contradiction, which is a deception, will lead to living a life of rules and regulations, an obsession with duty, an intensity of having to get it right, and the stress of a too demanding system, which will be undergirded by the ungodly vision of performance and perfectionism. In this environment, hearts get hardened and judgementalism becomes more apparent, which leads to the way of the Pharisee.

Grace is God saying to us, 'this is what I want to do for you,' which means, we haven't got to do anything to acquire His favour. Grace has nothing to do with, 'do better,' 'try harder,' or 'love deeper,' as it is free and unconditional, because we are his children and He loves us as such! I am very much aware that I am bad enough to need God's grace, but I still need to know that I am not good enough to do anything about it. All of my efforts are meaningless; they get me nowhere. God's outrageous grace, which includes His unconditional love, are tools to undermine and demolish our performance mentality and our striving to be perfect. Jesus was magnificent in not only receiving His Father's favour, but also in knowing how to rest in that with confidence, as He journeyed in His radical ministry. The place for us to start, is to rest in the Father's grace and favour, and to once and for all give up trying to meet conditions that are not there.

Summary

We are not called to a performance mentality to seek approval, to people please, to live under anyone's expectations, or to attain perfection, but to love God and to live in His pleasure. There are many times that I have said to God, particularly in difficult circumstances, 'what can I do?' Inevitably, the answer revolves around grace, and I am reminded by my Abba Father, that His grace is all I need. Paul went on to say that, *'my power works best in weakness. So now I am glad to boast about my weaknesses, so that the power of Christ can work through me,'* (2 Corinthians 12:9 NLT). Putting God in the centre of our lives and depending upon Him, are fundamental keys for the orphan hearted, therefore it is time to be honest and transparent, so that the areas that control us can be dealt with once and for all, and getting help is a priority for this. There is a clear difference between demanding perfection and peaceably desiring excellence; may God give us revelation to see it, apprehend it, and live in its benefits.

The Father

The parable that Jesus told which is known as 'the Prodigal Son,' about the father and his two sons, is probably the most well-known worldwide. However, its title leads us to focus more on the two sons and miss out on the heart of the parable, which is the father. It is an amazing story, with many twists and turns, but is particularly related to the father's attitude regarding the way he responds to the really difficult challenges that are raised by his sons. Luke describes those who were listening as tax collectors and sinners, along with the Pharisees and the teachers of the law (Luke 15:1) and it seems that judgement and criticism from the religious group provoked Jesus into telling the parable. It is not difficult to understand what Jesus was getting at when talking about either son, but what was radical was the way in which He talked about the father. When Jesus began His ministry with teaching about the Kingdom of God, it was regarded as extreme and, by some, revolutionary, but when He started to introduce His Father to them, it became too much for them to understand, for the concept was far beyond them; it was unparalleled and unique. However, Jesus persevered, and the Gospels show that He talked about His Father hundreds of times. The Old Testament, however, is very different, as God as a Father is mentioned in a personal way less than twenty times. Jesus introduced the people to a new concept, a new era, and a new beginning, in which a close and personal relationship with God as Father is not only necessary but essential.

The way Jesus talked about the father in the parable was quite remarkable because what was seen was a man who was not bound by culture, tradition, or religious principles, but was clearly free in the way he continuously showed grace, compassion, mercy and unconditional love. He probably broke every social rule there was at that time, and he certainly failed to meet the listener's expectations, particularly in the way he should have dealt [harshly] with his sons. What Jesus gave them, was a glimpse of the father's heart for his sons, something which was summed up in what he said to the older son, *'you are always with me, and all that is mine is yours'* (Luke 15:11). Could it be that the purpose of Jesus here was to show that eclectic group a deeper meaning to the story? Perhaps Jesus was describing the very nature of God as Father? He did not mention His Father while He was speaking, but is not it obvious that He juxtaposed His and our Heavenly Father with the father in the parable?

I cannot find another illustration in scripture that is a closer comparison to Abba Father than this, for this revelatory glimpse of God's heart becomes our guarantee that He is always with us, and of what He has given to us. As we look at the various circumstances and incidents that occurred concerning the two sons, we will consider how their father's reaction illustrates the way that our Father God would respond to us, whether affected by an orphan heart or not.

The Younger Son
Leaving Home Lost

Within a sentence of Jesus starting the parable, there was an absolute bombshell that came from the younger son. In an unfeeling, uncaring and callous way, he said to his father, 'give me my share in the estate' (Luke 15:12). He may as well have used the word 'now,' because that was what he meant, for he had already prepared in his heart to leave the family as soon as possible. Not only did this cause acute embarrassment to the father, but also deep personal shame which, when the word got out, would bring further shame on the whole family. What the young son was saying, was, 'I wish you were dead!' This caused the father deep distress, as it brought the realisation was that the son preferred him dead. Whatever the differences the listeners had with each other, they all would have been filled with shock and horror as they heard this incredible story.

The father was left abandoned, rejected, and humiliated, but most people would have wanted retribution for how the son had behaved. The father would have been well within his rights to protect his honour, and at the least publicly deal with him with a beating, giving him the choice to either submit or get out. However, nothing like that happened - there was no reaction, no justifiable expression of anger, no arguing, in fact, the father publicly shamed himself by horrifying everyone further as he divided his wealth between them! Amazingly, he included his older son, who was not there, and as we are aware, he still would have received a double portion under the Levitical law relating to the firstborn son, and for the younger son, it meant that he received a third of the inheritance. Could this mean that by accepting his part of the inheritance, the older son was actually agreeing with his brother about wanting his father dead?

In the midst of this family upheaval, the father showed an incredible sense of grace and unconditional love, as he symbolically laid down his life for his sons; surely his heart was broken. The word, 'bios' that is used here for 'wealth' or 'property' seems to be unusual in the NT Greek, and it means his living or his life, rather than his money or goods. The father made a choice and divided his life between his sons, it was almost as though he was saying, 'ok I will die for you.' Both brothers had completely misunderstood their father; the younger one saw him as dead and the older brother served his father like a slave who needs a wage. They did not see the goodness and kindness of his generous heart, for the two sons had no loving relationship with him, they were already lost to their father, for one was about to leave and the older son was always silent and never around. What pain the father must have had as he saw the division, heard the anger and felt the rejection.

There were further setbacks that amplified the shock to the listening group, for the younger son quickly sold his portion, probably cheaply, realising the cash because he had planned to leave home as soon as he could. He had little thought about giving further offence to his family and the community as he had disappeared as soon as he could to go to a Gentile country! In his opinion, the father had no choice but to let him go, and this decision did not affect the consistency of his love for him; it continued and was not lacking in passion. The challenge to the father was that he was expected by the people in the parable, and those listening, and even by the local custom and tradition, to behave in the accepted way. He did not, so how did he cope? Instead, he had his own distinctive approach to living, which was motivated by grace and unconditional love. It was so much part of him that even in his darkest moments he remained consistent.

What manner of love is this? It is of such quality, that it is almost above human understanding, and is the sort of love that disregards every transgression because it is redemptive love. As we will see, this is a love that will not let go; it is tender, compassionate, dignifying, and honouring, and even when everyone knew he had been abused, debased, and humiliated, it was still wonderfully consistent. The father continued to love his younger son even before he left home, and to the point of giving him what he desired - his inheritance. This probably meant that in granting him his part of the legacy, he identified with his son's 'transgression,' and was even prepared to share in his son's shame, thus tarnishing his reputation and the integrity of the family. It seemed almost impossible for this to happen, but it had, and the consequences were severe, as his relationship with his son was broken, his standing in the community severely damaged, and he was aware that no self-respecting Middle Eastern father would ever let his son leave and would certainly not welcome him back to the family home!

When considering this, as a recovering orphan hearted person, I am continually amazed and impacted by the love of God as my loving Heavenly Father. *'See what an incredible quality of love the Father has shown [lavished] to us, that we would [be permitted to] be named and called and counted the children of God! And so we are!'* (1 John 3:1 AMP).

The Younger Son
Returning Home Found

It was too much to expect the father to let go of his lost son, for he had not given up hope, and although he had left home, the father continued to pursue him in his heart, as he longed for his return. This is extraordinary love, and although it is not known how long he had been away, it seemed that every day the father looked out for him, watching and waiting for his return. Then one day he suddenly saw him, and he got up to go to him, but what was so surprising is that he started to run. His heart was overwhelmed with compassion and mercy and he could do nothing else but express his love by getting to his son as quickly as he could. *'But while he was still a long way off, his father saw him and was filled with compassion for him; he ran to his son, threw his arms around him and kissed him'* (Luke 15:20). There are some things to consider here because the father broke all the cultural rules in the book.

- Dignified Middle Eastern Patriarchs do not run, they wait at home from where they would exercise their authority.

- He saw him in the distance. What God has done for us is breaking down the concept of distance; that is why the veil in the temple was torn in two as Jesus died, to draw us close to Him. God is in search of humanity for love and relationship, and just as the father pursued his son, God is in pursuit of us!

- He needed to run to his son to reach him before the villagers, because of what he had done. They had the right to banish him from the village for good.

- How could a man of his stature run? He wore a long robe, which he would have had to hitch it up and show his legs! This is utterly humiliating and shameful, particularly going through the village with the people astounded as they looked at the extraordinary sight of a distinguished landowner running fast towards his son.

- The father was unconcerned about the state his son was in, with his dirty ragged clothes, and the strange smell about him.

- He threw his arms around his son and fell on him, holding him closely. In the Jewish world at that time, you would not choose to recognise someone 'deemed dead,' and certainly not touch them! The father took no notice of that.

- He kissed his son tenderly with passion and repeatedly, as a mother would. Showering him with kisses is not what the patriarch of the family would have done, however he did not care, as his excitement overwhelmed both of them.

As much as the son was surprised at the response of his father, it was clear that the focus was on the father, particularly in the way in which he responded to his wayward son. Even though the son had a prepared speech ready, the father took initiative, because he did not want to show love in response to the son's confession, and by his actions, publicly declared reconciliation and unconditional forgiveness. He treated his son as though he had never been away. This was a new day, a new beginning of redemptive grace and mercy with visible love, which penetrated the son's heart to the point, that he made an undeniable choice to change by accepting that he had been found and restored.

In the midst of this, the father continued the process of restoration by giving his son the best robe, a signet ring with the family crest and shoes for his feet. The son was always a son even when he was in another country but giving these valuable possessions to the son restored dignity, authority and liberty. The father then declared that the fatted calf was prepared (it was reserved for very special occasions) and invited all to join him because it was time to celebrate this great event. 'For this son of mine was dead and is alive again; he was lost and is found. So they began to celebrate,' (Luke 15:24). The perception of the father was resurrection, for the son had been lost but now was found; he was dead but is now alive. It was a new beginning and worth celebrating with a banquet for the father's sake because he needed to share his joy in that he had pursued his son and found him. It was an astonishing, but costly demonstration of love, that led to the complete forgiveness and restoration of his son.

The Older Brother
Lost at Home

The appearance of the older brother in the parable did not happen until after his younger brotherhood had returned home, however, his influence was there right from the time his brother asked for his part of the inheritance. He should have been at his father's side when the problem started, but was nowhere to be seen, which in itself dishonoured his father. It highlighted the issues of division and dysfunction in the family, which exposed a serious need in the older brother. Middle Eastern culture at that time would have required that he should have been mediating between his father and brother, but he neglected his responsibility and did not turn up when the father in his suffering needed the support. After the younger son had departed and the father was yearning for his return, he was very much alone because the older son was far away working in a field with little contact to home. All the father could do was to keep looking in order to see if the son was returning. In that culture, it was the responsibility of the older son to keep watch for travellers in order to offer them hospitality, but it fell to the father to do what the older son should have done, something which would have only increased his humiliation.

The parable finally gets to the place where the banquet begins and the music, laughter, and joy were loud enough for the eldest son working outside to hear it and ask a servant what was going on. As soon as he found out he became angry (Luke 15:28). The original Greek word can be translated as 'enraged,' which seems to be more in keeping with his character. It seemed that the pent-up emotions finally erupted, and it was mainly aimed at his father. The older son's selfishness prevailed as he refused to go into the banquet, which caused more trouble for the father.

Firstly, the custom at a banquet is for the older son to act as host, to look after and serve the guests, but he refused to take up this responsibility.

Secondly, he waited outside in the courtyard, fizzing with rage, his pouting face showing how self-centred he was, which in itself caused a ripple of astonishment to go around the guests.

Thirdly, it meant that the father would utterly humiliate himself, yet again in front of everyone because he had to go out and plead with his son to join the banquet.

For the older son to be outside having refused to go in and share in such a celebratory banquet, was an immense public insult to the father. Sadly, this led to a very difficult standoff outside the banqueting hall, and probably many heard or witnessed it. It was a great cost to the father, but that did not deter him, because his love for his son was that much greater. However, he probably was not prepared for the tirade of resentment and aggression from this lost son (Luke 15:29-30) or the following reactions:

- The dishonouring began with the son refusing to address him as his father, he said angrily, loudly and controlling, 'look!' This is a personal rejection from a rebellious heart.
- 'All these years I have been slaving for you.' The son saw himself as a slave, but the father saw him as a son and partner.
- 'I have never disobeyed your commands.' There is more than a sense of hypocrisy here as he had just refused to honour his father and attend the banquet.
- 'You never gave me even a young goat so I could celebrate with my friends.' This reminds us of the pouting son trying to manipulate to get his way. Did not his father favour him with a double portion of his inheritance?
- 'But when this son of yours.' This is very callus and hardhearted and speaks of a division with his father. He also attacked the family integrity, and he rejected his brother by his refusal to forgive. He made it clear that he wanted nothing to do with either of them; he said, 'you are both dead to me.'
- 'Who has squandered your property with prostitutes.' He showed his contempt for his brother with an unproven accusation. He was being economic with the truth by exaggeration to prove a point.
- 'Yet you kill the fatted calf for him.' In other words, you were manipulated by your cunning younger son.

This was such a mess, and it was made so much worse by the son's dreadful treatment of his father. There was no hint of love, any concept of grace, and certainly no sense of joy about his brother returning. This would have been more than enough to destroy his father, but his first response was to call him 'son.' The Greek word used here is 'teknon,' which amazingly indicated affection and intimacy. What can be seen here is the consistency of the unconditional love from the father, who was still pursuing him, which in these circumstances of such hurt and pain is astonishing! The father held his ground, he did not capitulate but came out with some astoundingly heart-felt words, to which there was no answer. They were words of covenant, as he wanted to express his utmost, but unexpected love to this son, as he had already done to his younger brother. He was steadfast, unyielding; and uncompromising as he sums up the truth (Luke 15:31-32) that he deeply felt about his son, which motivated an appropriate response:

- 'You are always with me, and everything I have is yours.' Nothing had changed, for what the father had wanted, was to share his life with his two sons. There was never a thought about changing what was in his heart.
- 'We had to celebrate and be glad; it was only right for me to celebrate for your brother, there was no other way.' In saying that, he far exceeded the social norms, including the expectations of the people; he wanted a celebration, it was in his heart, so it happened. What both sons motivated in the father, was more and more unconditional love and 'scandalous' grace, to the point at which the father would not cancel the banquet at the behest of his older son. There were no limits to the release of his goodness, and he knew that whatever was said and done by his older son, he would not submit to his demands. Celebration was part of the acceptance of the son coming home, and in the mind of the father was necessary.
- 'This brother of yours was dead and is alive again, he was lost and is found.' This is a declaration of resurrection and restoration, meaning new life, and a new beginning.

When Jesus started talking about the older brother, it seemed obvious that the Pharisees would identify with him more than with the others in the parable. He was dutiful, but legalistic, without any sense of love and affection to give to his father. The Pharisees would have understood the response of this son, such as his anger, rather than the grace, love and mercy of his father. They were leaders who did not understand either God's heart or the way in which He viewed them, for they were hard-hearted and self-righteous. What the older brother did in his self-centredness was to shut love out and inevitably became shut out of love by his own choice, which seemed pharisaical.

The parable finished abruptly, and surprisingly there was no final conclusion. It was left open-ended with no resolution, no sense of reconciliation and nobody knew what had finally happened! Was this a deliberate choice that Jesus made there, so that the listeners could reflect on the vital areas of truth that He shared in the parable, then take stock, and make their conclusions with right godly choices? Of course, parables are timeless and therefore they still challenge us today. There is much to consider and identify with, which includes both sons, but it is necessary for orphan hearted people to put into perspective the father's amazing response to the very difficult circumstances that he was placed in, into perspective.

The True Prodigal

If we define the word prodigal as someone who spent his money rashly and recklessly, squandering it foolishly, it is easy to focus on the younger son, for it was clear that his part of his father's inheritance was wasted. However, as we have previously seen, the word prodigal can be defined differently - as someone who gives lavishly, extravagantly, profusely out of abundance. This definition would be more associated with the father because he gave and gave ceaselessly out of an abundance of amazing grace and unrequited, as well as unconditional love. Many listening to Jesus would have said that it was pointless for the father to waste everything he had on these rebellious sons, yet he was prepared to lose it all to find his sons. He had pursued them in his heart, but that soon changed with him humiliating himself by running to the younger son, and later, under the judgemental eyes of the guests, by leaving the banquet to entreat his older son to join him and his brother.

The father was a man of integrity and righteousness motivated by compassion and mercy, who was not afraid to be extravagantly wasteful to two sons who would have been happy to have seen him dead. Yet, he said to his eldest son, amidst the disrespectful rant towards him, 'everything I have is yours.' For me, the father rather than the sons is the main character of the story - he never gave up, he never let go, but sought them out and continued to pursue them, even when rejection seemed to have the upper hand. What the father was doing was depicting the heart of our loving Heavenly Father - the heart of one who pursues us dramatically in seeking us out, as He comes from the heavenly realm to make His dwelling place amongst us (John 1:14). He willingly forgives, rejoices when we are found, and lavishes grace upon us, tenderly, through His limitless love.

The father is the true prodigal in the parable, and what we can see through his response to his sons, is a glorious picture of our loving Heavenly Father reaching out to us to release us from slavery, through a revolution of the heart, by adoption into sonship. He will not leave us as orphans, for we are sons with an impetus to enjoy our God.

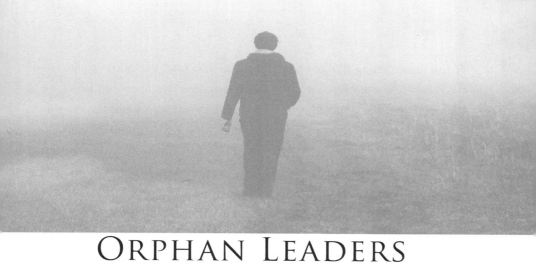

ORPHAN LEADERS

Why Leaders?

What I want to say in this chapter comes out of a journey during which I have seen a huge diversity of leadership styles. It sums up how people can be affected by their leader's decisions, attitudes and behaviour, for it seems that the way leaders have handled the people can create a mixture of blessing and encouragement, but regretfully there is also often much pain and hurt. There are various reasons why these things happen, however, I do believe that we are in a time where leaders need to be honest with themselves, as they consider their strengths and weaknesses, and particularly the condition of their hearts. For many, it is time to change. If we are amongst those who are looking for a worldwide move of God that we believe will happen, then surely it is imperative that we should be prepared for, and ready to, embrace whatever God wants to do. We have to be realistic though, for things do happen in leadership that are damaging, and denial or excuses are not the way to deal with these.

For over fifty years I have been in some form of leadership both in the church and in other Christian organisations, but despite having vision and strategy, I have found that handling and dealing with people has been one of the most testing things I have faced. As you read the gospels and see the different characters that Jesus called to follow Him, it cannot take long to understand the difficulties He had in leading them. An indicator of this is that when Jesus went to the cross, only John and a group of women, including His mother, were there. The other disciples were either on the periphery or had disappeared, yet a few days later they were together with the resurrected Christ, who prepared them for the promise of the Father at Pentecost (Luke 24). The same group of men who were with Jesus for over three years were, at Pentecost, dramatically transformed by the power of the Spirit, and began to do what Jesus did. Amazingly, they became the leaders of the new church, which inspired by all they learned from being with Jesus, released the people to impact the world with the message and demonstration of the Kingdom of God.

Just before He went to the cross, Jesus told them that He would not leave them as orphans, but would come to them, which He did, through His resurrection and in the power of the Spirit (John 14:18). The revelation of adoption through sonship came as the Holy Spirit began to reveal Abba Father to them (Galatians 4:6). As leaders, we are not exempt from needing this revelation, but rather have a greater responsibility in the way we look at our lives. For as much as we are called, gifted and anointed, we are also like the rest of humankind, being frail, fragile and flawed, plus there have been times when we fail (we are not failures), yet God continually accepts us through His amazing grace and unconditional love.

It is essential that, as we move on into our destiny in our relationship with God, we are aware of the effect that the orphan heart and orphan spirit can have on us. Knowing God as Abba Father is a core issue for the church, and, therefore, should be in the heart of every leader, whether it is understood and attained to, or not. We know that through Jesus, God has opened the way for us to get close to Him, therefore we each need to know the condition of our heart, so that we do not lose the closeness, affection and intimacy that we can have with Him. Because of the influence that leaders have in the church, it is fundamental that we as leaders understand that we are not immune from searching our heart but should in a consistent way lead the people by example into this amazing relationship with Abba Father.

There are churches with leaders who are driven to succeed and who have no hesitation in exploiting people, leading to a deterioration of relationships. There are reasons for this, which we will look at later, for it is something that cannot be met by ministry success or acceptable performance, because the orphan heart is so often motivated by the power of the orphan spirit, which can cause leaders to live in such a way that they do not have a safe and secure place close to the heart of their Heavenly Father. Being distant is their default position, which means that they struggle to have a place for affection, intimacy, affirmation, comfort, or belonging in their relationship with Abba Father. In many cases, it becomes a vicious circle with loneliness growing out of this, which, when coupled with independence, will lead to isolation. The result of this will be an inner drive to achieve more acceptance through performance, by trying to please everyone, including God! People can be manipulated, but not God. The fruit of all of this will be anxiety, stress, fear and frustration, often leading to anger, which will influence the leader to become even further distant from God.

Accountability

Being vulnerable and transparent is essential, however this is something that would be a challenge to orphan hearted leaders, as it is easier to hide or mask certain negative behaviour, such as fear, shame and insecurity. We do not build the church alone, for independence is not part of the Kingdom of God; it is interdependence that is necessary. In leading a church, I have realised that it is not my church, and I certainly do not know it all, for I need others to compliment me, particularly if they know things that I do not know about.

This leaves me with a choice, which is either to ignore them or to respectfully defer to them, if and when necessary, even if I am a senior leader. It might seem better to do everything on my own, but there is no doubt, that this would lead to an increase in stress which would be enough to affect my emotions, mind and behaviour, something which would will not be good for my health or that of anyone else. One of the principles in building a structure is the way the bricks or stones are laid in such a way that they create a strong and stable connection, known as 'bonding'.

They laid side by side, but halfway on top of each other forming an adhesive and cohesive unit, which is a united whole. Our strength is in our unity as we are built into a temple, which is the dwelling of God with the chief cornerstone being Jesus (Ephesians 2:20-22). Some leaders talk about risky living and would have no problem about their place of faith in God, and seeing Him move powerfully. However, when it comes to trusting people by opening their hearts unconditionally to give and receive love, something changes because they are only able to do that with difficulty. It highlights their fear of trusting others, for accountability is undergirded by trust, therefore we need to be aware that responsibility without accountability will bring instability.

Accountability starts by having an open heart to others, in particular to those who have a proven maturity and in giving them the right to ask 'the question' when necessary, such as, about a leader's style of leadership, or their difficult personality traits. These people would normally be in the leadership team of the Senior Pastor. I do not mean being open to any sort of abuse or control but being in a relationship where there would be mutual honesty, that becomes the impetus to deal with any sense of insecurity or fear that the leader has shown. Fear of rejection is a curse that will lock up a person to the reality of relationships, which ultimately will become non-productive. In itself, the vulnerability of the leader will bring security, that will bring peace to the congregation. What I have always enjoyed is wandering up and down the aisles talking, relating and interacting with the people before or after the service. Giving time to them is meaningful and certainly appreciated. It can be as important as the sermon itself, though unfortunately some leaders just turn up to worship and speak, but then disappear into the office without some, if any, contact with the people. Maybe we should consider where Jesus seemed to be happier. I say this with the utmost respect, 'the common people heard Him gladly' (Mark 12:37 NKJV). Surely accountability starts here.

Paradox

It is known, although rarely admitted, that [most] leaders have an enigmatic predisposition to be godly and yet can be dysfunctional at the same time. They live 'holy lives' being faithful to biblical principles, however, they are not whole, for subconsciously they are broken emotionally and mentally, because they still carry the wounds of yesterday hidden deep within them. They would see themselves as spiritually mature but are oppressed emotionally; they may be dynamic in prayer, but they can be just as strong in ungodly control. Their sincerity in loving God is not to be doubted, but do they know Him as Abba Father, the one who in His provision would cherish and treasure them with love and affection? In this situation, it is not difficult to cover over the deep-seated issues that still cause hurt and damage, which will create a veneer of spirituality. What this action leads to, is self-protection, which quickly becomes denial. These areas are never buried dead, they are very much alive, and even deep in the unconscious, they can still exert control in everyday circumstances.

There is a contradiction in many good leaders because they are still impaired in areas in their lives, which will ultimately lead to a deterioration in their behaviour and relationships. Often the emphasis is on pseudo-spirituality, which includes personal holiness, the functions of the church, family, etc, however, what is hidden, and therefore neglected or denied, can only be described as a dysfunction within the leader. This may show as self-righteousness, or anger, racism, sexism, and control. The deception of the enemy is powerful in these situations because some leaders would be adamant that they are not at all affected by any of this.

Where Are The Fathers?

'*Even if you had ten thousand teachers [instructors or tutors] in Christ, you do not have many fathers, for in Christ Jesus I became your father through the gospel*' (1 Corinthians 3:15). Paul is underlining the difference between his role as a spiritual father and the many who are teachers. The difference seems to be in the concept of relationship, as the heart of the father is closeness, affection and a godly intimacy. Paul was not saying that he was not a teacher or tutor, and we know he was, but what he was emphasising was that he fathered them through the gospel. However, fathering is not just leading a person to know Jesus, it is an ongoing journey with them of teaching and instructing them in how they live as they follow Him. Surely a pastor or shepherd should have the quality of a father, and in that would be able to influence and disciple a person in their walk with God. It is a fact that sheep know the voice of the shepherd and will come running to him when he calls. Is the voice of the shepherd the voice of a father? Shepherds care, provide, protect, with affection, as they lead the sheep, and I believe that is fathering. We are all made in the image of God to reflect His life and character to all we know and meet. A leader has a greater responsibility to do the same amongst his own group of people. Paul said, 'and you should imitate me, just as I imitate Christ' (1 Corinthians 11:1 NLT). He was saying, 'follow my directions and imitate my example.' Jesus is the perfect example, and Paul had caught the heart of Abba Father as he followed Jesus and was able to share this passion with the people. There are two challenges for leaders to consider as they endeavour to do the same:

Firstly, have leaders caught the heart of their Heavenly Father, so that they can lead the people by their personal experience of Abba Father? Those affected by the orphan heart would find this difficult, but what is needed is that they look at why they are like that, and then take steps to change.

Secondly, will the people follow their leader on the basis that they have the trust to do so, or have they seen and experienced something regarding the leader's style of leadership or behaviour that might dissuade them?

During my early years of leadership, I was told clearly by other leaders not to get too close to the people. This puzzled me because I knew I was a pastor and it was something that I did naturally as part my care for the people. The essence of Abba Father is closeness and it is not easy to do that when you have been directed not to get close! Years later, probably around 1990, I was at a conference in Harrogate. It was quite a time, and as the various sessions went on there was an opportunity for leaders to meet privately with some of the prophets [male and female] who were on the team to receive a prophetic word from them. I was fortunate to be asked, and as I stood there, one of them came out with a most peculiar word for me. It could have been construed as offensive, but I was more surprised than offended. He looked at me and said, 'you smell like a sheep' and stopped. Maybe he saw my eyes open wide with amazement, and then he said, 'Jesus smelt like a sheep' and stopped again before saying some other things. However, the revelation was there, and I understood; that was enough. If we are shepherds, we are going to smell like sheep because we spend time with the sheep, just like Jesus. He was just as happy with His 'sheep,' as He was with anything. We have a mandate to get close and share the heart of the Father, therefore dealing with the orphan heart and orphan spirit becomes more essential as we exercise our leadership.

Consider this version of 1 Peter 5:2-3 and ask yourself a question: 'Am I fulfilling Peter's mandate as a shepherd leader?' Being honest with yourself is the only option:

'Be compassionate shepherds who tenderly care for God's flock and who feed them well, for you have the responsibility to guide, protect, and oversee. Consider it a joyous pleasure and not merely a religious duty. Lead from the heart under God's leadership - not as a way to gain finances dishonestly but

as a way to eagerly and cheerfully serve. Do not be controlling tyrants but lead others by your beautiful examples to the flock.' (TPT).

The Past is Present

It is well known that our experiences and what we learn in childhood contribute to our development into adulthood, and whether they are positive or negative, they will affect us. Whatever context a child lives in, and whatever disposition they have, any trauma, hurts and wounds they receive will cause further damage to their future lives and relationships. It is also necessary to be aware that the emotional state or stress of the mother even before the child is born can affect the psychological development of the child. Past hurts that we carry will influence us today. We cannot change our past, but we can use our past to bring present stability, and also contribute to changing our future. Our past is a point of referral, not a place to live in which we allow it to continue to influence, or even control us.

While bonding with my mother in the womb, there was deep trauma as she was forced to leave her mother-in-law's house (her husband was away in the second world war) taking nothing with her, and then go to the unmarried mother's home (known as the House of Shame). She went through the birth alone, as my father did not even know she was pregnant, but later on, when he found out, he threatened her with taking me away if she would not marry him; he was an angry man. My mother was the emotional caregiver, and continued to be so, but was overwhelmed with the trauma, and my father's anger and control, as she struggled to make the right decision. She kept me, and after being divorced married my father. Children need security, and if they do not get it, insecurity will be a major influence throughout their lives. The early years of a child deserve special attention, and I think it was a struggle for my mother to give me that; but she did what she could and I am grateful. Good things do not happen to children when they should have, and bad things happen to children when they should not have.

There will be leaders that will understand this because of the unhealed childhood hurts in their own lives. Maybe some of you have wondered why you feel the way you do, and why occasionally your behaviour, your thoughts and your emotional reactions have not been conducive to the way you know they should have been. It is important to find out why this is so, because it is probable that any dysfunctional area will obstruct you from entering into God's best. The revelation that I had from God, which so clearly took hold of me regarding my past, not only exposed my orphan heart, but gave an impetus to do something about it. There is no doubt that this was a sovereign intervention, but I needed others to walk with me through it. One of the challenges to leaders is that of choosing to reach out to others who can help, and if you think there is no one, or you refuse to get help, you are only underlining the condition of your orphan heart! Humility is a necessity.

Children develop mentally and emotionally through learned behaviour. Unconditional love, affection, affirmation, protection and guidance to understand the difference between right and wrong all provide a safe and healthy place for this. It is sad, but it is not only abuse, neglect, or harsh words that damage. Children are like sponges, as they tend to soak in everything they see, hear and feel from those they are attached to. What they experience will affect their identity; love them, and they will feel good about themselves and behave accordingly.

During those early years, the child will begin to reflect from their parents or primary carers, either positive or negative behaviour. The challenge we face in adulthood is that when we are triggered by circumstances or events, we have a predisposition to reflect these images even though we are aware that our desire as Christians is to reflect the image of our Father God. My anger was a reflection of my father and grandfather, and along with other areas, such as insecurity and rejection, defined my orphan heart. This consequently affected my style of leadership.

David the Orphan King

Considering the life of King David can be helpful in a number of different ways. We see the mighty exploits that he did before and after he was king. We read that he was a man after God's heart (1 Samuel 13:14; Acts 13:22) but sometimes his actions communicated otherwise, which led to an abuse of power, dysfunction, conflict and instability in his family and the nation he led, which ultimately caused further problems generationally. Much of that is documented in scripture. It is important, therefore, to consider what and why this had happened, for it seems apparent that the events related to his pre-birth and childhood affected him considerably throughout his life. We will see that only a few scriptures highlight this, although they do give some indication that David's seven brothers as well as his father, Jesse, had considerable problems with him.

However, the traditional writings of the Jews, the Midrash and the Talmud, which are a compilation of biblical interpretation in Jewish religious tradition, including a rabbinic discourse of what the Torah (Hebrew Bible) means, connect the apparent problem to David's great-grandparents, Ruth and Boaz. Jesse was the grandson of Ruth (Ruth 4:17) and he would have certainly known her. After several years of marriage, and having raised many sons, Jesse began to entertain personal doubts about his ancestry, to the point of questioning the legitimacy of Boaz's marriage to Ruth. Boaz was a scholar who had had a different opinion on the general interpretation of ancestry regarding his relationship with Ruth, which enabled him to marry her, but sadly he died soon after they married, and he was unable to publish it.

During Ruth's lifetime, others also had doubts about the legitimacy of the marriage, and finally Jesse made a decision, which dramatically affected the life of David even before he was born. Jesse was sincere and his integrity compelled him to deal with his tormenting doubts. If his status was questionable, he knew that he was not permitted to remain married to a true Israelite because of the Moabite connection, so he separated from his wife, Nitzvet (who is not named in the Bible, but is also referred to in Jewish religious tradition) and no longer had marital relationships. He planned to have a relationship with a non-Jew, and that was his Canaanite maidservant. His sons were made aware of his decision and supported him. Jesse wanted another offspring, whose ancestry would be beyond doubt, and not contaminated by the ancestry of Ruth. However, the maidservant saw the anguish of her mistress and empathetically suggested that she would change places with her that very evening, just as Leah had done with Rachel, (Genesis 29:21-25).

That night, Nitzvet conceived, with Jesse oblivious to what had happened, and it remained that way, after the birth, for Nitzvet remained silent. Obviously, the truth came out and the incensed brothers wanted to kill their 'adulterous' mother and the 'illegitimate' unborn child, but Jesse persuaded them not to, and said, 'we will treat the child, not as a son and brother, but as a despised servant, and everyone will know that he is illegitimate and will not be able to marry an Israelite.'

His name was David, and as soon as he was born in Bethlehem, he was treated as an outcast and was even separated from the family at mealtimes. This is very much orphan language. When he was old enough, he was sent out to shepherd the sheep in certain dangerous areas, as the family hoped he would be killed by a lion or bear. When he returned home the whole town shunned him, as well as his own family treating him with the utmost contempt. It was ultimately accepted that all of the positive qualities of Boaz were in Jesse and his sons, while all of the negative characteristics supposedly in Ruth were attributed to the despised youngest son. Even from childhood David's life seems to have been full of loneliness, abandonment, rejection, and an orphan heart.

The scriptures are not quite silent on this dreadful scenario, as David releases his feelings in some of the Psalms:

'*Surely I was sinful at birth, sinful from the time my mother conceived me*' (Psalms 51:5).

'*Those who hate me without reason outnumber the hairs of my head; many are my enemies without cause, those who seek to destroy me. I am forced to restore what I did not steal*' (Psalms 69:4).

'*Even my own brothers pretend they do not know me; they treat me like a stranger*' (Psalms 69:8 NLT).

'*Even if my father and mother abandon me, the Lord will hold me close*' (Psalms 27:10).

From pre-birth until the time he began to reign as King, David was despised, rejected, and abandoned with derision, humiliation and contempt by his brothers and father. This was over a period of twenty-eight years, and it seems that Psalm 69 summarises the hurts, wounds and pain of those many years. No one cared that David was the innocent party of his mother's sin because at that time it was believed that the sins of the parents came upon the children, so David was pronounced guilty. After a period of time, an event happened, that not only changed the life of David but also the rest of the family.

The Prophet Samuel arrived in Bethlehem, sent from God, to anoint one of Jesse's son's as King of Israel. Jesse had all of his seven sons pass by Samuel and all were refused by God. 'Are these all your sons?' Samuel asked. Even though Jesse treated David as an orphan and had refused to give him status as a son, he had no choice but to reply that there was another younger son who was tending the sheep in a distant pasture. Samuel insisted that the younger son be summoned to see him, and as soon as he saw David, he anointed him king. Amazingly David was still a teenager, but had to wait until he was thirty before he began to reign over Israel (2 Samuel 5:4).

Not long after the anointing, the defeat and death of Goliath set David on a pathway in which he met King Saul, and it was not too long before Saul became enraged at the people who put David in a place above him. The seeds of jealousy were sown, and sometime later Saul tried to kill David who had to flee. The anger, hatred and jealously continued from David's family, which now included Saul, who contributed considerably to David.'s rejection.

The unconditional love and the grace of God were amazing in the life of David, for God as a loving Father took the orphan and treated him as a man after His own heart, like a son. However, as David married and had his own family, it was clear that the wounds and hurts from childhood remained through his orphan heart and carried into the next generation.

As leaders, we need to take heed of David's ongoing negative situation and be aware of the unhealed hurts that have affected us over the years, and not to be afraid of our vulnerability remembering that, '*my grace is all you need. My power works best in weakness*' (1 Corinthians 12:9 NLT). It is in God's heart to bring healing and change to us, as we submit to Him.

Insecurity

Insecurity will often manifest from the workings of the orphan heart by creating a conflict in how a person understands their identity. It will undermine their sense of value and self-worth, which in turn leads to a lack of self-confidence, uncertainty, anxiety and fear. This might cause a person to stall in their daily activity and motivated by self-doubt and self-pity they would feel an increasing need for reassurance, as their capacity to think and act effectively begins to diminish and indecision increases. An insecure person who recognises their unworthiness will often react with their words and actions in seeming opposition, in an attempt, on the one hand, to deny it, but on the other hand to drive themself, to prove to themself and others, how good they are, and that they are acceptable. All of this gives insecurity the right to become a controlling factor in their lives.

Being a Christian with this happening is certainly a challenge, however, if we consider that this was how a leader, senior pastor, apostle, or prophet was behaving, it becomes more serious because of the influence they have with the people they lead and the community they live in. it is important to realise that insecurity can be linked to trauma that has been experienced throughout childhood and on into the teenage years, particularly from those caregivers to whom we would have looked to provide security. Being denied, for example, by separation, rejection or abuse, means that any sense of remaining security remaining would tend to be diminished, leaving insecurity the right to take over.

Several areas need to be considered, as they indicate insecurity in a leader's life. It is important to be aware that we all feel insecure at certain times, but this is very different from actually being insecure. It is also necessary to ensure that gift and character are balanced and to be aware that we all have the ability to harmonise them. It is difficult to write this without sounding accusatory, which is not my intention, for this is a summary that will help give understanding to some of the traits. Please note that this is not a definitive list:

- Insecure leaders like to be first, in fact, they have to be first. They like the spotlight, and always want to be in the centre of everything, making sure people see how good they are.
- Self-pity with pity parties will lead to sympathy, not empathy, which by manipulation will lead to control.
- They have a fear of insignificance and would strive for significance through performance orientation and people-pleasing, which includes God. Self-promotion is manipulation.
- They will have a deep sense of self-doubt and uncertainty about their value and place in the world, which would include a tendency of being overwhelmed with self-consciousness.
- There are often trust issues in relationships, with themselves and with God as Father.

- Everything has to go through them. This sort of micro-management disables a team and stops gifted people from taking their rightful place.
- They consider anyone 'disloyal' who disagrees with them. Everyone has a right to disagree, but what is vital is a godly response. Rejection will finally lead to division.
- They look at those who work for them as employees, and not their team. We are sons not hired workers or slaves.
- They tend to surround themselves with people they can control.
- They mishandle conflict. Insecure leaders either avoid conflict through passive-aggressive means, or they look at every situation as a potential conflict. Secure leaders handle conflict with truth and grace working together because relationships matter more than being right.
- Insecure leaders can be easily offended, which may lead to a reaction of anger and rejection.
- Insecure leaders have problems when being questioned. They can become defensive when challenged and may also give 'the silent treatment.'
- They appear to shoot down or ignore good ideas.
- They make promises that they cannot keep or have no intention of keeping.
- Some leaders have a predisposition to be easily flattered.
- They limit opportunities for other gifted people; they feel threatened.
- Some have a weakness of being jealous of other gifted people.
- Insecure leaders tend to replace people rather than develop them.
- There can be a contradiction in the way leadership is handled with either passivity or intensity in micro-managing them.
- There is a need to compare themselves with others; they want to make sure they are better.
- They can cover up weakness and failure and would attempt to create an image of being strong.

- Insecure leaders are vulnerable to a victim mentality. Some always think that they are the injured party because they feel that they are unfairly treated. There is a tendency to blame shift.

Saul the Insecure King

The people wanted a king, but they found someone who was more like an insecure celebrity than one who could rule and reign with integrity and righteousness. God's advice was to look at the heart of a man, not his outward appearance. As leaders, we need to realise that we have the power to bring hurt and pain, and sometimes, bring further damage to people's lives by the way we behave in our own security. We have a serious responsibility to be and to remain accountable. King Saul is a prime biblical example of a genuinely toxic and unaccountable insecure leader. He was anointed, impressive, loved, and gifted, but his unbridled jealous insecurities prompted him to hate David and want to kill him. Saul's insecurities sent him down a twisted path of self-destructive behaviour, and tragically, when leaders like Saul fall prey to their insecurities, they can unleash a whirlwind of hurt. It got to the place where Saul, out of his driving sense of insecurity, anger and jealously attempted to kill David three times and sadly in the end took his own life.

Saul was a fine man who was very handsome, taller than anyone from the shoulders upward, He was physically attractive and wealthy and had a sense of responsibility (1 Samuel 9:2-3). He started well as a great leader, but things quickly went downhill. Maybe it was undergirded by what he thought of himself because he saw himself as very different, than other people did.

'Saul answered [Samuel], but am I not a Benjamite, from the smallest tribe of Israel, and is not my clan the least of all the clans of the tribe of Benjamin? Why do you say such a thing to me?' (1 Samuel 9:23). He could not accept what Samuel was saying, and even later in his reign, Samuel said

to him, '*when you were little in your own eyes, were you not head over the tribes of Israel? And did not the Lord anoint you king over Israel?*' (1 Samuel 15:17). What an amazing inferiority complex he had! Saul saw himself little in his own eyes, he had a very low opinion of himself, yet at the same time his mood swings showed that he was proud, self-centred and arrogant. His insecurity told him that anyone could be a threat to his kingdom. He was an enigma, full of conflict, and often gave the wrong impression with his erratic behaviour, which was becoming more public.

Saul's relationship with God was quite haphazard. Once, he met a company of prophets, whose influence released the Spirit of the Lord upon him and he prophesied. It was as though he became a different person as God touched his heart. Later in his reign, this happened again, but it left a bad taste in all who knew him, and with sarcasm, they said,' is Saul among the prophets?' (1 Samuel 10:9-11; 19:23-24). It could be that God was impressing him to change his heart, but in both cases, he quickly reverted to his more normal negative ways. The challenge to us, is that gift and character need to be in unity, and to remember that the gifts of God are given without repentance. This is the grace of God, but what is our response to it?

Samuel had drawn all of the tribes of Israel together, in order to anoint Saul king, but when he was called to stand before them, they found he was missing, and it was only God who knew where he was. He told Samuel that Saul was hiding in the baggage! (1 Samuel 10:20-24). His insecurity, fear of man, fear of failure, and a sense of false humility, in which pride is found, drove him there. Instead of welcoming his calling, he rejected it and ran away to hide in the baggage. It was Saul's baggage that was his downfall. We all have our own baggage and can easily hide in it and be controlled by it. Interestingly, David ran towards the battle line to meet Goliath, and as he lay on the ground hit by the stone from David's sling, he ran again to Goliath and cut off his head with his sword (Samuel 17:48-51). As sons, we have the ability through the Holy Spirit to cut the heads off the giants in our own lives and deal with our baggage.

Throughout Saul's life, his insecurity was very apparent. His behaviour, physical, emotional and mental was atrocious at times, so it would be important to consider the following:

- Saul had a difficult, indifferent, or even a non-existent relationship with God. He violated God's Word by offering a sacrifice instead of obedience, he was foolhardy in disobeying God. Samuel called it rebellion, which is like the sin of witchcraft, and ultimately, he met a witch and committed suicide (1 Samuel 15:22-23). Saul never took responsibility, he never owned his wrongs, and always had excuses, blaming everyone else, and even included God.
- Fear controlled Saul. He was a proud man, afraid of criticism and he loved and even craved popular approval. Because of this, he took credit for other's achievements. Saul could be impulsive, acting unwisely, he had a thirst for revenge and his intense jealousy of David drove him to the edge of madness.
- Saul was arrogant but anxious; he intimidated whoever was in his way, he was presumptuous and driven by paranoia, which sometimes included persecution.
- He easily broke relationships and promises, he lied, was irresponsible with a lack of humility and was self-centred.

It does seem, taking into consideration Saul's 'issues,' that there is a more than a hint of narcissism here.

The Cave

When Elijah was on the run from Jezebel, after the fire at Carmel, he finally ended up at Horeb, the mountain of God. Even though he felt discouraged, despondent, disillusioned and depressed, to the extent that he felt that he wanted to die, the miraculous was still very evident. He was strengthened supernaturally as he walked at least 250 miles in forty days and nights. As he reached Horeb he went into a cave. It was there that God spoke to him and asked, 'what are you doing here?' Elijah let go his pain of rejection and self-pity and told God that although he'd been very zealous, he was now the only prophet left (1 Kings 19:9-10,14).

Many orphaned and insecure leaders take refuge in their caves, but the cave is not the place where God wants us to be. Caves are places to hide and to isolate yourself in a self-indulgent way. It gives you a dimmed view, tunnel vision, with a wrong perception, so that you cannot see beyond yourself. All you have is the sound of your voice echoing around the walls of the cave.

Elijah was driven by insecurity and fear to a place where he wanted no one to find him. It is a place very suitable for the orphan hearted, and people notice. "Where is he?" they ask. "In his cave" come the response.

The cave is not the place for a leader to be, withdrawn, hidden and not wanting to speak to anyone. Then God spoke again and said, 'come out of your cave and stand on the edge of the mountain,' for that was the place where the presence of God was. Our call for risky living is standing on the edge, moving in the extremities, in the place of faith and not in a cave! We have an honest choice to make. Are we only capable to live in a cave, which is for the orphan, the insecure and allow our self-pity to feed the wrong information that there is no one else left except poor me? The cave was very close to the edge, but it was the wrong place.

Standing on the edge is where the presence of the Lord is, and that is where I want to be.

Diotrephes

The Apostle John wrote with some anger and despair to one of the churches about Diotrephes who was the leader. What John said is very telling and utterly upfront. Diotrephes wanted to be head of all things and lord it over everyone, which demonstrates a mix of at least pride, self-ambition and arrogance. He abused his authority and refused to acknowledge the authority of the apostle John. It seems he had no time to be hospitable or care with a servant's heart, but he was quarrelsome, slanderous, critical, power-hungry, jealous and antagonistic. This exposed a root of insecurity, because his behaviour demonstrated that he was easily threatened by anyone who, he perceived, would undermine his own pre-eminence. He refused to have anyone like that near to him and would never allow them any involvement in the church. Did Diotrephes really think that someone would want to enhance their image at the expense of his? It just confirms that he had no interest in anyone, except himself.

'I have written something to the church, but Diotrephes, who likes to put himself first, does not acknowledge our authority. So if I come, I will bring up what he is doing, talking wicked nonsense against us. And not content with that, he refuses to welcome the brothers, and also stops those who want to and puts them out of the church' (3 John 9-19).

'But understand this, that in the last days there will come times of difficulty. For people will be lovers of self, lovers of money, proud, arrogant, abusive, disobedient to their parents, ungrateful, unholy, heartless, unappeasable, slanderous, without self-control, brutal, not loving good, treacherous, reckless, swollen with conceit, lovers of pleasure rather than lovers of God, having the appearance of godliness, but denying its power. Avoid such people' (2 Timothy 3:1-5).

Reasons, Excuses and Blame

Taking the above comments into consideration, we are left with a challenge as to how we live and behave as leaders regarding how we see and treat ourselves and other people. Leaders, it is time to be honest with ourselves and examine our strengths and weaknesses, and particularly the condition of our hearts. We need to critically think about our style of leadership and know that if anything we have just read affects us, instead of passing over it quickly in denial, we need to move in humility and give serious thought as to how to deal with it.

It is here that the matter of trust becomes an issue, as we will need help from others. It is a big thing for some to be openhearted and vulnerable to others about unhealed hurts, wounds, and other issues in their lives. Are there mature people that we know well that we can trust to help us? If our style of leadership is still affected by past hurts, rejection, or some sort of abuse that has contributed to our orphan heart, we need to be prepared to get some help. It is important that we do not remain in isolation. Every leader needs help, wisdom, advice and prayer, and to remain humbly in peace, rather than to react with insecure behaviour, is the way forward. It is not a time to be angry or to feel rejected if godly people disagree with you. If God is speaking to us about our style of leadership, He will more than likely use people, and this is what we have to learn to cope with.

As leaders, we need to untangle excuses and blame culture from reasons. A reason can be an explanation or justification that satisfies everyone. The danger is that with an excuse, denial takes the upper hand, and a leader would say, 'that is just the way I am' or people may say about their leaders, 'that is just the way he is' That is not a reason to accept, but it is a self-defensive excuse, which says, 'I do not have to change!' Instead of taking responsibility for a wrong, it more often than not ends up being the fault of someone else.

It is not my fault, someone else is responsible for the way I am.' An excuse is an attempt to blame someone else, or an event or circumstance rather than ourselves. Some leaders will say that they just cannot help the way they are because they are descendants of others in their families who had the same problems. A generational curse will never be a valid excuse to not change our behaviour. Excuses are negative, deceptive and irresponsible, but reasons are a more natural, peaceable response and will lead to amenable behaviour. When we are unwilling to take responsibility for our behaviour and decisions, we are making excuses. When it went wrong in the Garden of Eden, Adam blamed Eve and Eve blamed the serpent, however, there was an implication that God was to blame too.

It is essential that we make the necessary adjustments in our leadership style and looking into our unhealed childhood hurts and trauma is the place to start. You will find that some of these issues will emotionally resonate. Childhood experiences are clearly at the root of many adult problems, but we know that the power of prayer in Jesus' name can bring healing and change.

There were times with me, as mentioned previously, where God moved sovereignly giving me a revelation of my past. So much was hidden from me over the years, and secrets and lies prevailed, but the time came when what actually happened was made known, and healing began within my orphan heart. At that time, I was in the leadership of a large church however, it was God's time and things began to happen, which has led me to write about my experience of healing. In all of this, the question that needs to be answered is, 'some things you have mentioned give me a feeling of familiarity, something that I can relate to, but it is not clear enough to deal with. What shall I do?' The following prayers are keys to this:

'Lord show me what I am not seeing about myself. Open the eyes of my understanding that I may be enlightened. Search me, O God and know my heart, see if there is any hurtful way in me' (Psalms 139:23-24).

This scripture in The Passion Translation sums it up:

'God, I invite your searching gaze into my heart. Examine me through and through; find out everything that may be hidden within me. Put me to the test and sift through all my anxious cares, see if there is any path of pain I am walking on, and lead me back to your glorious, everlasting way - the path that brings me back to you.'

HEALING THE HEART - PART 1

'For in You [God] the orphan finds love and compassion and mercy'
(Hosea 14:3, AMP).

Before progressing to the specifics of healing the heart with its mindset, there are several general, but important areas that need to be considered. These will lead to the principles of healing and deliverance which will continue in the next chapter. From my experience of working through these areas in my own life, I have found that there have been some key times when God has moved in a spontaneous and sovereign way, which has brought distinct revelation to me regarding personal issues related to my own orphan heart and mindset.

One of those times took place in a leaders' meeting in Toronto, Canada, in the midst of the renewal, where the tremendous worship released a powerful presence of God across the church and many were brought into a further release of healing, which for me was very cathartic.

God Looks on the Heart

First and foremost, God looks on the heart. 'The Lord cannot see things the way you see them. People judge by outward appearance, but the Lord looks at the heart (1 Samuel 16:7). God has the unique ability to see inside a person; He knows our true character because He looks at the heart. David was God's choice - imperfect but faithful, and always a man after God's heart. Appearances can be deceiving. The outward appearance cannot reveal what people are really like, they do not show their sense of worth, value, character or identity. *'Above all else, guard your heart, for everything you do flows from it'* (Proverbs 4:23). The keyword is 'everything,' which includes both good and bad.

It is clear that the very core of our life, our heart, can be affected and damaged by the orphan condition, and this requires a process of healing, transformation and renewal. The condition of our heart depends, firstly, on the things we intentionally allow in, and secondly, on the suddenness of the shock and trauma that can happen unintentionally. They afflict the heart, which can then become broken, that is broken into pieces or fractured - broken-hearted people are not uncommon. Jesus came to mend our brokenness and heal our fractures from deep distress, like pieces of broken earthenware or delicate porcelain, and to set them free from their unwanted limitations. He wants our orphan heart to be changed and transformed to be the heart of a son. 'He heals the brokenhearted and binds up their wounds (Psalms 147: 3 NJKV).

Lies or Truth?

The Scriptures clearly state that Satan is a father; Jesus called him the father of lies, *'you are of your father the devil, and your will is to do your father's desires. He was a murderer from the beginning and has nothing to do with the truth because there is no truth in him. When he lies, he speaks out of his character, for he is a liar and the father of lies'* John 8:44, ESV).

Satan told the first lie to Eve and has been continuing to undermine our identity with his lies since. Adam, who was next to Eve, watched everything without interrupting and stopping the conversation. Eve then drew Adam in and he believed the lie. To believe is to receive and as soon as they disobeyed God everything changed, for they lost their relationship with Him. Immediately, they saw that they were naked, and all they could do was hide in fear and shame, but most of all, an orphan mindset was seeded in them which has become a dark legacy to humanity. As much as we are aware of the power of sin in our lives and have understood the effect it has had upon us, we also need to be enlightened about the way the orphan heart has affected us. Satan is still the father of lies, and we have believed the lie, which has been established in us and has hindered us from fully entering into our destiny in God as sons and daughters.

What many have missed is that when Jesus came to preach and teach about the Kingdom of God, a great part of what He said related to His Father. Introducing His Father to the people was a core part of His ministry. It still is, but the enemy continues to attempt to deceive us in whatever way possible, and to deflect us away from the Father's love. Jesus came to challenge the lie of Satan with the truth. He declared that 'you shall know the truth and the truth [reality] will set [make] you free (John 8:32).

Truth is liberating, it will give us freedom; it is a promise that gives revelation because it is far beyond a principle, it is a person! 'Thomas said, we have no idea where you are going, so how can we know the way? Jesus told him, I am the way, the truth, and the life. No one can come to the Father except through me (John 14:5-6 NLT). As we submit to Jesus, He shows us the Father (John 14:9); as we receive the Spirit of Jesus, He reveals Abba Father to us (Galatians 4:6) because He is the Spirit of truth, and will guide us into all truth (John 16:13). 'Pilate said to Jesus, what is truth?' (John 18:38). He did not realise that he was looking at the incarnation of truth.

What David longed for was truth in his heart, '*behold, You desire truth in the innermost being, And in the hidden part [of my heart] You will make me know wisdom*' (Psalms 51:6 AMP). The enemy wants our orphan hearts manipulated and fed by lies, but, we, like David, can we seek after God, and see our orphan hearts healed and transformed. With truth rooted in our hearts, we will be in a place to receive the revelation of the Holy Spirit who will bring the wisdom that we desire to live in the Father's love. Enough is enough; it is time to deal with the lies of Satan and any tormenting and afflicting demonic powers that have been internalised in our orphan hearts, and with the help of the Holy Spirit know freedom to live in the reality of Jesus, who is the truth.

Event or Process

There have been occasions when God has dramatically moved in my life regarding my orphan heart and brought revelation that I was able to take hold of and apply to my life. Truth is more than theory, for it has to be known, applied, and put into practice. Minds need renewing. These one-off events are foundational to us moving into total healing. They can be spontaneous and sudden. It is up to us to have an open heart to the moving of God and trust Him in His timing.

In a previous chapter, I told of when I was in a leader's lunchtime and God broke into my life and released so much pain concerning my father. It was almost an ambush, but in the glorious atmosphere of worship I went with it and that, 'happening' was a key to further healing of my orphan heart. Initial breakthroughs are necessary and should be welcome, but we need to be aware of the process that flows from that. It was as though I went from step to step punctuated by the suddenness of God impacting me. More and more I have learned to trust the Holy Spirit as He tutors me by leading me into the truth of sonship. The danger for us is to try and work at our healing ourselves, however, this is not a time to strive, but to rest in what God is showing us. Performance comes out of an orphan mindset, as does attempt to please God by our actions. The credit is all His and nothing of us.

Taking Personal Responsibility

As we go further in the process of our healing, the issue of personal responsibility will begin to come into prominence. This always starts with a choice that comes from a willing heart, and even though you may be feeling vulnerable and insecure, your response will establish your intention in the spiritual realm.

First of all, we need to understand that it always starts with God and His initiative, and in that we trust Him to do what is right. As we open ourselves to Him in an honest and vulnerable way, we need to trust Him by giving Him the right to make us aware of the specific issues of the heart that need healing. The heart cry of David was, *'search me, Oh God and know my heart, know my anxious thoughts, see if there is any hurtful way in me'* (Psalms 139:23-24). Giving God the total right over your orphan heart and mindset is a necessary risk. Now is a crucial time to seek God and to open ourselves to Him regarding any revealed or hidden issues, such as the lies and the effects of internalised hurts and trauma that have formed the orphan mindset, and then begin to trust Him to release His hand of healing on us. We know that God is preparing a bride to show His glory to the world and to move in the power of the Spirit with freedom and purity. The day of the orphan is over, for He wants sons released into the fulness of their inheritance.

Recognition of all this is very important, and for the orphan hearted person to admit their deep need to God and also to themselves is very difficult, because, in their eyes, it shows weakness or vulnerability. However, if you have come this far already, your seriousness in dealing with the lie of the orphan, as you began to turn towards the truth and reality of sonship, is evident. Therefore, the only way to wholeness and freedom is to confess your spiritual poverty, impotence and personal inadequacies. Most orphan-hearted people struggle to receive anything without thinking that they would only deserve it if they were to then give something back, because they are convinced that they would be in debt as a result. However, we know that the very essence of Christianity is that all debts have been paid in full, and through God's outrageous grace and unconditional love we can now receive it. This now becomes the place of trust and may be the biggest challenge so far, because, on the one hand, God has made us give us His love, yet on the other hand, He has made us receive that love without any cost to ourselves. We can take action by intentionally and continuously making the right choice to go forward into God's purposes for us. Doing this will establish within us the fact that we refuse to give the enemy any ground to afflict and torment us in this vital situation. 'Faith is a choice I make and a position I hold.'

Facing the Past

Once we take personal responsibility, we can face the past particularly knowing that God is not just concerned about the future, but also, that He is committed to giving us relief, with His reassuring presence, from the pain of our past. 'You've gone into my future to prepare the way, and in kindness you follow behind me to spare me from the harm of my past (Psalms 139:5, TPT). Living in denial of the past will not dispose of its pain, for even though we attempt to forget these traumatic issues, all we do is bury the problems deeper within us. They remain alive and tend to surface suddenly. The way forward is to face the truth, that these damaging situations continually cause, and then begin to deal with them with the help of God. Knowing that God is with us gives us the strength and determination to take those first steps into liberty.

Empathy and Encouragement

Be encouraged, it is Jesus we go to for healing, for He is the one who identifies in every way with us in our pain and unhealed hurt. 'For we do not have a high priest who is unable to empathise with our weaknesses, but we have one who has been tempted in every way, just as we are--yet he did not sin.' 'For we have not an high priest which cannot be touched with the feeling of our infirmities; but was in all points tempted like as we are, yet without sin' (Hebrews 4:15 KJV).

When the enemy comes to condemn, torment, and attempt to afflict us further, we have Jesus who can identify with every painful issue, including the orphan heart, in our lives. When Jesus on the cross cried out to His Father, 'my God, my God why have you forsaken me' (Matthew 27:46). He could have said, 'my God, my God why have you orphaned me,' Compassion was a key and personal impetus in Jesus' ministry, for it poured out of Him in a release of divine power, healing the people. Jesus is not cold, emotionless and unfeeling; He is not distant and reserved, but is tender, kind and understanding.

Deliverance and Healing

There are two main areas related to healing and deliverance, and both are important to consider for both have their part to play. Principally, the heart will need healing, and any specific demon will need to be expelled from those being afflicted or oppressed. You cannot cast out an orphan heart, but what you can do is deal with the demonic spirits that feed it. The orphan heart will require healing, which is a process. In its unhealed state, the orphan heart will develop an orphan mindset. This mindset is a pattern of habitual thinking, mentality, and attitude, which often begins to develop in childhood, and includes learned behaviour. As we have seen in previous chapters, the heart becomes wounded in many ways through the circumstances and issues of life, including being affected by deprivation, separation and rejection amongst the many other negatives. This way of thinking will give the enemy a foothold (Ephesians 4:27) and the father of lies will plant a seed, which will entice the person to accept and believe it, and it could become a stronghold. The fruit of this will undermine the person's identity, destiny and purpose creating dysfunction in the way they live.

Jesus, after reading the appropriate portion from Isaiah 61 in the synagogue, declared that 'today this scripture is fulfilled in your hearing' (Luke 4:21).

Nothing has changed, the words of Jesus are as powerful today, as they were when He spoke them in Nazareth. 'The Spirit of the Lord is upon me, because He has anointed me to preach the gospel to the poor; he has sent me to heal the broken-hearted, to proclaim liberty to the captives and recovery of sight to the blind, to set at liberty those who are oppressed; to proclaim the acceptable year of the Lord' (Luke 4:18-21; Isaiah 61:1).

The setting of people free from the demonic is a sign that the Kingdom of God has come. This was so much part of the mission of Jesus to bring truth and freedom. *'But if I drive out demons by the finger of God, then the kingdom of God has come upon you'* (Luke 11:20).

Why the finger? This is the only time the word is mentioned in the New Testament, and is, significantly, found twice in the Old Testament. Firstly, when the Egyptian Magicians submitted to a higher power [the finger of God] when they could not reproduce some of the plagues (Exodus 8:19) and secondly when the Ten Commandments were written on stone by the finger of God (Exodus 31:18). As much as God is Spirit, the term finger must relate to the expression of God by the Holy Spirit, and it implies a concentrated power that is specifically applied. It is the release of the immense, unlimited and dynamic power of God, which, when focussed in a laser-like context, releases something which no human or spiritual agency can compete with.

When removing demonic powers from people's lives, we do what Jesus did through the Holy Spirit, the finger of God. *'And you know that God anointed Jesus of Nazareth with the Holy Spirit and with power. Then Jesus went around doing good and healing all who were oppressed [overpowered] by the devil, for God was with him'* (Acts 10:38).

Be aware, that Jesus gave no specific methodology regarding healing the broken-hearted, or delivering those from demonic powers, however, there are some specific points to consider in ministry, which we will look at later. Also, whilst the initial breakthrough of being set free from demonic oppression is often immediate, getting help concerning moving into a change of lifestyle is necessary, particularly in our attitude, and in the way, we think in daily living. The healing and ultimate transformation of the orphan heart and its mindset is no different; it too is an event and a process.

The Promise of Hope

'*Therefore, behold, I will allure her, I will bring her into the wilderness, and speak comfort to her. I will give her back her vineyards from there, and the Valley of Achor as a door of hope; she shall sing there, as in the days of her youth, as in the day when she came up from the land of Egypt*' (Hosea 2:14-15). What God is saying, is that He will attract and captivate His people with His grace, love and words of comfort. He wants to reassure us, to put us at ease and into 'shalom' living, as He speaks tenderly and affectionately to us. His promise is for peace, harmony, and fruitfulness in our lives, with healing happening throughout our being. He will return what has been taken from us, but most of all He will transform the Valley of Achor, which means trouble, into a door of hope. It is a door that needs to be open by us so that we can commune in our rightful place as sons with our Heavenly Father.

Taking Hold of the Promise

The promise of God to Joshua (Joshua 1) regarding the destiny of Israel going into the Promised Land needs personal consideration and application as we take hold of God's promises for our lives. God declared to Joshua that He would give him the land, and even described its boundaries (v3-4). Three times God said to Joshua, 'be strong and courageous' (v6,7,9) and twice said that He will be with him and would never leave him or forsake him (v5,9). God spoke about obeying Him and meditating on the scripture to know prosperity and success in the land (v7-8) and He encouraged Joshua not to be terrified and discouraged (v9).
All of this was a fantastic prelude to God's promise, but it was not enough,

because, despite it all, Joshua still had to go in and take possession of the land that God was giving him! We have a promise from God about our healing and freedom. God has declared it, and we can consider it, think about it and even preach it because we have been told it is ours, but until we possess it, everything is to no avail. In other words, nothing will happen! We are called to claim the ground in our lives; to clear the ground and then take possession; to take back what the enemy has stolen.

It is a fact that God has already accomplished that, and the triumph of 'tetelestai', which is Jesus declaring 'it is finished', puts the cross into its right perspective. We can overcome because He has overcome, and with love and grace, for He has given us the right to be sons and not orphans. Joshua succeeded, with God breaking through most amazingly and miraculously, which saw them across the Jordan to the destruction of the stronghold Jericho. God Has something much better for us! We can know victory in our lives as we move forward having claimed the promise of sonship.

Principles

It is said that only the broken become masters at mending. Several principles are essential and fundamental to your healing. They are not only a reminder, but a necessary provocation for you to look into your own life and take back what the enemy has stolen. These areas are vital to you in your preparation for healing (some of the specific subjects are described more fully in the two chapters on 'Consequences'. The challenge is to be vulnerable to the ways of God in order to discern the unhealed areas in your life. You will see that there are many issues, which are meaningful for the orphan hearted to consider. I am sure, like me, you will prayerfully consider whether you resonate with them and, if so, begin to consider how counselling and prayer ministry will help.

I trust that you will receive an understanding of why your painful circumstances happened. Once revelation, and an understanding of 'why' these things had happened to me, I found that I had an impetus to begin the process of moving forward into healing. In that sudden moment when the secrets and lies of my family were revealed, I became very much aware of my unhealed hurts and was able, with understanding, to make the right decision to come into healing. You may be aware, that each in one of these subjects there would be enough to form a book. Should you feel the need to investigate any of them in more detail, however, you would have no difficulty in finding the great amount of information that there is in books on the subject, and in other writings, papers, etc., which are available on the internet.

Repentance and Faith

'If we confess our sins, he is faithful and just and will forgive us our sins and purify [cleanse] us from all unrighteousness' (1 John 1:9). As we confess with a clear acknowledgement of our sin, the promise of God to release us will be imparted. God cannot be unfaithful to that which He promises. This means that God not only wants to forgive you because He is faithful, but that He has to forgive you because He is just. What never changes, is that He is there to forgive us because the death of Jesus has made it a matter of justice, that God would forgive. 'But if we are living in the light, as God is in the light, then we have fellowship with each other, and the blood of Jesus, his Son, cleanses [purifies] us from all sin' (1 John 1:7 NLT). The blood of Jesus is efficacious. It is effective to the point that all past sin is removed to free us to live pure lives. There is no stain that is so deep that the blood of Jesus cannot take it away, because there is no limit to its cleansing power.

- Repentance is a change of mind, a deliberate redirection, and a complete reorientation for the future. This is penitence, contrition and remorse, and a serious business.
- We turn away to turn, in utter trust, to God.
- Therefore, recognise and renounce the lie and deception of the enemy regarding the orphan heart.

- Sinning unintentionally (Leviticus 4:1-3; 5:14) is still sin and although it may not be a deliberate choice, sometimes our nature causes us to react in a way we did not expect, which could be surprising to us. It seems as though we were not aware of what was happening, it was not planned, it was inadvertent, but this is not the time for excuses, it needs dealing with, for it is still sin. God knows what is hidden within us more than we do, and even though we may be personally shocked, just remember that He knows about it anyway.
- Recognise the incredible fact that God's grace never changes - it is still outrageous, and His love is still unconditional. We are so gloriously accepted!

Forgiveness: Freeing Ourselves from the Past

When Jesus, in answer to Peter's question about how many times we forgive a person said, 'I tell you, not seven times, but seventy-seven times' (Matthew 18:22) He was talking about a perpetual lifestyle of forgiveness. Peter thought that he should forgive someone up to, possibly, seven times, but Jesus took it very much further, and so should we. Ask God to show you anyone you need to forgive, who was connected to any abusive event that you have been affected by.

Abuse can be verbal, emotional, physical, sexual or spiritual, and will be traumatic. Who do you need to forgive? It may be your father, mother, siblings, or someone else in your family, or those close to you relationally, as well as others who were in any way responsible for hurting and wounding you. It may be something that happened many years ago in childhood, but you can ask God to show you. He knows, as He was there. You will also need to consider forgiving yourself because of your negative reactions and feelings, that you spoke against yourself, including curses, vows, and pronouncements (see below). If you do not forgive yourself the personal shame and guilt will grow further within you. Consider the following:

- The greater the offence, the greater the need to forgive your offender. The past offence will control us until we let it go and forgive in Jesus' name. We cannot withhold from others that which we need ourselves.

- Continue forgiving until the peace of God overtake the pain and quells it. Being hurt deeply by someone means that we need to keep forgiving them until we know we are free from their influence.

- Grace means extending to others the same forgiveness that God has extended to us. God heals all of our iniquities [sins], Psalms 103:3. Grace brings restoration and resolution.

- Unforgiveness will continue to give the right to the pain to bring further damage.

- Unforgiveness underpins the judgement in your heart to the person that hurt you.

- Forgiveness releases you from the consequences of bitterness and judgement, which can be strongholds as they will ultimately become strongly attached. Do not give them the right to remain.

- It is important to understand that if you say you are unable able to, or you refuse to, forgive, you will find that this negative attitude holds a power, which will detrimentally affect you, as well as the other person. It will become a judgement and will continue to build up resentment and anger. Humility is a key for release, therefore keep short accounts.

- The power to forgive is personal, no one can give it to you, and no one can take it away. Forgiveness is self-healing, self-empowering and self-liberating. As they are mixed with the grace of God, and with the power that we have to choose to forgive, the transformation will take place. We can all afford to forgive, it is free.

'I call forgiveness the best revenge against the perpetrator,' a Second World War survivor of Auschwitz. (The Times, 25 April 2015)

From Victim to Perpetrator

The orphan-hearted person is a victim, who in all probability will develop a victim mentality through the orphan mindset. Amongst other things, their vulnerability underlines their sense of powerlessness, as it gives them a habitual way of looking at life being motivated by the feeling of being unfairly treated and taken advantage of. Believing that they are trapped drives them to act like a victim with a perception of being a failure in life. The temptation is to indulge in a pity party or attempt to elicit pity from anyone. The victim mentality rests on the following areas:

- It is not only that bad things happen, but that they keep happening!
- Other people, events, or circumstances are always to blame. Blame was apparent in the beginning when Adam blamed Eve, and unsubtly God, while Eve blamed the serpent (Genesis 3:12-13). It is easier to blame something or someone else.
- Even making the effort to change is fruitless, so there is no point in changing because anything that is done will not make any difference.

There is always a choice, which can either lead to healing and freedom, or the victim status, which can be used to seek and gain attention, sympathy, or feeling sorry for yourself. However, this will lead you to perpetuate the problem, which could mean that the next step is to become the perpetrator. You know you have been wronged, you know you have done nothing wrong, but hiding in your victim state, fed by your orphan mindset, will keep you in darkness. There is a better way, and once that is acknowledged, you can open up to the one who laid down His life as a victim and died in your place.

Generational Inheritance

It is clear that some of a child's learned behaviour can end up being hidden deep within, and although this behaviour may remain dormant for a while, it does not take much to trigger it and for it to cause a reaction, and so we may end up acting in the very same way as the person we vowed we'd never become! This reveals a pattern that happens generationally, such as in the case of a grandfather who, motivated by anger, is not able to show love and affection to his son, something which later ends up being replicated in his grandson.

It can mean the possibility of the orphan heart manifesting in at least three generations, and it demonstrates that families can create the same personality trait, over and over again, across generations, resulting in the victims becoming perpetrators and then, probably without even realising it, becoming like a member of the family that they would never wish to be.

The scripture is clear that God can visit the sins of the fathers on the sons and daughters. We can inherit sin and every kind of weakness to the third and fourth generations (Exodus 20:3-5, 34:5-7). Although we can exhibit the same behaviour as our parents, we need to know that all that Jesus did at the cross has the power to set us free from any of the negative traits inherited. Even though our ancestors' sins may have affected us, we are always held accountable by God for our own sins and behaviour. We can make the right choices and take responsibility. Why should we allow these issues to bring us into bondage when we know the power of the cross deals with any and every generational issue? Amazingly, our Heavenly Father God shows his love to a thousand generations (Exodus 20:6; Deuteronomy 7:9).

Soul Ties

A soul tie is a strong connection in the spiritual realm; it holds us in a relationship with people. They can be also linked to generational inheritance. Wrong emotional ties and wrong bonding can affect relationships, especially in families. Ungodly ties are formed through unhealthy relationships with those who wish to dominate, control or abuse mentally, sexually or physically. Godly ties are formed through loving and caring relationships, whether in a family or a strong friendship such as David and Jonathan, (1 Samuel 18:1-4). Evil spirits can affect people ancestrally because there is a connection through the spiritual ties in family and other relationships. We can apply the work of the cross to our lives, with repentance and confession, and deal with any negative family predisposition. We can bring the authority and power of Jesus' name to cut off the ungodly soul ties, including any demonic interference, as we bless the godly ties.

Rejection

Rejection is an important part of the context of the orphan heart and its mindset. You will recall from a previous chapter that it can be defined as the inability to give or receive love.

When Adam and Eve left the Garden of Eden they were separated and isolated from God and the power of rejection began to afflict them. This power became very apparent in the next generation with Cain the firstborn, as we have seen previously, murdered his brother and as God banished him from the land, declared him to be a restless wanderer in the earth (Genesis 4:1-14). Many rejected people are restless wanderers.

Three root areas undergird rejection and discernment is needed to divide between the orphan mindset and the demonic:

- Rebellion: This is an aggressive reaction displayed through anger, arrogance and criticism, and will in some instances erupt like a volcano intimidating many.
- Self-rejection: This is rejection turned inwards, causing self-hate and self-harm, including thoughts of suicide. The power of the mind and tongue can bring life or death, Proverbs 18:21.
- Self-protection: Rejected people are wrongly motivated to self-protect, as fear drives them to run and hide, which is a delusion.

Control, which can be simply defined as 'power over someone' has intertwined itself in all of the three roots. The fruit of control can be expressed in domination, manipulation and intimidation.

Rejection has a connection to abuse, which can be verbal, mental, emotional and spiritual. It is being deliberately hurt by someone else.

Abandonment coming out of rejection will cultivate the orphan heart and help to strengthen the victim mentality.

For a further detailed examination see my book, 'Rejection Hurts.'

Bitter-Root Judgement

One aspect of the bitter-root judgment is a judgment that a person makes at some time during their childhood against his or her father, mother, caregiver, or others close to them. Often, it is a subconscious judgment that has remained hidden for a period of time rather than a conscious one which is close to the surface. A root of bitterness comes from unforgiveness, and this will lead to resentment that will defile or poison others. *'See to it that no one comes short of the grace of God; that no root of bitterness springing up causes trouble, and by it many be defiled'* (Hebrews 2:15 NASB). These judgments are rooted in the past but will influence your present and future. Then, because of the law of sowing and reaping, the one who judges at some point in their lives, will sentence themselves to do the very thing that they judged in the past (Romans 2:1-3 TPT).

Look for patterns or habits, that you are aware of in your own life, that have manifested fear, doubt, rejection, heartache, jealousy or anger. These patterns may result from judgments that you have made against others, including your mother or father. God wants us to honour our parents, (Deuteronomy 5:16). This can mean to forgive, but most of all it means to accept their humanity. Are there situations where you repeat the same behaviour over and over? Through repentance and faith, we can deal with these roots once and for all in Jesus' name.

Pronouncement, The Curse, and The Inner Vow

These three areas are an amalgam of negative self-talk and self-sabotage, which leads to undermining any attempt even to consider a change. Because of the sense of betrayal, they can be fed by anger at yourself, as well as other people who have hurt you. We start by holding onto the judgement proclaimed, but ultimately, we find that they have a 'strong hold' upon us!

- A pronouncement is an authoritative and powerful statement of judgement, and that in itself triggers the curse or inner vow. It is a legal term that hands down a judgement, but when related to a curse or inner vow, it not only becomes established and empowered in a legal sense, but it also creates something in the spiritual realm, which gives the enemy rights. Parental pronouncements, such as 'you are useless,' or 'I wish you had never been born,' are abusive curses that can negatively affect a child for a lifetime.

- The term 'curse' may seem an antiquated word. It means a wish to speak, declare or pronounce evil, abuse, or misfortune over someone, something else such as land or property. It could mean appealing to a supernatural power to come and do harm.

- An inner vow is a promise made by you to yourself. For example, you have been hurt once again, and you get to the place in your pain and anger where you clearly and strongly speak into yourself with a vow. You are determined not to allow yourself to be hurt and wounded again so, you use the words, 'I will never…,' which makes a powerful and controlling pronouncement as you exercise the will. If you are angry with yourself, a thought or pronouncement such as, 'I wish I was,' will be very effective in cursing yourself.

- Be mindful that curses and inner vows go deep, and certainly if spoken in childhood can be forgotten about, but this does not mean they have disappeared. They may be triggered by circumstances or situations in the future. You reap what you sow.

These areas can be dealt with, as you acknowledge your involvement with repentance and forgiveness. Then, it is necessary to renounce the pronouncements and judgements made and cut off the power of those words in the name of Jesus. The price that Jesus paid at the cross has set us free from the power of every curse pronounced on us or that we have pronounced on others.

Emotions

- Emotions are critical in their contribution to the release of inner pain in the process of healing. They need to surface so that the pain can be released to our healing God.
- Many are easily trapped in a deep box of emotional pain; they feel like they are prisoners paralysed by fear, guilt and shame.
- Adam and Eve hid from God because of their fear, guilt, and shame, but God found them (Genesis 3:9-10). However, God in His mercy did something that pointed towards the cross. He took an animal (a lamb?) and sacrificed it to made garments to cover them. It was a blood sacrifice. We need no longer hide away, or hide our pain deep within our unconscious, because at the cross, Jesus, the Lamb of God, made a way for us to be released from all of the inner pain hidden in the emotions. Closing the heart and trying to bury the pain believing it will go away is denial, and therefore deceptive. You cannot hide away - it causes further emotional and mental pain. Your pain is real, so do not pretend it is not.
- 'He collects our tears in his bottle' (Psalms 56:8). Amazingly, not only does God know us intimately, but He also knows every tear that we release. He collects them, and not one will be lost. He also records them in His book of remembrance, meaning that He won't forget any of them. He understands the reasons why we are emotional, and the depth of pain that we feel - something which emphasises His care and compassion for us
- Therefore, do not be afraid of your unhealed emotions, but be

transparent and vulnerable as you commit them and yourself to God, trusting Him to bring the necessary healing.

- There may be a necessity to repent and ask forgiveness from your negative feelings, reactions, and attitude to those that have hurt you, as well as appropriately forgiving them.
- It is important to first separate the emotions from the effect that any demonic power may have. Then, deal with those powers before bringing healing to the emotions.
- Jesus Christ is the same yesterday, today and forever (Hebrews 13:8). As you invite Him by His Spirit to come into the situation, remember He transcends time and space. Therefore, He is able to come into the source of the pain and bring release and healing, whenever that was.
- Ask for a revelation of the Father's love to be released as healing takes place.

Catharsis

- In many cases, there will be a deep release of pain, which describes the process of the purifying, purging, relaxing and releasing effect of a dramatic emotional experience of the past. It is the conscious expression of repressed emotions.
- It is possible that the emotional release is linked to a desire to relieve the unconscious conflict in a process that will lead to restoration and renewal.
- 'Joseph wept so loudly that the Egyptians and Pharaoh's household heard him (Genesis 45:2).
- Weeping may remain for a night, but joy comes with the morning (Psalms 30:5).

HEALING THE HEART -
PART 2

The Battleground of the Mind
Deliverance

We have, in the previous chapter, considered a biblical basis for deliverance and seen how foundational it was in the ministry of Jesus. It was such a crucial part in bringing the good news of the Kingdom of God to the nation, as well as in giving that mandate to the disciples. Deliverance also continued after the resurrection of Jesus when the church began to grow. There are many examples in the gospels and Luke's testimony of the early church:

'And he called to him his twelve disciples and gave them authority over unclean spirits, to cast them out, and to heal every disease and every affliction' (Matthew 10:1).

'And the crowds with one accord paid attention to what was being said by Philip, when they heard him and saw the signs that he did. For unclean spirits, crying out with a loud voice, came out of many who had them, and many who were paralysed or lame were healed' (Acts 8:6-7).

'As we were going to the place of prayer, we were met by a slave girl who had a spirit of divination [Greek: python] and brought her owners much gain by fortune-telling. She followed Paul and us, crying out, these men are servants of the Most High God, who proclaim to you the way of salvation. And this she kept doing for many days. Paul, having become greatly annoyed, turned and said to the spirit, I command you in the name of Jesus Christ to come out of her. And it came out that very hour (Acts 16:16-18).

The power of Satan and his demons should not to be underestimated. Deliverance was a vital part of the ministry of Jesus, and as we follow Him it should be central to our calling too. Jesus spoke with an unparalleled and divine authority, and He was not the only first-century rabbi and teacher to cast out demons. The difference was in the manner in which Jesus ordered demonic powers out of a person's life, in a way in which demonstrated that the Kingdom of God was at hand. It was His authority (Greek: exousia) the right, and His power, (Greek: dunamis) the dynamic. This is not through human ability and strength, but through the power of the Holy Spirit and motivated by love and compassion.

There are many times in the Gospels where Jesus cast out demons, for example: 'Demons came out of many people' (Luke 4:41) and the scene in the synagogue at Capernaum where Jesus was confronted by a demon in a man as He was teaching. It was full-on with the demon crying out that it knew who Jesus was, 'the Holy one of God' (Mark 1:23-28). The people were amazed, not by the demonic, but by the authority, He had to make the demon obey Him.

The New Testament Greek word 'daimonizomai,' describes a variety of conditions of a physical, emotional, mental [mind] nature identified as a direct demonic influence. It can be defined as having the presence of a demon that has taken an opportunity to impact a person. This is not ownership, because as Christians we have given our rights totally to God. Before renovating a house, you need to own it, and if we have given ownership of our lives to God, then He can bring the necessary restoration.

It is amazing to know that the man who had over 6000 demons was later sat peacefully at Jesus' feet, dressed and in his right mind (Luke 8:35). This is the good news of the Kingdom of God.

The Demonic, the Emotions and the Mind

It is possible that the demonic can attach to emotional pain and affect the mind with its memories, thus causing distress. The demonic will attempt to harass, afflict and oppress through the various hurts and trauma related to the orphan heart and its mindset. Scripture warns us not to give the enemy an opportunity or foothold which can create an opening (Ephesians 4:27). It is obvious now that the enemy was able to take advantage of the circumstances surrounding the beginning of my life. My emotions and my thinking were influenced over the years by negative thoughts which triggered me to overreact in anger.

Demonic powers are often attached to the mind and the emotions, so it is important to first separate the demonic from the emotions and the orphan mindset. Then cast out the demon. Trying to bring healing to damaged emotions and the mind whilst it is still affected by the demonic could bring about some unnecessary confusion or disruption because the demon would still be free to torment. Declare a separation first, deal with the demonic, and afterwards pray for healing in the emotions and the mind as appropriate.

The Orphan Spirit - Definition and Process of Deliverance

The Orphan Spirit is the key demonic power that will ultimately create a stronghold in a person's life through unhealed hurts and wounds. These may be caused by the consequences of rejection, abandonment, fear, etc, by the primary carers, particularly the father, which would create a void when there is no love, affection, intimacy or acceptance. This would, in turn, allow demonic powers to attach to the mind and the emotions, and would lead ultimately to an orphan mindset. He or she would then be left with a wrong perspective in their relationships, and this is likely to make it difficult for them to closely engage with their Heavenly Father. In working through the process of seeing someone being set free from demonic powers, I have found through my experience that this need not be a long, laborious or meticulous process. There are, of course, some important points to always remember.

Firstly, the person being prayed for will need to understand:

- The orphan spirit and its purpose.
- The Holy Spirit is the tutor and teacher (Galatians 4:6).
- The nature of Abba Father.
- The promise of Jesus is not to leave us as orphans (John 14:18).
- Bring your past and present hurts to Jesus and reach out to Him for healing and release.
- Take responsibility for all wrong actions and attitudes.
- Repentance and confession, which are not an option.
- The efficacy of the blood of Jesus still cleanses and purifies sin.
- Ask God for forgiveness for embracing the attitude and behaviour of the orphan spirit including any anger, bitterness, blame, or other feelings against others, and crucially to yourself. He is faithful and just to forgive us.

Secondly, the person praying should take into account the following principles:

- Everyone has their own method of ministry, and no one has a monopoly on everything. Interestingly, Jesus cast out demons; the disciples saw Him do it, and then He sent them out to do the same, however, He did not tell them exactly how to do it.
- We have the authority and the power to deal with the demonic; the same 'right' and the 'might' that Jesus had. Not only has Jesus

given us a mandate for ministry, but also an impartation of the Holy Spirit to set people free. 'These miraculous signs will accompany those who believe: They will cast out demons in my name' (Mark 16:17).

- Have we missed a simple way to cast out demons? It is clear that the demons acknowledged Jesus not as their leader, but as the Son of God He was sovereign over them, and they knew that He had the power to cast them out. They had to submit to Him, and they never attempted to resist Him. Jesus evicted demons simply by a command, which showed the power of God's word. 'He cast out evil spirits with a word' (Matthew 8:16). There was no long formula.

- Therefore, in ministry, we can simply apply that delegated authority of the power of Jesus' name. He only used one word, 'go,' when dealing with the demons in the two men (Matthew 8:28).

- Jesus said that you know the Kingdom of God has come to you when I drive out demons by the finger of God (Luke 11:20). When we pray in His name, the authority of the Kingdom of God is with us, and demons have to go.

- Be open for any further revelation of the Holy Spirit, such as the word of knowledge. He will guide us into all truth (John 16:13).

- Repent from any judgements and inner vows and cut ungodly soul ties.

- Separate any demonic power from the mind and emotions.

- Jesus said, 'I will give you the keys of the kingdom of heaven; whatever you bind on earth will be bound in heaven, and whatever you loose on earth will be loosed in heaven.' The keys of the Kingdom that He has given us, include the authority that we have to declare His word to bind or loose in His name. We bind the power of the demon and set the person free.

- Tell the demon to leave the person in Jesus' name.

- Ask the Holy Spirit to fill them with His presence and to bring further revelation of adoption and sonship.

Points for Consideration:

- Jesus cast out demons wherever he went. To cast out means commanding the demon to come out of the person; to expel, to drive out, to call out, to banish and to send them away. Jesus did not always call a demon by a specific name, He sometimes used a more general name like a spirit of infirmity (Luke 13:11 NKJV), or an unclean spirit, (Matthew 12:43 ESV). The Holy Spirit will give you the appropriate discernment.

- The Syrophoenician Woman's daughter was demonized (Matthew 15:21-28; Mark 7:24-30) but the child was not with her mother, she was at home. The faith of the woman inspired Jesus to pray right there and then; a prayer by distance! 'He sent His word and healed them' (Psalms 107:20).

- Reaction to pain, triggered by hurts and wounds can make a person susceptible to other demonic intrusions. Rejection, for example, can bring deep wounding and as already explained, makes a person vulnerable to the demonic. There are three roots of rejection: Rebellion, Self-Rejection and Fear of Rejection or Self-Protection (see my book 'Rejection Hurts' for more of an in-depth study). There are other ways the enemy can afflict us, such as by fear, shame, etc. Each of these can be demons in its own right.

- Anger is a reckless and impulsive trigger to the orphan heart and mindset. 'In your anger do not sin: Do not let the sun go down while you are still angry' (Ephesians 4:26). We can be angry and not sin, which is legitimate, but if we constantly react in anger.

The Battleground of the Mind

It is easy to underestimate the powerful impact that thoughts can have on our lives. It is said that it is probable that a person generates an average of around 40,000 thoughts a day, which is one in less than every thirty seconds! These are a mixture of positive and negative thoughts, all of which contribute to our day-to-day life experiences and will influence how we respond and behave. Thought patterns that have been established over many years, often from childhood, will influence how we interpret life experiences, and the response to them. It is important to recognise the trigger points that can send a person into a spiral or cycle, ending in the comfort of the orphan mindset.

I have come to realise that manipulation, dominance and intimidation can affect someone with an orphan mindset. Mindsets are habitual patterns, and when triggered, they automatically operate in an unchangeable way. This is a stronghold, and it needs to be identified, understood and replaced through the renewal of our minds by God's transforming power. Some professionals would say, 'what you think you become.' As we think, 'orphan,' we will begin to behave like orphans, and ultimately live like an orphan. 'Your beliefs become your thoughts. Your thoughts become your words. Your words become your actions. Your actions become your habits. Your habits become your values. Your values become your destiny,' Gandhi.

In its unhealed state, the orphan heart will quickly reveal a deep-seated belief that God is distant and you feel separated and isolated from Him. The enemy would want us to be prisoners of our minds. King Solomon said, 'for as he thinks in his heart, so is he' (Proverbs 23:7). We have let our minds rule us, but there is another way, another set of values, a different framework, that instead of being entrenched in the deep wounds of the past, we can know liberty and freedom whereby orphan hearts can be healed with mindsets renewed by the power of God.

The Mind of Christ

'How long must I wrestle with my thoughts and day after day have sorrow in my heart? How long will my enemy triumph over me' (Psalm 13:2). All of us can identify with David's lament, but our gracious Heavenly Father has provided us a way though to overcome in the power of the Holy Spirit. All

that Jesus was and what He achieved on earth was as a result of him aligning his mind to God's word. There are many promises regarding the mind in the scriptures, however, there is one, which is fundamentally radical. *'For, who can know the Lord's thoughts? Who knows enough to teach him? But we understand these things, for we have the mind of Christ'* (1 Corinthians 2:16 NLT). There is a danger here, as we could take this scripture in isolation and make it something that it is not. Therefore, it is crucial that we look at the content and context from v10 to v16 in order to gain an understanding of what having 'the mind of Christ' means to us.

The text is pointing to the role of the Holy Spirit, and because God has sent the Spirit of His Son into our hearts, we have immediate access to Him. As we open ourselves to Him, we will have the opportunity to encounter God without the restrictions that our orphan mindsets endeavour to put on us. Our minds are in a process of renewal, moving away from the pattern of an orphan mindset towards adoption to live as sons. If we are sons, let's think like sons and act like sons. We can with the help of the Spirit, who gives us the incentive to listen to Him as He speaks, inspires, and illuminates us with the truth. He is the ultimate teacher, as He can search the deep things of God. For no one knows the thoughts of God except the Spirit of God, and we have received the Spirit of God that we may understand what God has freely given us. Therefore, we have access to the mind of Christ through the Spirit of Christ, which is the divine alternative of thinking about life that Jesus himself had! This is the only way we can radically affect our world, and it starts with us thoroughly reforming our fleshly and orphan mindsets to fully know the mind of Christ through the Holy Spirit dwelling in us. Choose to be intentional and align our minds with His, so that we begin to think as He thinks.

Promises

- ''Do not copy the behaviour and customs of this world, but let God transform you into a new person by changing the way you think.

Then you will learn to know God's will for you, which is good and pleasing and perfect' (Romans 12:2 NLT).

- 'Throw off your old sinful nature and your former way of life, which is corrupted by lust and deception. Instead, let the Spirit renew your thoughts and attitudes. Put on your new nature' (Ephesians 4:22-23). This is God's work through the Holy Spirit, to bring about a renewal which is continuous. He is in us, so we give him the right to work on our renewal, as we partner Him

- 'Do not worry about anything; instead, pray about everything. Tell God what you need, and thank him for all he has done. Then you will experience God's peace, which exceeds anything we can understand. His peace will guard your hearts and minds as you live in Christ Jesus' (Philippians 4:7 NLT). Guard, remember is night and day, for He never sleeps. It is a warlike word that garrisons or defends our hearts and minds with Jesus the Prince of Peace.

- You will keep in perfect peace all who trust in you, all whose thoughts are fixed on you' (Isaiah 26:3 NLT). Perfect means no inner turmoil, no anxiety or worry, and it relates to the inner rest and stillness being a peace above all peace. The core meaning of peace is an inward sense of wholeness. The word fix means to be focused. Do we focus on our circumstances or God?

Direction

It is important to understand that we have a part to play in changing the way we think. We have to take responsibility to move forward in the promises of God, and of course, it is a challenge.

- 'Those who live according to the flesh have their minds set on what the flesh desires; but those who live by following the Spirit have their minds set on what the Spirit desires' (Romans 8:5 NLT).
- 'So letting your sinful nature control your mind leads to death. But letting the Spirit control [govern] your mind leads to life and

peace' (Romans 8:6).

- 'Set your minds on things that are above, not on things that are on earth.' (Colossians 3:2). Set = to put in place, to give direction. We tell our minds what to do; we can choose to think differently, therefore we can retrain our minds.
- 'Finally, brothers and sisters, whatever is true, whatever is noble, whatever is right, whatever is pure, whatever is lovely, whatever is admirable - if anything is excellent or praiseworthy - think about such things' (Philippians 4:8).
- 'In your relationships with one another, have the same mindset as Christ Jesus,' or, 'have this mind among yourselves, which is yours in Christ Jesus' (Philippians 2:5 ESV).

Weapons of Warfare

There is a scripture that is foundational in challenging our beliefs and seeing them change: 'The weapons of our warfare are not physical [weapons of flesh and blood]. Our weapons are divinely powerful for the destruction of fortresses [strongholds]. We are destroying sophisticated arguments and every exalted and proud thing that sets itself up against the [true] knowledge of God, and we are taking every thought and purpose captive to the obedience of Christ' (2 Corinthians 10:4-5 AMP). This vital scripture shows us our responsibility as well as our authority in God to bring about change in our lives.

The affirmation and application of scripture are that both 'Word and Spirit' can be harmonised to be proactive, and we need to take the initiative in Jesus' name, as we go forward with the process of change. There are many specifics regarding the weapons of warfare, but our source fundamentally lies in the Gospel of the Kingdom of God, our relationship with Abba Father, and in trusting the Holy Spirit to release His powerful healing presence.

Mighty in God

One of the names of God is El Shaddai, which means the 'All Mighty One,' the All-Powerful, or All-Sufficient One, (Genesis 17:1-2; 2 Corinthians 6:18). What God has given us is divinely powerful; it is not ours, it is His, but He has given His infinite, dynamic power and authority for us to stand on. 'Not one promise from God is empty of power. Nothing is impossible with God,' (Luke 1:37 TPT).

Strongholds

The original Greek word for 'stronghold' is only mentioned once in the New Testament as a place of strength. Its meaning is a coastal rock fort, a dungeon, or fortress and these places can be resolutely defended. In this context, the stronghold is a thought or belief pattern, which controls and holds you in its grip, and not demonic per se, although there may be some demonic power that could influence. It is based on lies and deception and will oppose the truth of who we are in God. Strongholds are birthed in deception, and they cause us to think in ways that will attempt to keep us from God's best. They can be defined this way: 'A mind-set impregnated with hopelessness that causes us to accept as unchangeable situations that we know are contrary to the will of God,' Ed Silvoso.

The most important strongholds are mistaken or deceptive images in our minds of who God is and how He sees us, which includes the negative way we think about ourselves. The challenge is to surrender to God in these areas. Give the Holy Spirit the right to enable you to identify the strongholds in the mind that still affect you, and then in the power of Jesus' name reject them. We can overcome the resistance of the orphan mindset and make it ineffective. We can use the only weapon Paul mentions in his letter to the Ephesians, the sword of the Spirit, which is the word of God (Ephesians 6:17). '*For I can do everything through Christ, who gives me strength*' (Philippians 4:13 NLT).

Taking Captive Every Thought

We will need to remain alert to how the enemy will try to remind us of our old belief systems and undermine our relationship with God in any way he can. Satan has no right to whisper into our minds to challenge our identity in Jesus and bring condemnation and accusation. We have a right to stand against these negative beliefs, and to take authority over them in Jesus' name. Speaking in our prayer language can be important in these situations. This is not the time to back away and rebuild walls to self-protect, because that is a deception.

- We need to become more aware of negative thoughts and attitudes, which are contrary to God's will and purpose. It is not a sin to be tempted, it is what we do with those thoughts that matters. We need to think about what we think about; pay attention to what's going on in our minds. It is easy to let thoughts run away and become unrestrained.

- Satan and his demonic powers can and do put thoughts in our minds. Sometimes we think thoughts that we know are not true, but they feel like they are. Often, we do not realise how much we subconsciously hold on to negative thoughts. It is possible to get to the place where we refuse to let our past shape our future, as we recognise the lies that we have believed.

- We all experience negative thoughts. If we allow these thoughts to go round and round in our minds, they will become overwhelming, and we will lose a sense of perspective. Learn to identify the negative, tempting, unwanted thoughts, and take control to deal with them. As we acknowledge our negative and destructive thoughts, we come into a place where we will begin to be able to deal with them. We have the power to choose what we believe and what we allow into our minds.

- Recognise where you are vulnerable to certain thoughts and how they affect you. Some of our thoughts are like a heavy burden.

'Then Jesus said, come to me, all of you who are weary and carry heavy burdens, and I will give you rest. Take my yoke upon you. Let me teach you because I am humble and gentle at heart, and you will find rest for your souls. For my yoke is easy to bear, and the burden I give you is light' (Matthew 11:28-30 NLT). We need not be afraid to ask God for help if we are struggling with certain thoughts. We have the Holy Spirit within us, and He will come to our aid, and help us take these thoughts captive, as they have to obey Jesus.

- We can look at our patterns of thought and begin to change them so that we get to the place where we can challenge unhelpful and negative thoughts, and then learn to replace them with good and positive thinking. Personal breakthroughs will happen by our changing our beliefs - challenging them in line with God's purpose as sons.

- The very best strategy for removing negative thoughts from your mind is to replace them with positive ones. Positive beliefs are those that support you and challenge you to live to your full potential in God. We must intentionally accept and nurture them.

- As you do this, you start to restructure your mind. By dealing with the toxic thoughts that limit you, you will heighten your self-awareness. As your perception is enhanced, you will notice more of an awareness of the positive and/or negative words that you speak.

- Talking to yourself rather than just listening to your thoughts talking to you, is important. Do we allow our 'self' to talk to us, instead of us talking to our 'self?' When we wake up in the morning, we may have a sudden influx of thoughts bringing back, for example, the problems of the day before. You have not created them, but they are talking to you. David talked to himself, 'why, my soul, are you downcast? Why so disturbed within me? Put your hope in God, for I will yet praise him, my Saviour and my God' (Psalms 43:5). It is time the negative thoughts started to listen to us!

- Taking our thoughts captive is a process, but intentionality committing to this is an important start.

'Guard your heart above all else, for it determines the course of your life' (Proverbs 4:23).

Mephibosheth - From Orphan to Son

If there was ever a story in the Bible that has affected me over the years, it is what happened to Mephibosheth (2 Kings 9). It is more than an allegory, it is real-life, poignant account of tragedy and trauma to recovery and restoration. It is a miracle that this man survived beyond his early years. He did but was left with such pain; physically, emotionally and mentally. The narrative illustrates the orphan heart and mindset as well as the power of rejection (for a more detailed account of rejection see my book, 'Rejection Hurts'). We live in a season in which God is revealing His heart to us. He desires to draw us close to Himself as He restores our identity and inheritance. God wants to make us 'like one of the king's sons' (2 Samuel 9:11). In the same way that King David did for Mephibosheth.

All in a Day

Mephibosheth was born into the royal court of King Saul, who was his grandfather. Jonathan who was in covenant with David was his father. As a five-year-old, and seemingly an only child, he was suddenly hit by personal and traumatic events that shaped his life. His father Jonathan, and grandfather, the King (Saul), were killed in battle on the same day. Even though Mephibosheth was with his nurse, he was at risk as he was a prince. She was afraid that the enemy would come to destroy the rest of Saul's family, so she picked him up and ran to hide him. As she was running something happened that would have sent a shudder through any family; she dropped him! Mephibosheth became crippled in both feet for the rest of his life, because of this (2 Samuel 4:4). He was only five years old; he had lost his father and grandfather and was now crippled. He had lost his home and family (his mother is not mentioned), his identity and his inheritance. He became alienated in exile and was ultimately forgotten.

The problem for him was so overwhelming that he changed his name. He was not called Mephibosheth when he was born; He had a royal name, Merib-Baal (1 Chronicles 9:40) meaning opponent or contender of Baal, the false god. He changed his name to Mephibosheth. The complete meaning is 'out of my mouth proceeds shame.' It can mean 'greatly shamed,' or 'son of shame.' However, you cannot forget past hurts by changing your name. We feel guilt for what we do, we feel shame for who we are; shame emphasises what is wrong with us. Mephibosheth ended up hidden in a forsaken place called Lo Debar. It was a city characterised by its barrenness and wastelands, a desolate place known as a land of nothing, a place of no hope. Too far away to be noticed, and in the middle of nowhere, it seems he lived there for many years, maybe up to fifteen, and he married and had a son (2 Samuel 9:12).

The Call of the King

After David had become king, he remembered his covenant with Jonathan, and out of honour for him and respect for Saul, he wanted to bless their generations instead of killing them as was the custom in those days. This was a type of kindness that culturally was unheard of. It was shocking to the people, but David called it, 'the kindness of God' (2 Samuel 9:3). It opened a new sense of meaning involving the words covenant, loving-kindness, mercy and grace. David sought out Mephibosheth to extend his grace to him because he wanted to restore Mephibosheth to his rightful place. All the king wanted was for Mephibosheth to humbly accept his favour, because there was nothing he could do to gain it. He deserved nothing; that was grace.

What Mephibosheth must have felt, when the soldiers arrived to take him to the King, his life was turned upside down again, which after so many years, was inconceivable. The trauma and pain of the unhealed hurts of a five year-old would have certainly affected him even though he might not have remembered very much of what happened. He was probably extremely frightened and, no doubt, feared the worst. He had felt safe as long as he was hidden, but even in his conflict, he had no choice, because in that culture the king required obedience.

As Mephibosheth bowed before him, King David's first words were, 'do not be afraid.' From this, we see that he cannot want to hurt, kill or punish him, but has good in his heart for him, he wants to lift him up not put him down. *'There is no fear in love. But perfect love casts out fear'* (1 John 4:8). David was offering covenant love and grace, but Mephibosheth struggled to receive his favour and reacted by comparing himself to a dead dog, *'who am I that you pay attention to a dead dog like me?'* (2 Samuel 9:8). A dead dog was the vilest and most contemptible object possible. Mephibosheth not only believed the lie about himself, it had become part of him, and because of this, he had learned to live the lie. He would have stayed in Lo Debar forever if it was not for the response of David. His life became ruled by the power of his tongue, which had poisoned himself as well as others. *'Words kill, words give life; they're either poison or fruit - you choose'* (Proverbs 18:21 MSG).

David was able to give the same covenant of grace that he had received from God to Mephibosheth. When grace is released, healing begins to flow. The power of healing began for Mephibosheth even before he knew what was going to happen. It seemed that coming into the presence of the king brought up all the emotion and pain Mephibosheth had carried. *'God through His great love for us is rich in mercy,'* (Ephesians 2:4).

The Provision of the King

David wanted to show favour, in the same way that God shows favour, out of covenant love and not duty. This is kindness not justice, for there are no conditions with grace; it is as a result of unconditional love. Mephibosheth had not done anything to merit the favour or the kindness of David. David saw a man with shame and moved in the opposite spirit and honoured him. He did this by making an amazing offer to Mephibosheth (2 Samuel 9:7):

- He restored identity: David gave him a sense of worth, value and esteem.
- He restored inheritance: David gave back all the land that belonged to his grandfather.
- He gave him family: David said, 'you will always eat at my table.'
- He adopted Mephibosheth into sonship, 'so Mephibosheth ate at the king's table like one of the king's sons' (2 Samuel 9:11).

The story of King David and Mephibosheth is one of the clearest and most moving illustrations of adoption to sonship in the scriptures. For many years it has challenged, affected, and taught me so much, particularly about the unconditional love and outrageous grace of the Father, and the passion that Jesus had when introducing His Father to the people, and the wonderful role of the Holy Spirit, as He speaks Abba Father.

- God continues to extend His grace to us.
- He wants to restore what the enemy has taken, (John 10:10; 1 Samuel 30).
- His desire is to bring release from the orphan spirit, healing in the orphan heart, and transformation and renewal of orphan mindsets.
- He wants to restore us to a rightful place of sonship. 'The Spirit you received does not make you slaves so that you live in fear again; rather, the Spirit you received brought about your adoption to sonship. And by him we cry, Abba, Father' (Romans 8:15).
- He wants to make us part of His family whereby He can cherish (Abba) and provide (Father).
- He welcomes us to sit at His table as sons and continually provides. 'You prepare a feast (a table) for me in the presence of my enemies. You honour me by anointing my head with oil. My cup overflows with blessings' (Psalms 23:5 NLT).

Possessing Our Inheritance

For as much as many of us have believed the lie about how we see ourselves and how we see God as Father, it is time to start telling ourselves to live in truth so that it becomes part of us in our daily walk with God. The power of the Holy Spirit will give us momentum as our minds become renewed by truth. We need to be intentional, particularly as we take hold of the words of Jesus, *'you shall know the truth and the truth will set you free'* (John 8:32).

Firstly, restore God as Abba. We have the ability through the Holy Spirit to live in the reality of Abba Father. Always remembering that Galatians 4:4-7 is foundational to moving on in sonship. We can now take back that which has been stolen from us and enter into the fulness of our inheritance and destiny as sons.

Secondly, walk In Sonship. Adoption into sonship has not only been ordained by God but it has already been established in the process of redemption through Jesus. We can enter into the fullness of this revelation by embracing and owning the Spirit of sonship. God adopting humans! It is almost inconceivable, but it is the heart of the gospel, as it identifies us as belonging to the family of God. As we recognise the role of the Holy Spirit and submit to Him, we can, as image-bearers, reflect Abba Father's life, His character, and values as perfectly as it is possible. This is a daily walk with Him in the sonship He has purposed for us. God wants to walk with His family as He did in the garden with Adam and Eve (Genesis 3:8).

A Final Observation

This book has been a personal challenge to me, in study, research, writing and soul searching. It has been a lifelong journey so far, but I am confident that some of what I have discovered and written will help you in your own journey. The power and influence of the orphan heart and its accompanying mindset have been consequential in significantly hindering and restricting me in my relationship with God. They affected my journey, my mind set, emotions, spirituality and my reactions and behaviour.

I have learned that as I know the truth, the truth will set me free (John 8:32). The truth, primarily, is a person, and in knowing that Jesus is the door to freedom, together with the revelation of the Holy Spirit, there is, in turn, a revelation of God, my Abba Father. I am not an emotional and spiritual orphan living as a slave; I am a son and have access to the fullness of my inheritance in God. As I journey with the Trinity, I realise that, like you, I am not immune to the circumstances of life, but by His grace there is further understanding of it to help me to begin to make changes, as I commune and communicate with God.

As you move on in your own journey with God, please be honest with Him and with yourself. It is time to face those things that restrict you in your relationship with Him. Hiding these things only plays into the hands of the enemy, and denial will also feed your orphan heart mindset. *'But on Mount Zion [in Jerusalem] there shall be [deliverance for] those who escape, And it shall be holy [no pagan will defile it]; And the house of Jacob shall possess their [former] possessions'* (Obadiah 1:17 AMP). We can take back what the enemy has stolen, as David did at Ziglag, after which, everything was restored (1 Samuel 30).

'For it was always in his perfect plan to adopt us as his delightful children, through our union with Jesus, the Anointed One, so that his tremendous love that cascades over us would glorify his grace - for the same love he has for the Beloved, Jesus, he has for us. And this unfolding plan brings him great pleasure' (Ephesians 1:5-6 TPT).